MILITANT

G000117196

Also by Alice Beck Kehoe

North American Indians: A Comprehensive Account
(1981, 1992, 2006).

The Ghost Dance: Ethnohistory and Revitalization (1989, 2006).

Humans: An Introduction to Four-Field Anthropology (1998).

*The Land of Prehistory: A Critical History of American
Archaeology* (1998).

*Shamans and Religion: An Anthropological Exploration in
Critical Thinking* (2000), *CHOICE* 2001 Outstanding Title.

America before the European Invasions (2002), Italian translation,
Il Nord America Prima dell'Invasione Europea, translated by
Anna Tentindo (2006).

*The Kensington Runestone: Approaching a Research
Question Holistically* (2005).

Archaeology: A Concise Introduction, coauthored with
Thomas C. Pleger (2007).

Controversies in Archaeology (2008).

Expanding Anthropology, 1945–1980: A Generation Reflects,
coedited with Paul L. Doughty (2012).

MILITANT CHRISTIANITY
AN ANTHROPOLOGICAL HISTORY

Alice Beck Kehoe

First published in 2012 by PALGRAVE MACMILLAN®
in the United States—a division of St. Martin's Press LLC,
175 Fifth Avenue, New York, NY 10010.

Where this book is distributed in the UK, Europe and the rest of
the world, this is by Palgrave Macmillan, a division of Macmillan
Publishers Limited, registered in England, company number 785998,
of Houndmills, Basingstoke, Hampshire RG21 6XS.

Palgrave Macmillan is the global academic imprint of the above
companies and has companies and representatives throughout the world.
Palgrave® and Macmillan® are registered trademarks in the United States,
the United Kingdom, Europe and other countries.

Hardcover ISBN: 978-1-137-28214-9
Paperback ISBN: 978-1-137-28244-6

Library of Congress Cataloging-in-Publication Data

Kehoe, Alice Beck, 1934–
     Militant Christianity : an anthropological history / by Alice Beck Kehoe.
        p. cm.
     Includes bibliographical references.
     ISBN 978-1-137-28244-6 (alk. paper)
     1. Church history. 2. War—Religious aspects—Christianity. I. Title.
     BR148.K38 2012
     261.8'7309—dc23   2012022508

A catalogue record of the book is available from the British Library.

Design by Scribe Inc.

First edition: November 2012

10 9 8 7 6 5 4 3 2 1

For Mickie
Mary LeCron Foster, PhD
1914–2001
Anthropologist
She worked so hard, so long
to establish peace studies
not war
in the social sciences
and in the world

CONTENTS

ILLUSTRATIONS

ACKNOWLEDGMENTS

A shock, and a phone call, seeded this book. Shock, in 1974, hearing three men from Bob Jones University tell an overflow audience in a Wisconsin high school auditorium that Satan is always near us, don't trust anyone, not spouse, parent, child, neighbor, business person—all could be Satan incarnate. It's a dog-eat-dog world, red in tooth and claw; "ethics" will be found in Heaven, here we fight Satan. Then a phone call in 1983, my colleague Mickie Foster, asking me to fill a gap in a symposium she was organizing on religious doctrines on peace and war. Could I present Christian doctrines? I turned to two professors in Marquette University's Department of Theology, Daniel Maguire and Matthew Lamb. They launched me into the history of Christianity and pacifism.

Mary LeCron Foster—"Mickie"—worked for many years to establish peace studies as a subfield in anthropology. It didn't take hold. Studies of conflict resolution and war get funded; peace studies don't. This, in itself, struck me as a topic to be observed and analyzed from an anthropological approach. It led back in time to Bronze Age Indo-Europeans, through Constantine, Martin Luther, John D. Rockefeller, up to Rick Warren. A range of colleagues encouraged this sweeping view: Mary Foster, Lita Osmundsen, Robert A. Rubinstein, Peter Worsley, Paul Doughty, Dan Maguire, Matt Lamb, David O. Moberg, Kristian Kristiansen, Robert L. Hall, David Anthony, Solomon Katz, Sidney Greenfield, and Claude Jacobs. Bob Hall pointed out to me that the chi-rho looks like a battle ax with crossed spears.

Others who came in begin with Pastor Brien, who persuaded me to "debate" the Bob Jones team in 1974, and James Courtright, geneticist at Marquette, on my team that night. Laurie Godfrey, Eugenie Scott, and Andrew J. Petto kept me in the fold of *Scientists Confront Creationism* plus *Intelligent Design* (in our book's second edition). Thanks to Sol Katz, I met Kenneth and Elise Boulding, John Bowker, Philip Hefner, and Karl Peters at IRAS weeks on Star Island. Anthropologists Donna Brassert, William Beeman, Les Sponsel, and Rob Borofsky working in peace studies are valued colleagues. Nancy Peske, writer, shared her experience with popular spirituality books. Victoria Lewin-Fetter, MD, in Milwaukee fostered friendship with Frank Zeidler, Milwaukee's great Socialist, and Archbishop (retired) Rembert Weakland, who read and endorsed this manuscript.

I am grateful to Robyn Curtis, my editor at Palgrave, for recognizing there is value in this long-term anthropological approach to a literally vital subject. April Bernath, art-historian-to-be, drew the illustrations.

CHAPTER 1

———⋆≍◉≍⋆———

CULTURAL TRADITIONS

To understand today's militant Christian Right requires history, sociological analyses, semantics, and basic anthropological concepts to develop an understanding of this powerful American subculture. Anthropological study of religion has gradually moved from fascination with the exotic to engagement with our own society, yet the broad anthropological approach applied to American Christianity is still a small segment of contemporary research. It is, we might say, a herd of elephants ignored in the room of anthropology, among them the loudly trumpeting militant Christian Right. Thirty years of observing these fellow citizens has convinced me, a professor of anthropology, that the militant American Christian Right is a remarkable case of the persistence of cultural tradition, four thousand years and counting, of an ethos that continues to activate millions of our fellow citizens.

KEY CONCEPTS

Cultures, like languages, can persist through many generations of a society, so long as adjustments to changing environments are absorbed. Worldviews—the understanding of the universe and humans' place in it—taught within cultures, are basic and overarching cores of cultural traditions. They color our perceptions of the world around us. French anthropologist Pierre Bourdieu used the term "habitus" to indicate how the worldview instilled as children are socialized prompts them to recognize what is significant in their society and to act conformably.[1] *Habitus* derives from the Latin word for "lives in, dwells in." Habitus encompasses the natural world around a community and its members' social experiences. Languages reflect speakers' habitus, not only with words denoting what they see, feel, hear, taste, and smell, but also with metaphors often so commonplace we don't realize they are metaphors—for example, saying a person is "bright" compares illuminating intelligence to physical light illumination.[2] Religions incorporate worldviews and are part of the habitus a person experiences.

"Religion" is a broad term encompassing physical symbols and performances, beliefs taught to explain our existence and our world, and moral strictures. The word "religion" derives from the Latin *religare*, "to bind." Religious beliefs and practices bind humans together in communities, fostering cooperation. Perpetuated through natural selection over several million years, cooperative communities are the human way of life. A worldview and its religious expression that enhances a community's survival are likely to persist. Famous twentieth-century American anthropologist Margaret Mead researched a variety of societies around the world and found that cooperation, and means to promote it, are indeed basic to us gregarious mammmals.

A contemporary of Margaret Mead, the British anthropologist Bronislaw Malinowski described a function of religion he called "social charter." Communities teach histories that legitimate their cultural practices and territory. If such a history seems fantastic, we label it "myth" or "fable." For most Americans, the Genesis story of God creating the world in six days is myth. For Fundamentalist Christians, Genesis is absolutely true, and it legitimates manipulating the natural world as its stewards. A fascinating aspect of studying the militant Christian Right is seeing how its worldview structures its interpretation of familiar American situations and events, to the extent of demanding to rewrite the history of the Civil War and its aftermath (Chapter 13). Believing in a God-given charter, the militant Christian Right is firmly committed to its cultural tradition. For an anthropological observer, this subculture is unusually clearly delineated.

Culture is the core concept of anthropology, while not cultures but the individual is the focus of contemporary American society. Popular books on religion and textbooks on psychology of religion ask what the individual believer can get out of religion. A recent publication subtitled "A Theory of Religion" claims that religions exist to help individuals avert misfortune, overcome crises, and think they will achieve salvation.[3] Standing as a participant observer in our society, the anthropologist notes that Americans see each individual person as an independent actor, making his or her road through life. Americans are as blind to social class as they are alert to skin color, so particular to each person in our heterogenous population. As Canadian political philosopher C. B. Macpherson[4] put it, Americans look at people as individuals possessing certain definable qualities (beauty, ambition, intelligence, stupidity, work ethic, and so on). "Possessive individualism," Macpherson's term, is peculiarly congruent with capitalism; individuals' qualities are social capital. Yes, societies are aggregates of individual persons deploying their abilities as best they can to produce a good life, but however much we prize freedom, no one is independent of human communities and their cultural parameters. The perspective of anthropology of religion delineates the culture within which a religion is practiced. Its compelling strength is explaining how people are said to "have a religion" even if their participation seems no more than a social convention. That social convention is not superficial, it is what binds—*religare*—communities. In the case study of this book, the inculcated worldview binds both physically real communities and the greater "imagined" communities[5] tied by shared ideology.

THE ARGUMENT OF THIS BOOK

A distinctive worldview is embedded in Indo-European languages. It appears historically four thousand years ago, in Near Eastern texts and in Eurasian archaeological sites. By the standards of 2,500 years ago, it is abundantly documented, the language and culture of the expanding Roman state in the west and among Sanskrit speakers in India in the east. Beyond state borders, artifacts mutely bespeak Indo-European cultures throughout much of Europe and western Asia. Two thousand years ago, a radical Jewish sect caught on with Indo-European-speaking residents in the Roman-dominated eastern Mediterranean. Intervention by a bishop of this sect, interpreting an apparition seen by the Roman emperor Constantine, led to the sect, Christianity, gaining legitimacy in Rome, 312 CE. The powerful Indo-European worldview fueling Rome's military campaigns overwhelmed the sect prophet's pacifist egalitarian principles.

That worldview persists today, shared by millions throughout the globe. In the United States, adherents are major players in politics, education, and business. The actively militant segment legitimates its ideology by claiming it is Bible-based (i.e., a myth-based social charter). Its rite of passage is to be metaphorically, and often symbolically, "born again." The "battle-ax culture" ethos glorifying war and competition finds expression in capitalist economics as well as within megachurches and evangelical crusades.

Anthropology's holistic approach and breadth provide a perspective on the militant Fundamentalist segment of American Christianity, explaining its worldview and illuminating the remarkable persistence of its Indo-European heart.

CHAPTER 2

THE PAGAN CHRISTIAN ICON

In hoc signo vinces, BY THIS CONQUER! Emblazoned in the sky above Constantine's army, then painted on his shields and banners, the sign was chi and rho, the two first letters (χ and P) of *Christos,* "Anointed." So explained the Christian clerics writing of St. Constantine's miraculous victory at the Milvian Bridge, at the edge of Rome, 312 CE. The clerics wrote that Constantine, grateful for Christ's support, ordered that the Christian church be added to Rome's officially sanctioned temples. That order marks the institutionalization of Christianity in Europe.

What did Constantine see that day, marching through Gaul, probably 310 CE? Greek letters, or a more familiar image? The sign could have well been a battle-ax and crossed spears. These were traditional weapons of Constantine's forebears, not Roman but Germanic. The fourth century was the time of multiple invasions of the Roman Empire by Germanic nations, a time when German mercenaries were routinely recruited into Rome's armies, and the Roman emperors themselves could be Germanic: Constantine's father, emperor of the western sector of the empire, was from Dacia on the frontier.

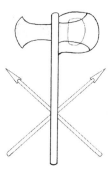

Figure 2.1. Battle-ax with crossed spears
Credit: Drawing by April Bernath.

Germanic religions as well as Roman cults and Christianity were familiar within the empire in 312 CE. Germanic ideology glorified the battlefield, the fighter, the man of action.

That exaltation of militancy became part of institutionalized Christianity. Today, the militant Christian Right carries on that pre-Christian ideology, paradoxically advocating violence in the name of Jesus of Nazareth.

CONSTANTINE ESTABLISHES CHRISTIANITY

What did Constantine institutionalize when he officially validated Christianity for observance and support within the Roman Empire?

Constantine (b. 271–273?/d. 337) was the son of Constantius, a Dacian soldier in the Roman army, born along the Danube, in present-day Rumania, and Helena, whose family operated an inn in Bithynia near the Bosporus in northwest Turkey. Helena traveled with Constantius as his common-law wife and gave birth to Constantine at Nish in Serbia. The family continued to live in the Balkans as Constantius rose in rank, first as a member of Emperor Aurelian's guard, then as a provincial governor, and then as an appointed caesar (junior emperor in the four-ruler system set up by Diocletian in 285).[1] When he received the office of Caesar of the West, Constantius was married to a daughter of Maximian, Augustus (senior emperor) of the West. Apparently, he had put away Helena, the innkeeper's daughter, although their son Constantine continued to honor her.

It is noteworthy that Diocletian's Tetrarchy, as the system of four rulers was called, was composed of men of Germanic origin from the Balkan frontier. Constantius and his household were headquartered in Trier on the Rhine, with visits to outposts elsewhere along the western frontier; Constantius died in York, England, in 306, with his eldest son Constantine in attendance. Months later, in 307, Constantine married Fausta, another daughter of Maximian (like his father, he put away the common-law wife, Minervina, who had borne him a son). Maximian had reluctantly retired in 305 when Diocletian decided to retire, but tried unsuccessfully to stage a comeback in 310. His son-in-law Constantine, who had given him protection when he was retired, magnanimously allowed Maximian to commit suicide rather than be executed.

This brings us to 312. Maximian's son Maxentius, claiming to be Augustus of the Italian half of the western sector of the empire, persuaded the Roman Senate to accept his leadership and to order statues of Constantine to be pulled down. Provoked, Constantine organized an army of 40,000 men, marched across the Alps into northern Italy, and took town after town without harming their inhabitants, thus gaining the people's goodwill. By October 28, Constantine's army stood on the bank of the Tiber outside Rome. Maxentius decided to give battle, seeing that his army outnumbered Constantine's. Meeting near the Milvian Bridge over the river, the armies fought and, *mirabile dictu* (wonderful to relate), Constantine won. Maxentius drowned in the

Tiber. On October 29, Constantine triumphantly marched into Rome, and the Senate decreed him Augustus of the West.

Two years before, Constantine had announced himself a devotee of Apollo the sun god, called Sol Invictus ("Invincible Sun"). On the way to Rome in 310, Constantine said he saw in the afternoon sky a cross above the sun, and the words *hoc signo victor eris* (by this sign, you will be victorious). What he saw was likely a sun halo with sundogs, the result of ice crystals in high cirrus clouds. A Christian bishop, Ossius of Cordoba, was with the army and may have interpreted the vision to Constantine, who recounted a dream the next night in which he was told to paint the sign on his battle flags and soldiers' shields. According to a biography written 25 years later by a bishop who had interviewed Constantine, the sign to be painted was not the cross but a monogram that the bishop explained was made up of the first two Greek letters, chi and rho, in the name Christos. Another Christian writer, a tutor to Constantine's son before the march to Rome, described the sign as the letter X with a vertical line drawn through it and curved around at the top, X with a P through it. The sign came to be termed the *labarum*, a Celtic word. Archaeologists have not found any carving, coin, or document depicting the labarum earlier than 327.[2]

Plausible as is the Christian clerics' interpretation of a chi and a rho in monogram form, the sign does look like crossed spears with a battle ax.[3] Battle axes and crossed spears are pagan icons; archaeologists have labeled a third-millennium BCE culture in southern Scandinavia the Battle-Ax Culture, from the frequent inclusion of a stone battle-ax in male graves, and postulated it to represent an early incursion of Indo-European speakers out of the Russian steppes.

Figure 2.2.   Scandinavian rock art
Warriors fighting with battle axes near their ships, Bohuslän, Sweden.
Credit: Tanum 12, Aspeberget, Bohuslän. Photo: G. Mílstren, Tlvll.
Source: SHFA_icl 23.

Figure 2.3. Warriors on horseback
Warriors on horseback, one with spear, one with battle-ax, on a belt plaque, 500 BCE, Slovenia.
Credit: Drawing by April Bernath, after illustration in W. Lucke and O.-H. Frey, 1962, *Die Situla in Providence* (Rhode Island): *Ein Beitrag zur Situlenkunst des Osthallstatt Kreises*, Berlin.

In the middle second millennium BCE, archaeological evidence is strong that northern Europeans identified the battle-ax with the war priest, who seems to have carried a real battle-ax and an elaborately decorated solid-hilted sword, in contrast to war leaders carrying more functional flange-hilted swords and battle axes. Appearance of the sword-and-battle-ax pair associated with a chiefly class in Scandinavia at this time indicates contacts, perhaps by traveling Scandinavian aristocrats, with the Carpathian region north of the lower Danube and the Black Sea-Pontic steppes region that, in turn, traded with Mycenean Greece and the Aegean. By Constantine's time, the Norse god Thor wielded the battle-ax and thunderbolts, and Odin/Wotan held the sword.

Triumphant in Rome, Constantine had the labarum carved on a statue of himself. Significantly, it was not carved on the great stone arch erected to commemorate his victory at the Milvian Bridge. That was due to the favor of Divinity, *instinctu divinitatis*. Christ Jesus is nowhere to be seen in the triumph. Instead, the name Christos appealed to Constantine because of its literal Greek meaning, "Anointed." Constantine believed his good fortune— the acclaim of his father's soldiers making him Caesar of the West upon Constantius's death at York; his successful campaigns in Britain, Gaul, and along the Rhine frontier; and the culmination, his defeat of Maxentius—testified that Divinity anointed him emperor. It was then incumbent upon him, after his final victory at the Milvian Bridge, to acknowledge the churches and worshippers of Christos *Anointed*, the Christians. He ordered that persecutions against Christians end, legitimated their churches and priests, and allowed them governmental support the same as enjoyed by pagan temples. But Constantine did not become a Christian. Not until he lay on his deathbed in 337, did he agree to be baptized.[4] Theologian Daniel Maguire remarks, "Constantine . . . sort of converted to Christianity. It is better said that Constantine converted Christianity to him."[5]

A compelling case made by Alistair Kee, professor of religious studies in the University of Glasgow, emphasizes that Constantine's goal and concern after attaining the prize of emperor of Rome, was to consolidate, pacify, and unify the empire. Rescinding persecution of Christians and placing their churches and clerics on the same legal basis as enjoyed by pagan temples and priests was a politic act in an empire with hundreds of thousands of Christians, including many serving as soldiers in the imperial armies (accompanied by bishops, such as Ossius of Cordoba in Constantine's army of 312). From this perspective, the vision on the march to Rome and the subsequent victory served to justify the political act. After his mother, Helena, made a pilgrimage to holy sites in the land of Israel, probably between 326 and 328, Constantine pleased her by paying lavishly for churches to be erected on the legendary sites. His generosity was a filial act rather than out of his own religious conviction (he didn't go to the new churches), but it also had the political effect of ostentatiously displaying his economic power in the eastern sector of the empire, which he had conquered from its Augustus, Licinius, in 324.

Professor Kee goes further than deducing that Constantine was not himself a Christian. Kee finds remarkably few references to Jesus or to Christ in a context that clearly means Jesus the Christ, even in texts written by Eusebius, bishop of Caesarea, the biographer of Constantine. "Savior," in these texts, in most instances could, or sometimes explicitly does, refer to God.[6] It was God (Divinitas) who saved Constantine at the Milvian Bridge, bestowing upon him the saving sign—the labarum. Where a Christian would be expected to inscribe a cross, Constantine has inscribed the labarum. Unquestionably, it served as Constantine's magic sign, enabling him to be anointed stage by stage, from conquering Rome in 312 to conquering the remainder of the empire in 324. Kee points to passages in Eusebius's *Oration* for the thirtieth anniversary of Constantine's reign that imply that Constantine believed himself the savior of the empire, under God his own Savior.[7] More surprisingly, perhaps, Constantine may not have rejected his 310 identification of Sol Invictus—*Apollo*—as his savior.[8] When after his 324 victory he promulgated a series of civil edicts, one of them was to make Sunday a day free of legal business, and the wording in the edict is *Dies Solis*, Day of the Sun: "It appears to Us most unseemly that the Day of the Sun, which is celebrated *on account of its own veneration*, should be occupied with legal altercations."[9] Raising Christianity to the status of an officially supported religion within the Roman Empire, Constantine neither banned existing pagan religions nor personally abjured his earlier devotion.

Christianity was institutionalized after Constantine conquered Rome in 312, yet in a real sense, Constantine's espousal of the God of the Anointed (i.e., himself) broke the legacy of Jesus of Nazareth. Can anyone imagine this valiant man of arms turning the other cheek to an insult? Did Constantine give away all his treasure? Live ascetically? Prefer the company of the poor, of the oppressed, of women, to that of men of power? Would Constantine have said to Peter, "Put up thy sword"? Constantine revolutionized Christianity, institutionalizing establishment of a bureaucracy of clerics living in palaces, carrying out public ceremonies in opulent basilicas, supporting secular rulers by attending them in war and in court, and promoting ferocious crusades against dissenters. The beatific strength of Jesus of Nazareth was forgotten in the churches of Christ the Anointed.

CHAPTER 3

———————⋇◉⋇———————

INDO-EUROPEAN CHRISTIANITY

THE FOUNDATION

Emperor Constantine, Caesar, and then Augustus of the West in the first quarter of the fourth century, institutionalized a church of Christos, the Anointed, embodying powerful, longstanding principles of Indo-European societies:

- Conflict is inherent throughout the natural and social world.[1]
- Competition is basic to human nature, and war—competition writ large—is therefore normal and inevitable.
- Loyalty to one's leader is the highest virtue.
- Fighting is the greatest occupation; glory is to be won on the battlefield; and death in battle takes one into heaven.

Bundled with these principles is recognition of the individual as the basic unit of society, recognition of three social classes, and a pantheon of deities ruling human fates but amenable to petition. Originating, it seems likely, on the steppes of Asia Minor, Indo-European culture is well suited to pastoral peoples subsisting on grazing herds plus trade.[2] Such an economy in semi-arid grasslands is risky, requires households to respond to risk and danger quickly and independent of others, and at the same time, to maintain multiple ties with other households and be ready to join them defending common territory.

Pastoral economies dependent on large herd herbivores seem to display these qualities whether or not they speak an Indo-European language—for example, East African nations such as the Masai, Asian nations such as the Mongols, and American First Nations such as the Crow and Blackfoot. Threatened constantly with physical danger from rustlers, wolves, and enemies, pastoral societies tolerate a high level of violence. They have an ethos of ostentatious generosity from leaders to followers, pragmatically reinforcing the virtue of loyalty to one's commander. Because of the risks both natural (drought, blizzards, livestock diseases) and social (rustling, raids, debt indenture if a household loses its herd), wealth is considered fragile, and giving it away in exchange for prestige is smart.

Beyond the factors arising from a pastoral economy, Indo-European societies had, and still have, a strong proclivity for the magic number three. The most familiar example is the US government divided into three branches: judicial, executive, and legislative. According to the twentieth-century classicist Georges Dumézil, the American tripartite structure reflects the ancient Indo-European conception of three sectors of society: that of priests and judges; that of the king, his counselors, and his army; and that of the producers and merchants of food and goods. Each branch is a necessary function for society (hence, Dumézil called them the three "functions"). No one function should dominate over the others, because each is so necessary. The US government embeds a set of checks and balances to ensure the three functions remain coequal. Richard Nixon's effort in 1973 to make his executive branch more powerful was successfully countered, in a dramatic showdown, by counsel Archibald Cox refusing to subordinate the judicial and legislative branches. The Founding Fathers at the Constitutional Convention, well versed in Classical, especially Roman, law and politics, used a tripartite structure already more than two thousand years old that proved still viable in the 1970s.

Over against the magic number three, seen trivially in our frequent enumeration of three items (every Tom, Dick, and Harry; bell, book, and candle; man, woman, and child; noun, verb, object; and so on) is the Indo-European belief in conflict and competition, which posits a duality of combatants—man against nature, men and women, master and slave, two by two. Christian theology incorporates both structures, holding the Divine to be a trinity, and opposing God and Satan in eternal conflict. Note that "threes" (the magic number) are good, whereas "twos" are the opposition of good and evil. A nation built of three segments is good, while dyadic relations within a society are premised to be inherently conflictual—king versus subjects, nobles versus commoners, officers versus enlisted men, husband's authority versus wife's wishes, parent controlling child, teacher dominating pupil.

In order to maintain and defend, and ideally to extend, its territory, an Indo-European society needed to defuse conflict within the group. Among the Germanic nations (those speaking languages of the Germanic branch of Indo-European, which includes Norse as well as German dialects), this was done through a pair of constructs, one being the loyalty pledged to a leader who reciprocated by sharing booty and granting land, the other being an assembly of the free men to discuss plans and issues. Although leadership was basically hereditary within royal and aristocratic lineages, it was not automatic, but required acclamation by the free men, as when Constantine was acclaimed Caesar of the West by his father's soldiers upon his father's death. Within a leader's retinue, his men vied with one another for his favor (and his gifts) and to be respected for valiant deeds. It was glorious to die in battle protecting one's lord, and shameful to survive a battle in which one's lord was killed.

The role of king in Indo-European societies was ambiguous in that the king controlled the military and enforced laws, but was himself subject to judicial decisions and bound to regard the welfare of the populace. Almost inevitably, kings overstepped the fragile balance. Indo-European mythology describes second-function (executive branch) heroes suffering from either a lust for power or fatal indecision. This was, in part, because kings often were said to be descended from a god, which gave them a charisma and capability to perform great deeds but was coupled with human weakness. Germanic kings would claim descent from Woden ("Odin" in Norse; equivalent to the Latin Jupiter). When Constantine facilitated councils of bishops—for example, the Council of Nicaea of 325 that produced the Nicene Creed, which is fundamental to Christian theology—he showed genius in using his executive, second-function power to keep in balance the priestly/judicial first-function power. At the same time, under Roman law that he did not alter, as emperor, he was pontifex maximus: high priest of the state's official religions. Constantine's many edicts meant for the welfare of the populace, particularly once he overcame his rival Augustus Licinius and became emperor of the entire Roman Empire, similarly speak to his understanding that an Indo-European king must curb the seduction of power and strive to maintain the balance of the three segments of society.

Indo-European myths, brilliantly compared by George Dumézil, attribute fatal lapses from moral judgment to second-function figures—kings or warrior heroes. Carried away by lust for power, they betray other lords or ferociously murder rivals; unmindful of marriage commitment or respect due a host's wife or daughter, they seduce women; bedazzled by gold, they take bribes. The point seems to be that a man of action, a quality necessary in a military leader with executive function, can be neither as judicious as a priest or a judge nor as steadfast as a farmer or a craftsman. This insight is not limited to Indo-Europeans, as witnessed in the narrative of King David in the Old Testament. Second-function heroes are all too human, even those said to be descended from gods.

Constantine was a man of action par excellence. His political genius guarded against any "fatal flaw" by adroitly spinmeistering his maneuvers and co-opting, rather than slaughtering, groups of the first and third functions. From the standpoint of Christians, he was a great and good man. They could overlook the executions of his wife, Fausta; his son, Crispus; and his young nephew Licinius Jr. Since he claimed they were dangerously disloyal to his lawful rule, not just his person, having them killed was his second-function duty, not a fatal flaw. Constantine had not the benefit of Georges Dumézil's analyses of the Indo-European tripartite structure 17 centuries in the future, but his heritage of Germanic and Hellene parentage and lifetime of experience on the empire's frontiers fine-tuned his understanding of political diversity and the questionable status of moral certitudes.

This understanding of human leaders partaking of divinity, formulated by Indo-Europeans, so thoroughly a part of Constantine's socialization among Germanic people on the frontier as well as Roman ideology, would have molded his reception of Christian doctrine. If Christ incarnated in a man, and this man was a leader, chief of a loyal retinue, then he would be not unlike Constantine himself, Anointed by Divinity. Christian bishops' fulsome adulation of the great emperor, preserved for us in Eusebius's orations and biography of his ruler, shows us that those princes of the church attending the court saw how their bread was buttered. Rather than upbraid the emperor for ignoring Jesus's advocation of poverty, meekness, and brotherhood, the bishops pragmatically encouraged him to extend favor to Christians and assist conclaves of bishops to resolve disputes. The upshot was that Indo-European values persisted, and Jesus of Nazareth virtually disappeared.

It is the argument of this book that Indo-European values, particularly as developed within Germanic nations, persist today in the militant Christian Right.

Figure 3.1. Parashurama
Indo-European ideology of battle: Hindu god Vishnu's avatar Parashurama killing Kshatriyas
Credit: British Museum.

Figure 3.2. Greek queen Clytemnestra killing the prophetess Cassandra, knocked from her seat in Apollo's shrine
Credit: Drawing by April Bernath, after painting on Greek vase, c. 430 BCE, in Museo Nazionale di Spina, Italy.

THE "DARK AGES" AND THE CONVERSION OF EUROPE

Constantine set the pattern for Christianizing Europe. Rulers decree national religions, and if rulers change their religious affiliation, so go their nations. Missionaries endeavored to enter the courts of kings and nobles, in many instances (according to the histories) winning over the queen or noblewoman and, through her persuasion, gaining the ear of her husband. As with Constantine, the pattern in Europe was for a king to wager that if he wins an impending battle, then he will accept Christianity and favor it for his kingdom. Clovis, king of the Franks, is one storied example of this pattern, declaring himself willing to be instructed by a bishop and baptized after calling upon Christ to give him victory in battle in 496. We are told, by a bishop writing a century later, that three thousand Frankish soldiers followed their liege lord into Christianity.

Europe was officially converted to Christianity during the centuries between the later Roman Empire (the "Decline and Fall of Rome," as the eighteenth-century historian Edward Gibbon phrased it) and the Middle Ages (in Latin, medieval). Conventionally, these are the Dark Ages of Europe, when good government, general literacy, manufactures, and trade deteriorated. Rome in her final two centuries was overrun, again and again, by barbarian Germanic armies plundering her cities and farms, until finally, like a boxer at last unable to rise after blow follows blow, the empire collapsed, and Europe reverted to petty kingdoms with subsistence economies. The Dark Ages end when Christianity is established to the farthest ends of Europe, Iceland and Greenland, in the eleventh century.

Actual histories, so far as they can be gleaned from documents, traditions, and archaeology, are far more complicated. The Roman Empire collapsed, slowly, by merging hundreds of thousands of Germanic people into its provinces until the Rhine and the Danube no longer made sense as frontiers. After the achievements of the original caesar (Julius) and his successor Augustus (44 BCE–14 CE), in extending and consolidating the empire, a number of later emperors were ineffectual or worse. Marcus Aurelius (d. 180 CE) is generally considered the last of the capable emperors of Roman lineage. Diocletian's ascendancy to emperor, 285, ended a century of instability, but Diocletian was not a Roman by parentage; he, like Constantine after him, came from a soldier's family on the Balkan frontier. The strange tetrarchy he instituted was one of those rational plans that looks good on paper (or in this case, papyrus) but disregards human emotions. Constantine, after reunifying the empire, arranged to segment it again so that his three sons by Fausta, his noble second wife, could each have a sector to rule. Back to square one, we might say, back to rivalry and instability.

Rome began as a republic absorbing small nations[3] in Italy. From the mid-third century BCE to 149 BCE, Rome battled other Mediterranean powers for supremacy. Her devastating defeat of Carthage, a North African offshoot of Phoenicia in Asia Minor, in 149 gave Rome a huge territory that required standing armies to defend it and thousands of bureaucrats to administer it. These tax-devouring institutions undermined the relatively democratic republic, culminating in Julius Caesar's takeover. He was, of course, assassinated for his hubris. His grand-nephew Octavian Augustus fought rivals and foreign states to solidify Caesar's empire, terminating the shift from citizen rule to the machinery of a state led by a potentate.

By the third century CE, numerous Germanic nations along the north and east of the Roman frontier of the Rhine-Danube were moving through the frontier into Gaul, Italy, and Illyria (the Balkans). Serving as mercenaries in the Roman armies, provisioning and servicing frontier garrisons, trading both in frontier towns and with Romans journeying into Germanic lands, Germanics were familiar with Roman customs and material goods. Occasionally, soldiers with their families or a leader with his retinue who had lost against a rival petitioned Roman authorities to grant lands to settle on the Roman side of the border. Frequently, a Germanic lord with his warrior band raided into Roman country, out to gain glory in each others' eyes and booty to take home. They could, and did, raid other Germanic regions for glory and slaves, but the riches lay in Roman towns and estates.

To Romans, the nations of "Germania" were uncivilized because they had no real cities. They were described as living in trackless forests. They seemed unwashed, uncouth, bearded. They fought fiercely in scrimmages rather than in disciplined ranks. They were illiterate; dressed in skins; and wore trousers, not togas (so they couldn't make graceful sweeping gestures with yards of cloth). They gobbled chunks of meat instead of elegantly dressed dishes. Taking a Greek term, Romans called them "barbarians." They made good mercenaries and allies against other barbarians, but the main thing was to keep them in their cold lands, where neither the olive nor the wine grape would grow.

Retaining much of the pastoralist culture of the Late Bronze Age Indo-Europeans, their ancestors, or conquerors who had imposed their languages upon Late Bronze Age Europeans, Germanic people's primary organization was the warlord with the men pledged to fight with him. If a leader did not plan raids or could not carry them out successfully, he failed his side of the unwritten contract with his men, and they could leave and join another nobleman's band. This "liberty" contrasted with civilized Romans' stable, solid organization where a household paid taxes and the state provided security, markets, and circuses. Throughout the third, fourth, and fifth centuries, swarms of Germanic-speaking Franks, Goths, Vandals, and Alamanni harassed Rome. The empire continually battled barbarians, plus Persia in the East and insurrections and civil wars within. After 313, when their churches gained empire support, Christian clerics were obliged to pray for Roman victories, as did the priests of pagan temples. Thousands of Christian men served as soldiers. Emperors gave palaces and money for ecclesiastical households to bishops, who felt they needed to display wealth to impress laity with the power of their Christ. Constantine's institutionalization of Christianity was perhaps the greatest feat of co-optation the world has ever seen. A slowly growing threat to the empire from the followers of Paul, the founder of Christian congregations, was negated. Indo-European values were protected within the empire as Christians accepted the dominant hegemony, and beyond the empire among the Germanic peoples still living in looser societies like their ancestors.

"The fall of Rome" happened more than once. One date is 410, when the Goth king Alaric invaded the city. He and his army continued on south, planning to take Sicily and North Africa, but failed to make the sea crossing to Sicily and returned north to winter around Naples. Alaric died that year, a Christian as he had lived. In his lifetime, Roman use of Germanic mercenaries, settlement of Germanic bands and families inside the empire's frontiers, and affiliation of the Goths to the Arian division of Christianity had thoroughly muddied distinction between Roman and barbarian. "Barbarian" came to mean, in the Whig[4] histories written by the winning division, adherents to Bishop Arius's interpretation of the Trinity, the deadly issue that Constantine tried to resolve by convening the Council of Nicaea. (Arius taught that God created his incarnated son, whereas the winning faction—Catholics—argued that God and Christ were basically the same, "of one substance.") The Goths of Alaric's time were heretics according to the Catholics, but they did not think themselves pagans.

Huns enter the swarms during Alaric's lifetime. The name may derive from "Hsing-Nu," a Chinese label for barbarians beyond its western frontier. Steppe pastoralists like the Indo-Europeans millennia before them, Huns, possibly speaking Turkic languages, were not a single nation. Their several, loosely organized raiding armies were moving into the eastern Roman Empire in the fourth century, attacking along the Don River in Russia in 375.

Encountering eastern Goths, Hunnic bands sometimes allied with them, as in the 378 defeat of Rome at a battle in the Balkans where the Hun cavalry convinced the Goths that wars would be won by mounted troops. Alliances were so common that the famous Hun leader Attila has a Goth name. It was noteworthy among the Romans that Attila dressed modestly and ate from wooden dishes and cups, although the fellow Huns in his court luxuriated with fine cloths and silver and gold utensils, part of the wealth the Huns extorted from Constantinople as payoff to refrain from sacking the city. Still, Attila followed the custom of allying with every village and band by taking a lady from it for wife, and indeed, died from a heart attack in the arms of his latest young bride in 453. His remarkable empire stretching from Russia through Hungary to Scandinavia culled huge quantities of gold through tribute from kings conquered by his mobile nation.

While Huns and Goths were marching through Italy, another Germanic nation, the Vandals, marched through Spain and across the Mediterranean into Africa, taking Carthage in 439, from which a Vandal army recrossed in 455 and captured Rome. Meanwhile, others of the Germanic nations fought each other and Roman armies, by this time looking to the emperor in Constantinople rather than the western emperor in Rome as principal power. By 476, the world saw the "last Roman emperor" of the West, a child, Romulus, installed the year before when the adult emperor accepted his realm's weakness and retired to Croatia. The boy was allowed to live with his mother after his father, the leading Roman general, was killed by the Germanic king Odovacar in 476—history's official end of the (Western) Roman Empire.

Germanic wars cost the Roman Empire in two ways. Obviously, battles were costly in loss of men and arms, and the frequent Germanic victories let their troops plunder Roman settlements and capture Roman people to sell into slavery. The wars also cost Rome in demanding more and more tax money spent on frontier garrisons and soldiers, their expensive weapons, their upkeep, and their salaries. At the same time, tax collections were reduced; because plundered towns and estates couldn't pay, the state declared tax relief during rebuilding and might spend money distributing food and assisting recovery. With personal income diminished, manufacturers and markets were weakened. Businesses failed; craftspeople lost employment; local people had to make what they needed instead of purchasing mass-produced cloth, pottery, and tools; and tax revenues from commerce disappeared. This slow economic collapse during the fifth century, making it more difficult to support frontier garrisons at full strength, pushed the Roman government toward more and more alliances with Germanic kings, to combat other Germanic kings. With so much danger within the broad zone of the frontiers, many Germanic bands sought grants of land to settle on the Roman side. The deposition of little Romulus in 476 was almost an anticlimax.

Less than two centuries after Constantine's victory at the Milvian Bridge, most of the people within the Roman Empire were professing Christians (however much they may have actually understood of the religion), Roman Catholics in the West and Arians in the East. Goths—including Vandals,

Burgundians, and others, as well as the Ostrogoths (East Goths) and Visigoths (West Goths)—were mostly Arian Christians. Regardless, their kings, like Constantine, ruthlessly put to death rivals, enemies, and their own next of kin who might have been ambitious. Odovacar had concluded a truce with Theodoric, king of the Goths, in 493, the two agreeing to be coregents of Italy; a few days later, as they ate together, Theodoric signaled his servants to hold Odovacar and thrust his sword through him. Germanic kings continued to trace their royal descent back to the Germanic god Woden, the original *rex* ("king") of a warrior band.[5]

In the mid-fourth century, an Arian bishop had translated the Bible into Gothic. Having a Bible in their own language, which became a lingua franca among the Germanic nations, made it seem natural for most Goths to profess the Arian creed. The translation also appealed to Germanic peoples because the bishop chose words and images familiar to them, so far as he could. Arian Christianity thus seemed not to be foreign. Clovis, king of the Franks, chose rather to be baptized a Catholic, perhaps because Franks and Goths often warred with each other. Although by the seventh century, Arianism was heresy and Roman Catholicism dominant, a structure dichotomizing Catholic Roman Latium from non-Catholic Germanic Christianity reappeared in the sixteenth century with Protestantism. This is a fundamental cleavage stemming from the establishment of Catholicism in the urban, civilized, literate, law-governed, bureaucratic Roman Empire, and the establishment of an opposing version of Christianity *and of society* among the "barbarian" Germanic nations beyond Rome's frontiers. In 1893, American historian Frederick Jackson Turner applied this model to the United States, identifying its frontier as the zone of liberty where a Germanic sense of community united for defense and, in its simple economy, bolstered American democracy. Turner was wrong—he didn't bother interviewing old homesteaders, one of his first students groused[6]—but his model appealed to America's self-styled "Anglo-Saxon" elite and became what today's historians call the myth of the frontier. For Europe as for America, the reality was complex political stratagems and military excursions as alternative economic and social ways of life, developed by once far-separated nations that met, melded, and modified each other. One great difference intervenes between the Roman-barbarian frontier and the Anglo American and Indian frontier: both Romans and barbarians (except for the Huns) were Indo-European, sharing a powerful ancient worldview. After Constantine, it was labeled "Christianity."

CHAPTER 4

EUROPE'S PAGAN CHRISTIANITY

Jesus of Nazareth was a radical Jew living in a Roman province. He taught,

> Blessed are the gentle, for they shall inherit the earth. Blessed are the merciful, for they shall obtain mercy. Blessed are the peacemakers, for they shall be called God's sons . . . You have heard that it was said, 'An eye for an eye and a tooth for a tooth.' But I say to you, do not resist injuries, but whoever strikes you on the right cheek turn to him the other as well. And if anyone wants to sue you for your tunic, let him have your robe as well. Love your enemy and pray for your persecutors . . . Do not lay up for yourselves treasures on earth. But lay up for yourselves treasures in heaven, for where your treasure is, there will your heart be also. (Matthew 5–6)

Jews have seen themselves to be the Chosen People; their forefather Abraham had accepted a covenant with G-d that He would "make thee exceeding fruitful, and I will make nations of thee, and kings shall come out of thee" (Genesis 17). Abraham's God is frequently wrathful, smiting directly or through armies. He sets up kings and allows social classes and slavery. Within traditional Judaism, a vision of a better world was voiced by many prophets, particularly Isaiah: "Nation shall not lift up sword against nation, neither shall they learn war any more" (Isaiah 2:4). Jesus of Nazareth preached the antithesis of traditional society, whether Judaic or Roman, hence Christianity's initial appeal to lower-class persons. His antithetical creed seemed to forbid his followers to use violence or to serve as police or soldiers, and it was not until well into the second century that Christian congregations would accept soldiers. Constantine's Savior was like Abraham's G-d, a Late Bronze Age lord of storms, quite different from Jesus's heavenly father.

Anthropologist Anthony Wallace developed a model of prophetic religions and their routinization. He focused on times of cultural change when conventions no longer worked well, in his selected case (Iroquois) due to invasion, conquest, and displacement. A prophet would arise, speak what he asserted had been revealed to him in heaven, and attract disciples. Evangelizing the new creed, disciples modified it to conform better to the people's existing culture, more clearly addressing the discontinuities causing stress, and lessening any radical tone. Wallace's model fits Christianity well, with the first generation after Jesus (Mark, Matthew, Luke) presenting his radical preaching and Paul subsequently institutionalizing the early church in a manner permitting Christians to continue living normal lives in the Roman world. Normalization continued after Paul, among other changes first accepting Christian policemen performing their duties so long as they did not deliberately kill, then going farther and permitting Christians to be soldiers and kill in war. The Christianity that Constantine accepted already had gone this far from Jesus's teaching.

With Constantine, the Christian church shifted from proselytizing individuals and forming congregations, to winning the favor of rulers and instant conversion of thousands of their subjects. Mass baptisms came before instruction in the religion. This was efficient in terms of manpower for missions, but it did not necessarily follow that priests were deployed to catechize thousands. Exacerbating the theological naiveté of the largely illiterate populace, translators of the Bible and creeds into Germanic languages had to choose which words would best convey the gist of a passage. Where the New Testament in Latin (familiar to bishops and missionaries) uses *Dominus*, "head of a household" (*domus*, "house"), for "Lord," the first translator of the Bible into Gothic, Bishop Ulfila (c. 310–83), carefully used Gothic *frauja*, "head of a household," rather than *drauhtins*, "military leader, warlord" (and omitted the book of Kings from his translation, because "these books contain the history of wars, while the Gothic people, being lovers of war, were in need of something to restrain their passion for fighting rather than to incite them to it," an early historian explained).[1] By the eighth century, Germanic culture prevailed over this scruple, *Dominus* being usually translated with cognates of drauhtins such as Old High German *Truhtin*. Christ the Lord is pictured wielding a spear against Evil, in the guise of a serpent, on a Frankish tombstone,[2] remarkably like the Indo-European god Indra—who, in being basically androgynous, is rather like the celibate Jesus familiar with women as well as with men.

Between mass baptisms and too few priests to instruct the converts, and the tendency for conventional Germanic concepts to take over New Testament translations, little stood in the way of persistence of Germanic ideology in Christianized Europe.

Most of the Christian bishops and missionaries in Europe not only were comfortable with mass baptisms but also tolerated rural people's continued reverence for holy places. Given the missionaries' few numbers, the church preferred to avoid confrontations that might become violent. Instead, people were told they had not known the true God to be worshipped, and they should now understand that they were worshipping the Christian God, or Christ, or Virgin Mary at the shrine formerly devoted to Wotan, Thor, or Freya. It was a policy to erect churches on the sites of pagan shrines and temples. Such a mild, conciliatory approach was certainly Christian in terms

Figure 4.1. Indra, Hindu god of war, riding a sea demon
He holds his iconic weapon, the vajra, a short iron hammer.
Credit: Banteay Srei, Angkor; photo by Alice Kehoe.

of Jesus's "Blessed are the gentle, for they shall inherit the earth," but it tended to make Christianity a reinterpretation rather than a real replacement among Germanic nations.

Violent enforcement of the new religion was by no means rare, carried out by kings as part of their conquests. Leofwine, also known as Lebuin, was an eighth-century Englishman working as a missionary to the Saxons in Germany. He preached, "Accept the God of the Christians and 'He will confer benefits upon you,'" but if they did not accept, "there is ready a king in a neighboring country who will invade your land, who will despoil and lay waste, will tire you out with his campaigns, scatter you in exile, dispossess or kill you, give away your estates to whomsoever he wishes; and thereafter you

will be subject to him and to his successors" (quoted in Fletcher 1997: 214).
So it came to pass. In 782, Charlemagne battled the Saxons, killed 4,500 of
those he took prisoner, and sold many more into slavery. Three years later,
the Saxon ruler capitulated. A Saxon then could be executed for refusing
baptism, eating meat during Lent, failing to observe Sunday Sabbath and to
attend church that day, or performing rituals marked as pagan. The populace
had to tithe to the church and build, or pay for, churches. These measures
were hailed as a triumph for Christianity.

An eighth-century English bishop mentoring some of the missionaries
to what is now Germany advised talking calmly with pagans, leading them
to realize their devotions are "absurd." Say to them, he counseled, "[i]f the
gods are almighty and beneficent and just, they not only reward worshippers, but also punish those who scorn them. Why then do they spare the
Christians who are turning almost the whole globe away from their worship and overthrowing their idols? And while they, the Christians, possess
fertile lands, and provinces fruitful in wine and oil [the Roman lands] and
abounding in other riches, they have left to them, the pagans, lands always
frozen with cold" (quoted in Fletcher 1997: 242). Sensible pagans should
see which side their bread is buttered on.

Evangelizing Germanic Europe was a slow, jerky movement taking 11
centuries, up to the baptism of Grand Duke Jogaila of Lithuania in 1386—a
political act that allowed him to marry the Christian princess of neighboring Poland and become king of Poland. Technically, there yet remained
non-Christian Saami (Lapps) in the far north, of little interest to the church
because their cold lands were good only for hunting, fishing, and rein-
deer herding. It seems clear that the majority of conversions were forced
by conquest and law. Kings became Christians, the chronicles tell, to win
wars. How many pagans opted for Christianity because it promised material
prosperity, we have no way of knowing. We can be reasonably sure that very
few were taught the radical precepts of Jesus of Nazareth. A hint of how
little Jesus mattered can be seen in the index to *The Conversion of Europe*, a
tome of more than five hundred pages for which there is no entry for either
Jesus or Christ.

WAR

Conversion of the Germanic kingdoms to Christianity brought a church
structured in Roman-style administration, with bishops and their bishoprics as the equivalent of Roman prefects and the provinces they governed.
Clerics were educated in Latin and often the only literate persons in a local-
ity. As an educated and cosmopolitan class, bishops and their clerics were
important to Germanic kings' courts and government. Insofar as "civilization" and "Roman" were practically synonymous to Europeans at the time,
the church "civilized" as it Christianized Germanic barbarians. Busy with
administering church personnel and estates, and advising secular rulers,
most bishops had little time to ponder the import of Jesus's words. It was

easy for Indo-European values to persist among the elite, as it was easy for practices to persist among peasants.

Developing out of the late Roman Empire's practice of creating *foederati* ("allies") by granting land to barbarians when they had served in the army or to recognize military alliances, feudalism became the basis of medieval Germanic Europe. This was entirely congruent with the Indo-European heritage of warlords reciprocating the loyalty of their soldiers with food, booty, and land. The feudal tenant, or vassal, pledged loyalty to his lord and was obligated to serve in his army when called. The obligation went up a hierarchy of vassals and lords to the king. Intertwined with the hierarchical system of *feus* ("fiefs") was the dominance of cavalry in warfare, a contrast with the Roman Empire emphasis on disciplined infantry. The Huns had shown Europe the power of a cavalry charge against infantry; they had relied on short composite bows that Asian steppe nomads had refined for mounted shooting. By the eighth century, use of the stirrup to brace a rider thrusting with a lance made the cavalry charge of mounted spearmen formidable. Bowmen then used longbows to let fly their arrows far in front of the cavalry onslaught.

Figure 4.2. Monasterboice, Eire, West Cross, with an armed Christ and armed apostles in the center of the cross, sculpted in the late ninth century CE
Credit Photo by Alice Kehoe.

Mounted spearmen needed heavy armor to protect them both from the arrows from these great bows, and later crossbows, and from the enemy's mounted soldiers. Handcrafted from fine-quality steel, armor for man and horse was very expensive, plus the breeding and upkeep of warhorses capable of carrying the load was expensive, so in the hierarchy of lords and vassals, an upper class of mounted men with equipage—knights—differentiated from a commoner class of infantry and bowmen. Vassals might be obliged to pay money for all this, in addition to or in lieu of service. The military core of the feudal system reflects earlier Indo-European society, to which the bureaucratic Roman Empire was an innovation that endured, after the fifth century, within the church.

Throughout the medieval centuries, more or less 800 to 1500, the church worked with kings to maintain its economic base in landholdings, and kings looked to bishops and the pope to legitimate their claims to rulership. Charlemagne, for example, already king of the Franks by inheritance, was anointed Holy Roman emperor in Rome by the pope in the year 800, acknowledging his extensive conquests from Spain to Denmark. Bishops blessed the warlords to whom they were affiliated through the *feus* they held. In 1095, Pope Urban II announced that God had told him to raise an army for Christ. Soldiers of the Cross—hence, Crusaders (Latin *crux, crucis*)—would be absolved of the penalty of their sins. Their God-given goal was to recover Jerusalem and the Holy Land from the infidel Muslims who had taken it more than three centuries earlier. An immediate threat was the advance of Muslim Turks from central Asia, hired as mercenaries by Muslim kings and now marching under their own sultans against Constantinople.

The Crusades climax the political conversion of Europe to Christianity, in actuality overwhelming Gospel Christianity with the Indo-European ethos of war. In 1053, Pope Leo IX had personally led an army against Normans in Sicily, and his successor Gregory VII in 1074 tried to raise "St. Peter's army" to fight against Muslims for Jerusalem, should they get that far east. Although many bishops and theologians protested that popes should not actively participate in war, when Urban II called for *milites Christi*, "soldiers of Christ," he garnered enthusiastic response from the churchmen assembled for a council at Clermont, France, and very quickly from laymen all over Europe. Born into an aristocratic northern French family, Urban II had been raised and educated in Indo-European languages and concepts. For the Lord God, Dominus, to call up his vassals to fight for his territory would have seemed natural. Lord God had to reciprocate his men, and Urban II believed that as Lord God's deputy, he could take care of this obligation by declaring that "if any men among you go there not because they desire earthly profit but only for the salvation of their souls and the liberation of the Church, we, acting as much on our own authority [as pope] as on that of all the archbishops and bishops in the Gauls [in council at Clermont], through the mercy of almighty God and the prayers of the Catholic Church, relieve them of all penance imposed for their sins, of which they have made a genuine and full confession" (quoted in Riley-Smith 2005: 12–13).

Building on the idea advanced by Gregory VII, Urban II postulated that soldiers of Christ would suffer so severely in traveling and fighting that the experience would match any other penance a priest might impose on a sinner. Furthermore, a "penitents' war" allowed noblemen to remain in character, bearing arms and leading troops. Urban II perfectly captured the Indo-European second-function warrior, a man of action prone to sin, and made him a soldier of Christ.

Medieval theologians could read, making for some discomfort with the notions of penitential war and soldiers of Christ. Half a century after Urban II, the monk Gratian, compiler of the first extensive handbook of canon law for the church, opined that maybe a Christian doesn't have to *physically* turn the other cheek. One century more, in the mid-thirteenth century, Thomas Aquinas carefully explained that if one's prince commands one to take a sword, loyalty and obedience override any scruple about Jesus's saying, "Return your sword to its place, for all who draw the sword will be destroyed by the sword" (Matthew 26): neither prince nor follower need expect to be destroyed by the sword because both merely used the tool put into their hand by God. These medieval theorists drew upon Augustine, bishop of Hippo in the fifth century, who wrote, "The natural order which seeks the peace of mankind, ordains that the monarch should have the power of undertaking war if he thinks it advisable . . . the man [must] be blameless who carries on war on the authority of God . . . by the authority of his sovereign" (quoted in Marrin 1971: 61).

Augustine said, "[I]t is obvious that peace is the end sought for by war," so "every man seeks peace by waging war."[3] From Augustine, Aquinas codified the Catholic principle of the just war, which requires three (ah, the Indo-European magic number!) elements: that the war is commanded by a sovereign authority, that he do so for a just cause (the enemy is at fault), and that he and his soldiers intend to advance the good of the common weal. Aquinas did not demand that an impartial arbitrator should judge how just the cause. Waging war to achieve the end one asserts to be just appears, to an Indo-European, to be natural.

"Christian knights" are routinely depicted in medieval church art, for example, on cathedral portals as at Chartres and Reims. Their reference is to Paul's admonition: "Put on the whole armor of God . . . the breastplate of righteousness . . . the shield of faith . . . the helmet of salvation . . . the sword of the Spirit" (Ephesians 6:11–17). Christ himself supposedly said to John the Baptist, "You entrusted to me sword and armour, helmet and battledress."[4] Armed thus, he was *Christus Victor* ("Christ victorious"). That image remained seductive through the sixteenth century, when the Catholic Hapsburg Holy Roman Emperor Charles V and his son Philip II, king of Spain, had themselves portrayed as the *miles Christianus* ("Christian soldiers"), Charles shown holding Charlemagne's fabled holy lance with a nail from the cross. There was also a popular "Armed Man" mass using a melody associated with the figure.

Bizarre though it sounds, medieval churchmen argued that crusaders expressed Christian love when they fought. The word they chose was *caritas*, love of God and love of one's neighbors shown by actions benefiting them. European Christians' neighbors in Spain, the Balkans, and Asia Minor were threatened or already conquered by Muslim infidels, so to go fight Muslims demonstrated *caritas* toward fellow Christians. Urban II's message was, in the words of a man who obeyed it, "if anyone, with a pure heart and mind, seriously wanted to follow God and faithfully wished to bear the cross after him, he could make no delay in speedily taking the road to the Holy Sepulchre" in Jerusalem.[5] The cross was the connection between Christ who accepted death on it to redeem humankind, and medieval soldiers of Christ going to war to redeem eastern Christians and the Holy Land.

THE MILITARY ORDERS

To most purely express Christian *caritas*, a *miles Christi* could join a militia of Christ such as the Swordbrethren, the Knights Templar, or the Teutonic Knights. The medieval military orders were like monasteries in that members vowed poverty, chastity, and obedience to superiors, but unlike monasteries in that they were not sequestered from the secular world. Templars originated the form, organized around 1120 in Jerusalem to guard pilgrims traveling to the city captured in 1099 by the First Crusade. ("Templar" refers to the temple in Jerusalem.) Quite quickly, Templars extended their function to fight Muslims on the battlefield.

In line with churchmen's interpretation of *caritas* to include going to war against infidels and heretics, and Urban II's promise that becoming a crusader was full penance for sins, the military orders saw themselves as men who gave up worldly gains to gain merit with God: "In our time God has instituted holy wars, so that the equestrian order [knights] and the erring people, who like ancient pagans were commonly engaged in mutual slaughter, might find a new way of meriting salvation. They are no longer obliged, as used to be the case, to leave the world and to choose the monastic life and a religious rule; they can gain God's grace to no mean extent by pursuing their own profession, unconfined and in secular garb" (quoted in Forey 1992: 13). Indo-European pagan ethos overwhelmed the message of Jesus of Nazareth.

The Order of the Hospital of St. John of Jerusalem began at the end of the First Crusade—at the beginning of the twelfth century—administering a hospital and orphanage in Jerusalem. Brothers and sisters of the order saw themselves, as did Mother Teresa in the twentieth century, as servants to the poor. They dressed simply, like the clothing they provided to their patients, while giving patients the luxury of private beds and good food. After the Knights Templar had extended their mission to active fighting on the battlefield, the Hospitallers of St. John followed suit, so that after 1136 they took responsibility for series of castles on the frontiers of the First Crusade's conquests. They did continue administering hospitals, building new ones in Europe and running field hospitals during wars. Hospitallers' rationale for taking up arms was that if it is meritorious to humbly care for the poor and sick, how much more meritorious it is to risk, or lose, one's life in battle to protect Christians' settlements. And just as their hospitals employed paid help to supplement the order's brothers and sisters, the Hospitallers led, and paid, mercenary troops in battle.

To pay for the enormous expenses of armored, mounted knights, including their houses and castles; their mercenary troops; volunteers and their weapons; thousands of saddle horses, pack horses, mules, and wagons; farms for breeding their warhorses; and of the Hospitallers' hospitals as well, the military orders were given grants by the church, donations of land and money by lay persons, and for the Teutonic Knights in Prussia and the Baltic, rights to land they conquered from pagans. The orders became almost global institutions profiting from estates all over Europe and western Asia, formidable on account of their economic power as much as their military might. They were independent of any particular secular ruler and could choose to fight other Christians—for example, Germans against French—in alliance with secular armies.

Inevitably, the military orders provoked anxiety and jealousy. In 1307, Philip IV of France charged the Knights Templar with heinous crimes: denying Christ, spitting on the cross, and sodomy. Supposedly, these horrible actions were required of new recruits in an initiation ceremony. Philip had Templars tortured to exact confessions, and most of those interrogated did confess, although many then tried to retract their confessions. The pope, Clement V, did not believe the charges were justified. King and pope challenged each other, until in 1312, Philip marched with an army to the French town where Clement was meeting in council with his churchmen. Clement gave in, announcing that the Order of the Knights Templar was terminated, its possessions to be given to the Hospitallers. This order managed to maintain itself even after crusading to the Holy Land frittered out in the sixteenth century, ruling the island of Malta until 1798. When Protestantism was established in northern Europe in the sixteenth century, estates of the military orders were secularized, and Teutonic Knights' grand masters were made dukes. The Teutonic Knights continue to the present, converted to an order of priests with only pastoral duties after World War I.

MARTIN LUTHER

Martin Luther was born in1483 into a commoner family in the German province of Thuringia. He loved school and was destined, his parents hoped, for a career in the law. Instead, at 21, he chose to enter an Augustine monastery in the city of Erfurt. A lightning bolt in a terrible thunderstorm had frightened him, he said, into vowing ascetic monkhood. Explaining his decision to his father, Luther was upset by the older man remarking, "God grant it was not a lying and devilish specter."[6]

Not long before Luther became a monk, a new university had been established in the small town of Wittenberg by the ruler of the principality of

Saxony, Frederick the Wise. The head of the Augustinian order was named dean of theology, and in 1508 appointed Luther to its faculty to teach the Bible. To do so well, Luther believed he needed to add Hebrew and Greek to the Latin he had been schooled in, while he equally felt compelled to use vernacular German to communicate knowledge to his students and the congregation he preached to weekly. His pastoral duties made him painfully aware that parishioners were exhorted to buy indulgences, church-approved letters remitting a soul's time in purgatory. Supposedly, the pope had power to affect remission. Selling indulgences was the principal money-raiser for building churches and monasteries; maintaining hospitals; and supporting priests, religious houses, and universities. Historian Ronald Bainton remarks, "They were the bingo of the sixteenth century."[7] Luther's meticulous scholarly study of the Bible indicated no authority for a human priest to remit sins, certainly not in exchange for money.

By 1517, after preaching several times in 1516 against buying indulgences, Luther felt compelled to more publicly state his concern. He prepared a Latin document outlining the outrage in 95 points ("theses"), essentially, the huge expenditure to build, out of indulgences sales, a stupendous basilica of St. Peter in Rome; the lack of any biblical support for the notion that priests have power to remit punishment for sins; and the danger that people neglected charity and righteous living on the false expectation of buying their way into heaven. The printed document was posted at the Wittenberg Castle Church, a conventional venue for publicizing theological news and issues. Luther sent a copy to Prince Albert of Brandenburg, who had been selling indulgences to pay the pope to appoint him archbishop of Mainz, head of the church in Germany. Albert forwarded the document to the pope, who considered it rant but let the Augustinians know that their brother should be punished. Meanwhile, others in Wittenberg quickly translated the Latin into vernacular German, printed it, and distributed copies widely.

Frederick the Wise told Luther he would protect him from extradition to Rome, and a hearing was organized in Germany, at Augsburg, before a papal representative. Luther had hoped to dispute his theses as an academic with a learned representative, but instead he was ordered to recant. Refusing to do so, Luther escaped by night from Augsburg, returning to Wittenberg. Frederick, a sincerely pious man, listened to his university scholar, concluding, in a letter to Rome, that the doctor of theology had convinced him that scripture did not recognize selling indulgences as a means of saving one's soul from punishment. The Augustinian order released Luther from his vows. Still a faculty member, he formally debated his theses at the University of Leipzig. From this debate, his sermons, and tracts he wrote, eagerly published and read by many Germans, Luther's position became clear: only God can save humans, by grace through Christ. Right living and contrition for one's sins are important, but not sufficient to guarantee salvation, because we cannot know God's intent. No human authority can override God or scripture, and in the same coin, reading scripture makes every man his own priest.

Luther's brilliant exegesis of the Bible and formidable talent for debate, to which he brought a manly presence and clear voice, catalyzed German dissatisfaction with the venal rule of the Roman Church. Significantly, in 1518 a papal emissary had requested the German princes to fight in, and support by taxes, a new crusade against the Turks. Meeting in Worms, the princes rejected the pope's call, complaining vehemently against the way their tax revenues already were flying over the Alps to Rome. Dr. Luther's scholarly denunciation of the Roman Church's self-anointed prerogatives had a ready audience in Germany. It helped that he liked to speak colloquial German, ready with pithy peasant proverbs and lusty beer songs. He was a man of the people, a proud Northerner, fearless not only in asserting scriptural truth but also in phrasing his convictions in remarkably earthy epithets.

There is a strange inconsistency in Martin Luther. His knowledge of the New Testament and his devotion to God manifested in Christ should have made him charitable to all, yet he denounced rebellious peasants in the crudest language, urging the German princes to put them down with harsh measures. Somehow he could not see the parallel with his own defiant rebellion against his prince, the pope. The Protestant Reformation that Luther sparked, and its mainstream churches continuing today, preach the worth of the individual and, simultaneously, obedience to constituted authorities. Recall the tenets of Indo-European culture (Chapter 2):

- Conflict is inherent throughout the natural and social world.
- Competition is basic to human nature, and war—competition writ large—is therefore normal and inevitable.
- Loyalty to one's leader is the highest virtue.
- Fighting is the greatest occupation; glory is to be won on the battlefield; and death in battle takes one into heaven.

Martin Luther thoroughly ingested these tenets, questioning only the last: that death in battle gained one entry to heaven. Throughout his life he was obsessively anxious over his soul's salvation, realizing that the New Testament taught that heaven was to be gained exclusively through Christ. Luther could not recognize that his Germanic culture was, to a large degree, still Indo-European, nor how deeply that tradition molded his life and his teaching.

Oppositional duality, in other words conflict, structures Luther's thinking and legacy. Constantly he saw the devil working against godly men, himself among them. He could square his defiance of the Roman Church with his glorification of loyalty by aligning the pope and his adherents with the devil—not unjustified considering that pope was a Medici, Leo X, inordinately indulgent in gambling, hunting and exorbitant living. Luther's Germany was *nominally* Christian, with most people little conversant with even a basic Catechism (which Luther attempted to remedy by writing one to be taught to every child). Everyday life was rife with folk religion beliefs and practices, commoners wearing knives and aristocrats swords, horrendous tortures imposed by ordinary civil authorities, and warlords contesting territories and revenues, even buying bishoprics. The Reformation cut northern Europe free from the Roman Church, the better to continue its Battle-Ax Culture.

THE REFORMATION

The Protestant Reformation from which today's militant Christian Right derives was the theological cap to Europe's early modern revolution against medieval feudalism. Luther's rebellion against Roman authority was protected by his liege lord, Frederick (the Wise) the elector of Saxony—a feudal position—yet it was Frederick's "modern" goal of building up his towns into economic and intellectual centers that motivated him to protect the Wittenberg theologian. The Reformation is often described as an urban movement making towns significant political actors. With schools, printing presses, a largely literate populace, and a money economy, sixteenth-century towns could contest the power of landed barons. Peasants on nobles' and church estates were often bound by serf status from which their "surplus" offspring (more than the peasant holding could support) could escape by moving to towns. Martin Luther's father was such a migrant. Like him, numbers of poor people achieved financial success in burgeoning towns.

Did the Reformation need a revolutionary theological doctrine? That is, population increase after recovery to its level before the mid-fourteenth-century Black Death, stimulating market production, money, and credit, plus unprecedented opportunities to extract wealth from the New World, might have been sufficient to revolutionize Europe. Luther's "priesthood of believers"[8] went along with multifarious changes in relations between lords and subjects, in subsistence versus capitalist economies, and in the development of a middle class (like Luther's own family). A trio of economists argues that the Protestant Reformation needs to be seen as introducing market competition against a costly monopoly (the Roman Church), facilitated by inexpensive printed pamphlets and books that advertised the new opportunities.[9] Analyzing the Reformation from a pragmatic, anthropological standpoint, rather than an intellectual one, makes Luther's theology almost a red herring. "Reform" became a slogan to wave over radical changes in political relations.

One fact leaps out in looking over Protestant reform movements in sixteenth-century Europe: *cuis regio, eius religio* ("who rules, his is the religion") doesn't change. Rulers, including councils in towns, could continue to decree that all their subjects accept their religious denomination. Just as Clovis could make his Franks Christian, Elector John of Saxony, successor to Frederick the Wise, could institute Luther's German Mass in 1525. Albert Duke of Prussia, grand master of the Teutonic Knights, similarly imposed Luther's reforms in his domains. Therefore, Protestant Reform was not so much reform in the hearts and minds of commoners, as political acts by the constituted rulers of principalities and bishoprics.

Behind Martin Luther lay two centuries of strain between the feudal order of the Middle Ages and a shift toward individual liberty, first gained in towns. Severe depopulation by the Black Death (bubonic plague), beginning in Europe in 1348, undermined the power of the landholding nobility, including estate-owning churches and religious orders, because fewer peasants meant lesser revenue. (It also became easier for peasants to find unoccupied land.) Many aristocrats desperately responded by raising rents and sharecropping payments and requiring peasants to put in more labor on the lord's estates. This, of course, produced grievances, sometimes expressed in riots and rebellions. All the aristocrats professed Christianity, and, by default, their subjects were nominally Christian, without either class appearing to find incongruity between being a Christian and using violence.

Towns gained populace, as population increase in the countryside sent them a steady stream of men and women who could not be accommodated on the rural estates. Townspeople required markets for artisans to earn their livings selling products and to buy food, tools, clothing, and other necessities artisan families did not themselves produce. Merchants invested in goods, developing trade with other towns and abroad. Shipping and freighting expanded. So did monetary and credit systems. Merchants and guild masters—the burghers of the city—demanded freedom from aristocrats' rule and had the economic clout to get it. In reaction, aristocrats saw their class interest balancing out their competitions with one another. Those who spoke German dialects conceived of "Germany" as a country that could have political reality giving its nobility and burghers strength to resist Vatican demands and encroachments by neighboring states such as France. There had been a Holy Roman emperor more or less since Charlemagne, but not until Maximilian I became emperor (1493–1519) did the title carry weight. Already, in 1486, the phrase "Holy Roman Empire of the German Nation" had been introduced. Maximilian convened a parliament of German nobles in 1495, the *Reichskammergericht*, in the city of Worms (also known as the Diet [Council Meeting] of Worms). A major accomplishment of the first meeting was its decree abolishing feud, up until then an acceptable means for one family to seek vengeance on another.

"Princes of the Church" at this time meant not a church hierarchy parallel to the secular hierarchy, but precisely men who were members of the secular aristocracy as well as clerics and who ruled territories belonging to a bishopric or religious house. Younger sons and nephews in a princely family would be given a church estate, and it was not unusual for such princes of the church to ignore ecclesiastical duties in favor of the pleasures of the flesh. As far as territorial subjects were concerned, a lord bishop would be no different than a baron. Contenders for an archbishopric raised armies to battle rivals' armies. Burghers of a city might enter the fray, demanding liberty for their town from autocratic rule. During the century before Martin Luther, the growing economic power of towns forced feudal lords to more systematically administer their estates in order to regularize income and expenditures; and as warlord grabs met more effective resistance, politics was enhanced over brute attacks—Machiavelli's time had come. Still, as von Clausewitz said, "politics is the source of war." The transition over two or three centuries from feudal to capitalist state political economies and structure led to more law and order and also to better-organized, more effectively supplied armies. There was also an outside threat pushing Europeans to invest in armies, the threat of Ottoman Turk takeover. Suleiman the Magnificent attacked Vienna in 1529 and fell back only as far as Budapest, holding the Balkans. He was the infidel always lurking at the frontier, ready to invade if Christendom weakened. Luther and others feared that corrupt church leadership and lawless commoners might tempt God to let the Turks scourge Europe.

The Protestant Reformation liberated northern Europe from Vatican control, elevating local aristocracies. Prince-bishops were (gradually) replaced by kings and queens as titular heads of national churches. Congregations had more voice in managing their funds and accepting pastors, within the national church hierarchy of authority. Especially in Germany, people thought they were reverting to the freer, more democratic "tribal" way of life Tacitus described for their ancestors. Tacitus's writings had become known through Renaissance revival of classical texts. Germans liked to link their late-medieval Holy Roman Empire to the Roman Empire through Charlemagne and Otto, a tenth-century king of Saxony who conquered Lombardy and central Europe and was crowned Holy Roman emperor by the pope in 962. Rome, the Carolingians, and the Otto dynasty served to justify sixteenth-century Germans' ambition to forge a real nation out of the multitude of German-dialect principalities, a great nation that could refuse Vatican control and might dominate Europe as its alleged forebears had. One contemporary of Martin Luther, Ulrich von Hutten (1488–1523), from an aristocratic family in Hesse (central Germany), popularized Tacitus and especially the Roman writer's admiring portrait of a brave Germanic leader, Arminius. Like Luther, Hutten railed against the corruption of the popes, the way the sale of indulgences beggared pious Germans in order to embellish the Vatican and its high-livers. Hutten was even more intemperate than Luther, to the point that, by 1523, he had to flee Germany, taking refuge in Zurich where he soon died from syphilis (another difference from Luther, who kept chaste and married a former nun).

Both Hutten and Luther personally knew the Dutch philosopher Erasmus of Rotterdam, a man dedicated to classical scholarship and peace-seeking middle grounds. Erasmus urged princes to be merciful while administering justice, to be upright, and to strive for their subjects' welfare and happiness. Refusing to break with the pope, although critical of his indulgences—personal and those for sale—Erasmus made his German friends angry. The falling-out between the two Germans and the Dutch scholar makes clear the nationalism entwined with religious doctrines in the Protestant Reformation. Luther's denunciation of the Church of Rome was the tipping point for northern principalities' shifts from vassalage toward modern nation-states. Nationalism often wears the battle dress of militancy. For northern Europe, Martin Luther was the prophet of revitalization of Germanic Indo-European allegiance to a local prince, a rejection of the classical Roman superordinate structure channeling power and wealth away from the bruderbund—band of brothers—fighting and feasting with their chosen leader.

CHAPTER 5

————✦————

PROTESTANTISM FITS THE STATE

Protestantism was the capstone of a gateway between the medieval world of feudalism and the Catholic Church, and the modern world of capitalist states. Martin Luther's challenge to the church legitimated seizure of vast ecclesiastical estates in northern and western Europe, estates that became windfalls for rulers centralizing authority and power in territorial states. Feudal nobles had placed younger sons and nephews in church offices, making an interlocking directorate of aristocratic families protecting aristocrats' privileges and private revenues. Breaking up half of this edifice of power enabled principalities to demand taxes from nobles' domains, extend their rule of law, take over social welfare programs, support capitalist enterprises, and not least, maintain armies. Luther's heresy succeeded because rising populations (recovered from the Black Death of the mid-1300s) attracted capitalist investment. Regional markets were strengthened, challenging feudal baronies. Wise rulers such as Frederick of Saxony realized that repudiating Rome gave them the upper hand in managing economic policies as well as in enforcing territorial laws. Luther supported such revolution from the ruling class.

In 1905, German sociologist Max Weber published the essay "The Protestant Ethic and the 'Spirit' ['*Geist*'] of Capitalism." Weber was stimulated by a senior colleague's history, titled *Modern Capitalism*. Reading this two-volume tome, Weber first noticed methodology that seemed questionable, or at least debatable, and upon further reflection, he perceived a failure to adequately consider the context of capitalist development following the Reformation. What the older economic historian called the "spirit of capitalism," Weber identified as an ethic of *Protestantism*, more specifically the teachings of John Calvin (1509–64) that the good Christian is ascetic, eschewing entertainment and sensual indulgence. The good Christian is also supposed to work hard, so, abjuring spending money on entertainment and luxury, he accumulates capital.

Calvin himself, a French lawyer invited to govern the Swiss city of Geneva, would have been surprised that his uncompromising dictates on personal probity and unflinching obedience to Reformed Church authority should be less noted than their economic effect. In theology, Calvin is remembered for his conviction that salvation is predestined by God (if God is omniscient and omnipotent, then God must know whether a person will be saved or damned, and it must be God's will). Although predestination would seem fatalistic, rather than an impetus to hard work and ascetic living, Calvin maneuvered around this by taking one's God-given *capacity* for hard work and ascetic living as part of God's plan and therefore *necessary*. Because hard work and ascetic living usually produce economic reward, achieving economic success is a sign that one has been fulfilling God's design. It logically follows that poverty is predestined damnation. This "Protestant ethic," in Max Weber's estimation, drove most people in Protestant countries to work hard, live frugally, and save money in order to be recognized as among "the elect" (God elected these people to be saved), rather than seen to be damned.

Weber's essay is a turning point in social science interpretation, insisting on discovering historical contingencies instead of postulating intangible "forces" driving societies, for example, his older colleague's "Spirit of Capitalism." Spurning the mystery-laden concept did not automatically produce an indubitable explanation for empirical data: which data are significant, and whether selected data are sufficient to cause the phenomenon, bedevil the researcher. Twentieth-century sociologists and historians laud Weber without necessarily accepting his emphasis on Calvinist ethos. British historian R. H. Tawney examined the thesis in his 1926 *Religion and the Rise of Capitalism*, bringing in more detailed familiarity with medieval and early modern English history than Weber had commanded. Tawney saw tension between Calvinist doctrine and capitalism, in that Calvinist Puritans stressed discipline and capitalism did not—the capitalist takes risks. Puritan leaders ordered businesspeople to remember Christian imperatives to succor the needy, lend them money without demanding interest, and restrain cupidity, working enough to secure a comfortable income for the household but not avidly to procure riches. Weber, who had died in 1920, would not have disagreed with Tawney, for he was quite aware that he did not command as deep a knowledge of Calvin and Puritan life as he needed to powerfully validate his interpretation. Weber's essays were addressed against nineteenth-century ideas of social development *sui generis* ("unique to itself"), from which historical facts fall out. To the contrary, Weber and Tawney asserted, history is a picture of human activities provoked by some circumstances, constrained by others, motivated sometimes by kindness, sometimes by greed, a picture in which "religion," "economics," and "politics" are abstracted distinctions.

PROTESTANT STATES

Protestantism is known for its emphasis on individuals, their means of personal salvation and direct communication with God. The Roman Church's hierarchy of sainted and human intercessors is rejected, along with its hierarchy of this-worldly power and authority. Protestantism fits the modern

Western belief in "possessive individualism," to use political philosopher C. B. Macpherson's term.[1] That is, persons are seen as individuals possessing innate and acquired qualities and abilities, without regard to social factors influencing them. Martin Luther and John Calvin both stressed the importance of fulfilling one's "calling" (*Beruf* in German), in the sense that God calls us to our vocations (the word derived from Latin *vocare*, "to call"). A person in a liberal democracy might see this as carte blanche to follow one's dream, but to Luther and Calvin it meant accepting one's place in society, in occupation and class. So long as people worked hard and honestly at their jobs, they deserved God's grace and humans' respect. Protestantism, then, is not in itself politically liberal or democratic.

Luther upheld the authority of secular princes, and Calvin instituted an authoritarian government in Geneva. The critical feature of the Reformation was its legitimation of secular rule, with the ruler titular head of the national church. Instead of economic policies and revenues bifurcated and contested between the Roman Church and secular rulers, they were consolidated under the latter. The notion that monarchs were given God's mandate to rule, even that their anointing at coronation imbued them with magical power to heal, persisted to the nineteenth century as Western democracies gradually built representative structures and extended the suffrage. Reformation states were not revolutionary but part of the centuries-long transition from feudal to modern[2] political systems, of which the crux was the shift from disbursed power in feudal societies to centralized power in modern states. In the longer view, they formed after a millennium of accommodations between Roman law and Germanic customs, complicated by power plays between the Catholic Church headquartered in Rome and principalities beyond the Alps.

Power was the issue. Power needs economic support. So long as the church drained money from northern principalities, it crippled their power. During the Middle Ages, barons raised military units by conscripting their vassals and tenants, and maintained them from their own revenues, or by borrowing money. When battles were over, soldiers returned to their ordinary employment. Baronial domains kept their own courts of law and punishment—hence the efforts of merchants and artisans to govern their towns themselves, legally free. Kings engaged nobles as vassals, buying loyalty and service, including providing fighting men and weapons, in exchange for grants of land and privileges. As we see in Shakespeare's historical dramas of the Wars of the Roses in medieval England, kings were *primer inter pares* ("first among equals"), competing against other nobles for loyalty and military capacity. Success in battle let them seize losers' land and bestow it upon their own vassals. Who was on top was volatile. At the other end of the social scale, in many territories peasants were serfs, bound to an estate whoever might take it. Towns fought, often literally, against ensnarement in these politics.

The Black Death at the end of the 1340s drastically cut Europe's population, killing one-third to one-half of the people in its regions. Huge areas of farmland became vacant, giving surviving peasants opportunity to obtain or expand farms with minimal obligation to the aristocrats. Wages for labor went up, rents down. Populations rebounded but economic and political relations had shifted. Raising armies to go on crusades no longer appealed to most Europeans; commerce appealed more, promising wealth through calculations of business potential instead of by looting infidels' castles. Families like Martin Luther's looked for lucrative openings to escape the grind of peasant farming. Production rose from mines and workshops, increasing the number of managers and merchants, the use of credit in business dealings, and the number of consumers buying food, cloth, tools, and services such as building construction. A network of part-time and home-based craftspeople linked village inhabitants to markets—for example, spinners and weavers in cottage industries selling to wholesalers. The trend was toward more and more organized production and marketing, so that, by the seventeenth century, it was common for jobbers to bring wool to spinners' cottages and regularly pick up spun thread or to bring thread to weavers' homes and pick up cloth and then bring that to fullers who would finish it for market. Transportation routes had to be improved, cartage expanded, robbery controlled, and so on, undermining barons' power and incomes. By the late fifteenth century, the medieval system of vassalage was going under, swamped by growing towns outreaching to peasant producers. Business was in the ascendancy.

With commerce demanding rights and protection and promising economic returns, shrewd rulers decreed their territorial laws and courts would supersede barons' private systems of law and courts. The territorial state could work with free towns, merchants, and producers' guilds, receiving fees and taxes. Territorial princes appointed salaried bureaucrats to manage the business-based economy, often hiring impoverished noblemen for the positions. As bureaucracies grew, barons' power declined. Rulers paid for their own armies instead of relying on soldiers raised by their vassals. Armies are expensive, especially if they are disciplined rather than freebooters. The Roman Church was a principal obstacle to territorial princes' power. Not only did it siphon off money by selling indulgences and sending tithes to Rome, but its religious orders owned vast estates independent of local princes. Worse, bishops in many principalities could vote along with their brothers, the secular nobles, to nominate, accept, or reject the territorial prince. Breaking away from the Roman Church, confiscating clerics' estates, enormously fattened state coffers and, at the same time, did away with threatening political opponents.

Taking advantage of increasing populations providing more labor, more producers, more consumers, and more trade, sixteenth-century German princes built two pillars for their states: a civil bureaucracy and an army. Both were supported by taxes, making commerce vital to the government as well as to the populace. The sixteenth and seventeenth centuries were the period of development of modern disciplined standing armies, particularly in the Protestant—that is, largely Germanic Indo-European—nations. Bureaucrats and soldiers were cogs in the machinery of the state, enforcing its dictates. Keeping order within and endeavoring to expand territorial control at borders, the state could be a benevolent, if stern, paterfamilias to its producers and merchants. The sixteenth-century Reformation was pragmatically a reformulation from medieval baronial political-economic structure to modern, centralized, bureaucratic states. That this reformulation did not require a religious reformation is shown by those German states, such as Bavaria, that remained Catholic while transitioning to modern secular bureaucratic structure.

State power was greatly enhanced when the state became, by default, enforcer of moral behavior. Without the apparatus of church surveillance, town fathers and civil officials had to decree the limits of acceptable behavior and punish transgressors. Secular authority also had to take care of the poor, the sick, and the orphans, defining who merited its care. It is interesting to see how Protestant congregations and then, as they became established, Protestant state churches took over these civic obligations. Protestant rulers even instituted their own inquisitions, arresting and torturing dissidents—John Calvin had a rival reformer, Michael Servetus, burned at the stake in Geneva. Max Weber emphasized Protestantism's promulgation of self-discipline, but the discipline wielded by Protestant governments was the stronger, because it hit every resident, regardless of their personal beliefs. Thus, by deposing what could be (though seldom was, due to the interlocking aristocracy) an alternative authority—the Roman Church—the Protestant Reformation promoted singular centralized authority, the basis of modern states.

Connection between Protestant state and modern army is clearly seen in the English Civil War of 1642–48 and the restoration of King Charles II in 1660. Protestants protesting Catholic king Charles I's disregard of Parliament raised several local armies commanded, in medieval style, by aristocrats. Coordinating these as "Parliament's army" proved difficult, so leaders proposed merging the troops into a new national army. Initially, all existing officers (aristocrats) were to resign and the ranks of officers filled without regard to civilian status, but this principle had to be compromised to obtain Parliament's approval. The New Model Army, as it was formally named, was organized on a rational plan of regiments of infantry armed with muskets or pikes and cavalry armed with pistols and swords, plus an artillery unit. Instead of leaving soldiers to forage for food, they were to be paid a daily wage. Command staff included an officer to supervise procurement and distribution of supplies and a scoutmaster-general to manage military intelligence. Oliver Cromwell emerged from the New Model Army Command as its best military strategist, taking the title "lord protector"—the republican equivalent of king—of England in 1653. After Cromwell died in 1658, his successor, who was his eldest son, failed to lead, and in 1660, Charles II was restored as king. Charles continued the innovation of an English standing army, ritually disbanding the New Model Army in 1661, only to immediately reconstitute it as England's army.

Protestant states assumed that wars can be justified. It was during the sixteenth and seventeenth century that philosophers and theologians laid out principles for "just war"—that is, justification for war—principles that had been debated by Cicero, among Romans, and formulated by Thomas Aquinas in the thirteenth century. A just war should be in response to an aggressor, should be carried out by legitimate governing authority, should aim to restore an equitable peace, and should not harm noncombatants. None of this can be found in the words of Jesus of Nazareth, who repudiated war; if scriptural validation is sought, it can only be by inference from the Old Testament and the books of the New Testament written after the Gospels. There were, and are, Protestant sects, notably Quakers, abjuring war under any circumstances, but these are a tiny minority of professed Christians, and many were persecuted by the majority. Compatible with Luther's preaching, Protestant rulers believed it was their God-appointed duty to impose law and order upon all their subjects. Aggrandizement for mercenary ends might be wrong, but to extend lawful rule was justified. Protestant states carried out sectarian wars—for example, the devastating Thirty Years' War (1618–48) against Catholic states. They carried out civil wars such as England's (1642–51), and they invaded and subjugated overseas lands from Ireland to America. Over and over, they justified their wars as Christian missions.

PROTESTANT MILITANCY

Martin Luther was the man for the time, son of a commoner family owing its prosperity to mining and business. He handed territorial princes a theologically valid reason to break with Rome, and during the Peasants' War confirmed their authority. The Peasants' War provoked Luther to call for bloody repression, urging everyone to "smash, strangle, and stab" the "gangs of peasants."[3] Commentators have excused this most unChristian exhortation by supposing that Luther's focus on salvation carried with it a lack of concern over earthly conditions of life. This may be true, yet Luther's passionate cry for violence fits his Germanic heritage. A nineteenth-century German historian declaimed, on the occasion of celebrating Luther's birth, that he had "this power of overwhelming anger and this intensity of pious faith . . . this profound mysticism and this *joi de vivre*, this uncouth roughness and this tenderheartedness . . . We Germans do not find any of this an enigma, we simply state: this is blood of our blood. Out of the deep eyes of the unspoiled German peasant son flashed the ancient 'Teutonic heroism which does not seek to escape from the world but seeks to dominate it through the power of the moral will.' "[4]

Luther saw the world a battlefield between godly men and Satan, and himself heroically embattled. His intemperate vituperations sound like the rage of the *berserker*, the Germanic warrior who fights like a bear, ferociously, carried away by lust for blood. Luther's character epitomized Germans' ideal, making him an icon of German nationalism. Embodying that persistent Indo-European battle-ax ideology,[5] Luther reinforced its manifestation in Protestantism.

Germany in the sixteenth century, and indeed until Bismarck in 1871 united 25 principalities and free cities under a kaiser, was not a state but a conglomeration of territories using dialects of German and more or less acknowledging the "Holy Roman Empire of the German Nation" with its emperor *elected* by its princes. The adjective "German" signified its difference from French-speaking polities equally descended from Charlemagne's eighth-century Frankish Holy Roman Empire. Lacking political unity compelled the German principalities and imperial cities to use claims of common heritage to sanctify their Holy Roman Empire of the German Nation; hence Luther's remarkable translation of the Bible into a vernacular furnished a means and symbol for the Holy Roman Empire of the German Nation. For Germans, Protestant Reformation repulsed Roman domination just as their forebears had done a thousand years before; the parallel became well known when a new edition of Tacitus's descriptions of the Germanic tribes appeared in 1515. Brave, stalwart, strong, and indomitable in battle, Germans had held the Roman Empire at the Rhine. Once again, the warrior ethos echoed in Luther's challenges could resist the foreign power.

Looking back from today, six generations after Bismarck's unification of Germany and two world wars where "Germany" was the enemy power, it is difficult to see how fragmented "Germany" was until 1871. That political fragmentation underscores the importance of the Germanic ideology and remembered heritage in maintaining a sense of unity, a peoplehood (*Volk*). Luther's translation of the Bible and a barrage of printed pamphlets and books in the sixteenth century furnished a common language among the Germanic dialects. In that Luther's sermons and voluminous other writings circulated widely through the Germanic-speaking regions, the Protestant faith fostered their sense of a German community. The medium that proselytized the faith simultaneously reinforced the ideology of battle that Luther expostulated. To be Protestant was to gird for battle against Catholics, sinners, infidels, Turks, Jews, peasants, witches, dissidents—to raise an army against the Foe, the Antichrist. This is not to deny that Catholics, infidels, Turks, and peasants likewise waged wars; the point is that the militancy embedded in Indo-European culture, and specifically its Germanic glorification of the battlefield, persisted as strongly through Luther's Reformation as it had through Constantine's acceptance of Christianity.

COMPETITION

One face of Indo-European militancy is the armed horde bearing down upon the enemy. Its other face, the obverse of the first, is opposition to others. Glorification of battlefields will have no truck with diplomatic compromise. As Thomas Hobbes put it when he translated his *Leviathan* into Latin, if not for social contracts, men would naturally live antagonistically, *bellum omnium contra omnes* (war of all against all). To live in this Indo-European world, boys are encouraged to pit themselves against other boys, to play at war and compete to be top dog. Teamwork might be the best way to compete against opponents, still focusing on coming out on top. Looking at medieval guilds and merchants' associations, for example the Hanseatic League, what appear to be cooperative organizations can be seen, from an

Indo-European worldview, to be strategies to best opponents. Guilds aimed to prevent outsiders from entering production in the local market, and merchants' associations won privileges from rulers and protected their members from lawlessness. These strategies allowed members to compete with one another for the market.

Social historian Robert Wuthnow described Reformation leaders as "Competitors . . . at war with one another, struggling to assert the priority of their own ideas and to see these ideas adopted in wider segments of the larger movement. The image of war is indeed apt, for one sees all the tactical maneuvers, skirmishes, and escalation of conflict usually associated with physical battle . . . [and] efforts to gain allies, stake out rhetorical positions, launch attacks, and engage in counterattacks."[6]

Battlelines included positions on tolerance; appointed hierarchies versus democratic participation; and integration, or refusal of it, with state authorities, as well as theological interpretations. One persisting thorn was whether it is Christian to profit through commerce transactions, generally seen to involve competition between sellers and between buyers. If profit-seeking is moral, to what degree is the good Christian expected to use his profits for the good of fellow Christians?

Protestants debated the propriety of working for wealth. Puritans in Massachusetts Colony were ready to excommunicate businessmen who sold goods at high profit. Families who did well economically were enjoined to help less fortunate. Massachusetts, after all, was designed to be a commonwealth, where government by citizens promoted the "common weal" (well-being). The critical feature was that commonwealths were bounded. They had rules for admitting persons to citizenship, and could outcast transgressors. Those outside the commonwealth were competitors, godless and therefore without rights—Richard Tawney remarked that Massachusetts Puritans quoted scripture when enforcing fair dealing among themselves, while disregarding it in taking land from Indians.[7] Puritan commonwealths, Calvin's Geneva or Massachusetts Colony, were embattled redoubts zealously persecuting dissenters and backsliders from their rigid discipline. The New England Puritans tried to convert Indians into baptized workers, definitely second-class citizens compared to the English, and waged brutal war against Indian sachems daring to resist. Too small to maintain standing armies, the colonies relied on militia to keep their expanding borders, but even militia required some outlay of public monies. The Calvinist doctrine of hard work without any reward of luxury channeled productivity into the commonwealth.

At the same time that Puritans built commonwealths, they rejected communism. Instead of from each according to his ability, to each according to his need, from communal resources, Puritans kept private property as the foundation of their economies. They assumed their citizens would strive to expand their properties, and that frequently such desire would produce conflict. Puritan towns spent a great deal of time discussing how to reconcile Christian love with individuals' pursuit of gain. They regulated not only prices, wages, and business practices but also expenditures by forbidding "men and women of meane condition" from wearing extravagant and expensive fashions—which were permitted to "gentlemen . . . of greater estates, or more liberall education."[8] Preserving social class distinctions in this way was meant to maintain harmony; the need perceived for sumptuary laws reveals the instability built into the authoritarian Puritan colony by its coupling of private property with its ethic of hard work, producing opportunity for lower-class entrepreneurs to gain status through wealth.

Competition for land and business fostered aggressive individualism, however much the Massachusetts Bay Colony promoted the ideal of a united commonwealth. The aggression seething within the colony erupted horribly in its 1637 Pequot War and its 1676 war against the Wampanoags (King Philip's War). Indiscriminate slaughter, with Indian survivors sold into slavery into the West Indies, nearly exterminated the native nations. To the Indians, the Puritans would have appeared very like the battle-ax-wielding Indo-European invaders of Europe four millennia earlier and the Germanic hordes marauding across Roman frontiers.

CHAPTER 6

⸺✦⸺

CAPITALISM

The militant Christian Right and American capitalism are like Siamese twins, joined at the hip and sharing vital organs. Max Weber hypothesized that Calvinist Protestantism begot modern capitalism from its work imperative and ethic of deferred gratification. It wasn't that simple, as a plethora of historians and sociologists have demonstrated with examples of capitalism in German states that remained Catholic—Counter-Reformation Catholic, to be sure— or debates about defining capitalism. To pursue the linked American Christian Right and capitalism, I'll take these characteristics to identify capitalism:

- a money economy—that is, commodities exchanged for specie
- economic structure with opportunities to profit by investing money
- economic opportunities for individuals to profit and for individuals to join together in profit-seeking corporations

Additional characteristics commonly occur in capitalist societies, including stratified social classes and markets. Competition is thought, by some economists, to be inherent in capitalism; be that as it may, an outlook for expansion seems to mark capitalists.

Beginning with the not-yet-Christian Norse who tried to colonize eastern Canada in 1000 CE, America was invaded by waves of European capitalists. It is particularly significant that Columbus's mythologized "discovery of America" happened only 25 years before Martin Luther kicked off Protestantism with his 95 Theses. Columbus's first voyage was financed with money and holdings confiscated by Spanish monarchs Isabel and Ferdinand from Spain's Jewish and Moorish residents (Columbus set sail at dawn the day after the last Jews departed from Cadiz harbor). Twenty-five years after Columbus began pillaging the Caribbean, Spain was rebuilding its economy with American gold, soon to be enormously augmented by Cortés's overthrow of Aztec Mexico (1521) and Pizarro's conquest of Tawantinsuyu, the Inca empire, in 1533. For two centuries, treasure galleons sailed with bullion from America to Spain's court. This pattern of extracting resources from the Americas to ship to European courts extended from Spain to Portugal and France—nations that remained Catholic.

By contrast, the Holy Roman Empire of the German Nation had neither real imperial power nor American possessions. German states in the politically fragmented "nation" had to encourage merchants to bring in money. The windfall gained by German (and English) rulers taking over ecclesiastical possessions at the beginning of the Reformation was a one-time coup strengthening the Protestant states at that critical juncture to continue independent of Catholic power. For the longer term, they had to foster economies that would produce taxes.

England was the major Protestant contender against Catholic imperial regimes. Queen Elizabeth I commissioned privateers to harass competing shipping, with Francis Drake making the most spectacular voyage around the Americas to reach Spanish California, continue northwestward along the Pacific coast, then out across the Pacific, eventually completing a circumnavigation of the world via Africa and back to England (1580). Although Drake and his crew seized several Spanish treasure ships, bringing Elizabeth an enormous gift of gold and other wealth, sending out pirates could not be a long-term strategy. Elizabeth's successors, the Catholic Stuarts, instead encouraged capital investment projects, beginning with Jamestown in Virginia in 1607, succeeding the first, unsuccessful Virginia colony at Roanoke, 1585–87. England (more formally, Britain, and legally, the Crown) claimed dominion over all North America by right of Francis Drake's circumnavigation and landing in California in 1579. The Crown granted territory and certain rights, for example, for commercial exploitation and governance, to investment groups, generally by issuing legal documents called charters. The Crown hoped to profit from its citizens' business successes leading to further business ventures, in addition to receiving revenues from shipping duties and other transactions. To this end, Britain favored agribusiness plantations, in Ireland as well as the Caribbean and America, rather than small family farms. In North America, collecting and exporting furs was an alternative business requiring capital investment in ships, agents (traders), and trade stock—not only in Canada, where the northern climate ruled against agribusiness and luxury furs were obtainable, but also in Carolina, where finely tanned deer hides had been a precontact major trading product; export of skins handsomely paid the English proprietors of the chartered companies.

John Locke (1632–1704) was the great spinmeister for Protestant Britain, so great a rhetorician that his treatises are taught as philosophy. Seen in the context of his employment by the Earl of Shaftesbury, first lord of trade in 1672–76, and then a leader of opposition to Charles II, Locke's treatises are elegant arguments for Protestant capitalist policies. Most of his principal writings were published after the "Glorious Revolution" of 1688 reestablished Protestant domination of England. Locke supported property in land as the basis of value, declared that ownership of land depended upon a written title that could be exchanged for money, and stated that input of labor raised the value of land. His elaborately detailed exposition is couched in universalist terms[1] but clearly relates to the debates of his time over the legitimacy of two contemporary movements, enclosing common lands in Britain and taking over American First Nations' territories. Enclosures took away peasant village commons and resources in forests, heaths, and fens, turning the lands into agribusiness enterprises by aristocrat estate landlords. Sometimes the labor "improvements" took the form of tearing down peasant buildings to make pastures for wool-producing sheep. A major result of enclosures was displacement of rural workers, forcing them onto the roads, as the phrase went, and into low-wage manual labor in mines, on farms, on docks, and in proto-industrial manufacturing such as weaving. Earlier in the seventeenth century, venture capitalists invested in North American colonization to produce raw materials such as cheap food for Caribbean plantation slaves, naval stores, and tobacco. By the end of the century, the number of landless, unaffiliated laborers in Britain frightened the upper class into looking at America as dumping ground for the mother country's "surplus" population—not only Australia but also Georgia Colony were sent shiploads of convicts.

Locke's neat trick of specifying that title to land rested on written title exchangeable for money nicely excluded all the Indian nations in Anglo America from any legal right to their territories. (Locke had no reason to discuss Mexican First Nations, which did have written titles to land and used money. In the sixteenth century, many Mexican native lords produced these documents to claim rights to their ancestral estates.) There can be no question that John Locke molded England's economic, and particularly colonial, policies: he had been secretary to the lords proprietors of Carolina Colony in 1669–75 and served as secretary-treasurer to Britain's Council for Trade and Plantations in 1673–74 and again beginning in 1696, when the council was reorganized as the Board of Trade (formally, "His Majesty's Commissioners for Promoting Trade of this Kingdom and for Inspecting and Improving His Plantations in America and Elsewhere"). Locke personally invested in Carolina Colony and the African slave trade. With his patron Shaftesbury, he wrote the rules for governance in Carolina, creating (on paper) a hierarchy of feudal estates. Like the Enclosure Acts in Britain, the legal structure for Carolina strengthened a landed aristocracy, autocratically dispossessing people whose communities had worked the land for millennia. In seventeenth-century America, it bought into precontact Indian slave trading and augmented it with raiding for captives to be sold. Indians, proving poor workers under conditions of European-bossed slavery and unable to survive on tropical Caribbean plantations, were being replaced by Africans by the end of the seventeenth century.

The "Protestant ethic" was piously intoned in the Treatises of Government,

As much land as a man tills, plants, improves, cultivates, and can use the product of, so much is his property . . . God and his [man's] reason commanded him to subdue the earth . . . He gave it to the use of the industrious and rational (and labour was to be his title to it).[2]

Employed workers, whether enslaved, indentured, or legally free, had no right to profit from their labor. With the assertion that "the turfs my servant has cut . . . become my property without the assignation or consent of any body,"[3] Locke appropriated the virtue of labor to the master. God in his infinite goodness shouldn't care who profits from tilling, planting, and cultivating.

"Agrarian capitalism" is the name given to agribusiness. For Locke, it was a policy to perpetuate the English political structure that gave gentility to his impecunious country family. Enclosure continued the feudal relationship of estate owners over tenants, a relationship he and Shaftesbury planned to establish in their retrogressive structuring of Carolina Colony. Locke's emphasis on tilling the soil—regardless of who actually labors in the field—privileges landed property over other forms of wealth. His own behavior reveals the degree to which his treatises were political propaganda, for in 1672, he invested in a Bahamas company but chose to not improve his land, heeding advice from a brother of one of the lords proprietors of Carolina that he should simply hold the property until he could sell his company stock at a profit.[4] Joint-stock companies were, in fact, the rule for English colonization in America. Neither "agrarian capitalism" nor "mercantilism," conventionally said to be the dominant economic form for seventeenth-century western Europe, describes English and Dutch business mode in this early modern period. These two small Protestant nations looked to their seaports for economic growth and to consortia of businessmen and wealthy landowners for capital to develop ports and shipping. Already in the 1480s, entrepreneurs in Bristol outfitted ships to fish the great cod banks of the north Atlantic, probably the Grand Banks off Newfoundland, as a correspondent of Columbus reminded him after that "Admiral of the Ocean Sea" boasted of his 1492 discovery. By Locke's time, chartered companies such as the 1660s Carolina and 1670 Hudson's Bay Company were primarily venture capitalism.

Both England's southern colonies (the southern United States and the Caribbean), which were based on plantation agribusiness, and the northern colonies organized by Puritan yeomen initially faced major threats from First Nations. Land was not free for the taking. Settlements had to be garrisoned. Thus the cost of defense was added to the costs of ship transportation and supplies of tools and clothing for colonists, obviously a considerable capital outlay. To reduce cost, rather than purchasing and transporting large supplies of food from the homeland, proprietors assumed that colonists would buy or seize food from the aborigines. Advancing the frontier from the seaboard colonies again would require capital investment in weapons and transportation, tools and clothing. The result was capitalist speculation in land, in laying out towns, in transportation routes, and in selling supplies to settlers who would bear the major costs of colonization. During the nineteenth century, the US government sold land cheaply to pass the costs of territorial expansion on to investors, many of whom bought huge tracts to divide into parcels to sell. The 1862 Homestead Act, passed early in the Civil War when

Southern secession removed planters' opposition to reducing land speculation, gave western land to homesteaders who "improved" and lived on it. Similar generosity had been the United States' means of rewarding armed forces veterans, beginning with those from the American Revolution. After the Civil War, railroad developers continued the practice of initiating towns and selling parcels from the six-mile-wide rights-of-way granted them by the government, and they and their banking associates profited from homesteaders defaulting on high-interest-rate loans, taking the debtors' farms with their improvements.

American land policy was framed in capitalist terms almost from the very beginning of Anglo colonization. In 1618, the Virginia Company decreed that every person who came to Virginia at their own expense, or paid for others' passages, could claim a "headright" of fifty acres per passenger. A well-to-do investor might pay for any number of indentured servants, and even slaves, and build a large plantation from the consolidated headrights of the laborers whose work he owned. When in 1622 the British Crown dissolved the Virginia Company on grounds of mismanagement, and Virginia became a Crown colony, headright continued. Carolina Colony used the same principle, varying the headright claim between twenty and eighty acres. A prospering planter in these colonies could expand his enterprise by having his agent in London send over another batch of indentured servants, each then adding fifty acres to the Virginia plantation or to a new plantation their owner or his associates might develop. Indentured servants who had completed their indenture term could become sharecroppers or tenants on their former master's, or another's, estate, or purchase from one, or from a speculator's claim in the frontier region, or squat on unoccupied land, gambling that no one with good legal title would contest their occupancy.

Against this Lockean economy based on private property in land was the purer mercantilism of producing and shipping raw materials in exchange for buying finished goods. The planters, of course, did produce tobacco, cotton, rice, and indigo to ship to Europe and bought European manufactures with their profits (or, strictly speaking, on credit with their London agents). The ease of expanding property by headright claims and opening plantations on the frontier, and the straight profits from land speculation, made better-off colonists prefer Locke's ideas. From the standpoint of London, such an economy brought two serious problems: it allowed considerable freedom to the distant, more or less self-sufficient colonists, and it precipitated Indian wars. The Crown was quite aware that its claim to all of America from sea to sea, derived from Francis Drake's circumnavigation, was tenuous in the international arena where Spain and France based claims on sixteenth-century settlements, and in America where First Nations were increasingly coming to understand Europeans' irrational notion that individuals could own bounded parcels of land, and meant to own theirs. London saw its interests best fulfilled by encouraging trading with Indians, letting them produce valuables such as furs and fine deerskins to sell for what Europeans considered cheap— metal kettles and utensils, coarse cloth, and glass beads. The Crown gained by taxing revenues. Its garrisons were more to confront Spanish and especially French excursions than to protect against Indians, to deal with whom the Crown sent diplomatic parties to make treaties. War with France bounced along through most of the eighteenth century until conquests in Canada gave Britain power to conclude it on favorable terms in 1763. Then the Crown was forced to declare a policy on colonization. It did so in the Royal Proclamation of 1763, establishing all public land to belong to the Crown and that west of the Alleghenies to be Indian territory, to be exploited only by licensed traders under Crown regulation. After the American Revolution, the United States continued the principle of dominion over "unclaimed" land west of Euro-American settlement, a principle that necessarily involved negotiating with First Nations. The British Crown's clash between a purely exploitive mercantilism and a Lockean privileging of private property in land continued to foment dissension in America after the Revolution.

CAPITALISM BEFORE INDUSTRIALIZATION

Puritan dominance of New England gave a peculiar slant to American capitalism. Coming from an England struggling with strong-willed Henry VIII's legacy of Protestantism, now under a Catholic king, the Massachusetts Puritans wanted to create a commonwealth covenanting with the Reformation's God. The very concept of a covenant has a business ring to it: it is a contract. The norm for Massachusetts Colony settlement was a business venture financed by a capitalist selling shares in a town. The entrepreneur selected "unoccupied" land, hired surveyors to lay out lots, negotiated with Indian neighbors, recruited families and skilled workers—including by advertising with printed tracts—and appointed or hired a manager. Some of the settlers (or their parents) had invested in the town corporation and could participate in its governance through the town meeting, which was usually restricted to shareholders. Most of the settlers could not, and were liable to be outcast if their behavior failed to conform to the town's demands, although tolerance often was shown to those with needed skills such as iron-working. The New England town was democratic only as a corporation is a democracy of shareholders.

Because labor was scarce in American colonies, the European model of yeoman farmers employing servants and seasonal laborers could not become common. New Englanders imported indentured servants and slaves, sometimes buying New England Indians who had been sold to West Indies plantations and then resold into their homelands. Farm productivity was diminished by a harsh climate (the Little Ice Age had begun) and hilly, stony, and nutrient-poor land outside a few major river valleys. The English ideal of the yeoman citizen, independent because he owns or rents his farm free of any servile obligation (i.e., paying quit-rent instead of fulfilling feudal duties), had to be modified in the colonies because indentured servants were free once their seven years or so of obligation were over, and few remained servants when recruiters sought settlers for new towns. If the settler could not make a go of his farm, he could try another farm or find work in the new town, rather than establishing long-term employment with his original master.

Southern colonies were originally more like the West Indies than New England, in that their proprietors openly sought profits; though piously mentioning spreading Christianity to the heathens, they didn't provide for missionaries. With climate and topography generally favoring agriculture on the scale of plantations, they managed the labor problem by importing slaves to supplement indentured servants, and as the latter left after their terms, the efficiency of relying on permanent bondsmen reduced planters' interest in paying passage for European labor. Plantations are capital intensive, out of the reach of the usual freed indentured servant, leading these to squat on marginal lands or respond to recruiters for new frontier ventures. There was less need for free skilled workers as plantation owners trained slaves to do blacksmithing, carpentering, sewing, and other crafts. Class differences were more pronounced in the South, capitalism more blatant, than in New England before the American Revolution. Nevertheless, what met the eye exaggerated social difference, for if Massachusetts Puritans denounced silks and laces, a discerning taste noticed the fine cloth and tailoring of sober Puritan leaders. Class distinctions as well as capitalist economies pervaded all the Anglo colonies.

Markets were very much a part of the colonies. Most everyday needs were produced locally, because long-distance roads were expensive to build and maintain. Local though they might be, tools and supplies were bought with money, and itinerant peddlers brought the market to farms and village homes. Thomas Jefferson's ideal yeoman farmer would be self-sufficient in regard to raising grain, vegetables, fruit, and livestock, and might wear homespun, but he and his wife would buy implements for farm and household, cloth, dishes, some furniture, and a few good books. Scrabbling a bare living out of a forest clearing should be only a matter for a first year or two on the frontier. Land speculators and town founders who pushed the frontier westward lived in a market economy and very much desired extending markets by investing capital in roads (sometimes toll roads), bridges, and waterway improvements, including canals. They built and operated steamboats and barges early in the nineteenth century, then railroads by midcentury, carrying manufactures, food, lumber, minerals supplied by rural producers, and passengers who often were engaged in commerce. A thorough market economy was slow to develop because it depended on developing transportation for bulk shipments beyond the capacity of Indian trading trails and canoes, but the drive toward a market economy was there from the earliest Anglo settlements.

Over and above colonization along an ever-moving western frontier, integral to the United States' strategy to dominate the continent for military security and a growing capitalist economy, there were major capitalist enterprises along the Atlantic seaboard. Southern plantations are one obvious type, selling food, cotton, and tobacco to the Caribbean and Europe. The fur trade, especially beaver pelts, was another transatlantic commerce involving heavy capital outlay and management. Timber and naval stores, not to mention cotton canvas sails and hemp rope, were big business in this age of wooden ships. Shipping itself soon became the really important commercial enterprise in New England, with captains from that region carrying on the triangular trade to the Caribbean, or round Cape Horn to China and back; whalers also sailed thousands of miles to bring back thousands of tons of whale oil for lamps and industry. Shipping on this global scale meant the American colonies were definitely capitalist.

Historian Jon Butler noticed that with the third generation in the colonies, after about 1680, communities began to build substantial churches. The first two generations, in Massachusetts as well as in less religious colonies, met for worship in unpretentious structures. When, with three generations of residents, towns and trade had developed a sense of stability, congregations wanted to exhibit—and advertise—their material blessings through impressive architecture. New Englanders employed professional builders to erect tall wooden edifices, middle colonies to construct substantial ones in brick or stone, and southern colonies in stucco over wood. Interiors were beautifully finished with fine woodwork, brass, and velvet. Southern and middle colonies were assisted by the Anglican Church in England after a 1692 decree established the state church in the colonies, supporting trained ministers and, beginning at the turn of the eighteenth century, using the Society for the Propagation of the Gospel in Foreign Parts and the Society for Promoting Christian Knowledge to send books and guidance. Handsome churches reflected handsome homes of southern planters and northern businessmen, higher social classes using congregational membership to differentiate themselves from hoi polloi who could not afford to buy pews or donate to church building campaigns.

When the thirteen colonies revolted in 1776, the "triangular trade" carrying rum and sugar from Caribbean island plantations to Britain, manufactured goods from Britain to West Africa, then African slaves to the Caribbean, was well established—in 1632, Charles I had chartered a company of London investors to transport slaves from Africa. Virginia exports of tobacco and hemp sometimes made a fourth port of call for triangular-trade ships, and an alternative for rum processed in the Caribbean was to take sugar to New England rum mills to produce a superior liquor. Victory in the Revolution opened opportunities for American vessels to extend trade to China, formerly the exclusive privilege of Britain's East India Company. Ships would visit British Columbia to trade for furs that they brought to China, returning with Chinese luxury goods. Although rum, fine silks, and china are hardly necessities, demand in America and Britain was great enough to yield fortunes to astute New Englanders, money that could be invested in land speculation or, as the nineteenth century opened, in industrialization.

"Industrialization" was a trend in early modern nations to control goods production by managing labor. Initially, it took the form of putting-out, organizing cottage households to work enough, and regularly enough, to have ready a set quantity of the product to sell to the jobber when he came to collect. How many people in the household worked, how often each worked was their business. The jobber likely provided credit and raw material so the household could work without much interruption for subsistence farming and could pay rent to its landlord. Putting-out was decentralized industrialization; it did not require much initial capital outlay since the laborers worked in their own buildings. For the laborer, it was quite a shift from a household economy dependent on its own food and cloth production managed by the farming couple—or on waged agricultural labor, perhaps with a small house made available—to dependence on a market and management by an entrepreneur. The next step, to centralized production in factories, hugely transformed landscapes, but in terms of labor arrangement, it was not so radical. It was a logical step in rationalizing manufacturing. Profits from shipping allowed this logical step to materialize by building factories. Southern planters had another strategy for wealth, investing in more cotton, tobacco, or rice acres and more slaves to work them, moving west as soil was depleted. Both North and South had businessmen engaged in profiting from selling slaves: both increased land speculation.

What would Jesus do if he visited America around 1800? The nation professed Christianity, from time to time in Great Awakening enthusiastic outpourings of piety. But day to day? Slaves were dehumanized, treated like livestock. Social classes were only too obvious in the refinement of the upper and the long hours of labor for the lower. Violence was every day, schoolmasters and parents whipping children, husbands beating wives, drunks brawling, even duels such as the one in which Aaron Burr killed Alexander Hamilton. Indians were being dispossessed still in the former colonies and on the frontier where President Jefferson's policy of trading with them on credit to drive them into debt underlay ostensibly legal treaties, wherein selling their land settled the demand for debt payment. The millennia-old Indo-European cultural pattern of competition and its doppelgänger, conflict, had crossed the Atlantic and flourished.

CHAPTER 7

————⚬✦⚬————

ANTEBELLUM AMERICA

For Indo-European culture-bearers, wars are the greatest events, the turning points of history. Americans label the first 62 years of the nineteenth century the antebellum period. The Civil War was the breaking point in a century-long contest between an agrarian capitalist South and a mercantile-industrial North. More to the point here, a professedly Christian nation threw millions of men and money into the most horribly devastating Armageddon ever seen on this continent.

Before the Armageddon, a determinedly expanding nation invented the slogan "manifest destiny." Somewhat surprisingly, this sentiment didn't appear until 1845. It was a newspaperman, John O'Sullivan, who popularized the notion that America obviously has been destined to cover the continent.[1] O'Sullivan favored conquering Mexico to achieve our destiny; other Americans could not see why we should take over a neighboring Christian (albeit Catholic) country. We didn't have California, but we did have access to the Pacific in Oregon Territory, ours in 1846 through a negotiated settlement with Britain dividing what had been jointly used. Americans had already begun settlement in Oregon, traveling with wagons and cattle the two thousand miles from the 1840s frontier in Missouri. The federal government spent millions between 1829 and 1860 for army engineers to construct, and protect with forts, wagon roads between Missouri and the Southwest, California, and the Northwest. Global commerce stimulated demand for these roads, for the alternative for linking Atlantic and Pacific trade was sailing entirely around South America, rounding dangerous Cape Horn near Antarctica. Although an ox team lumbers only ten miles a day, with an experienced drover it could make steady progress along the Platte Valley and through the Rockies at South Pass in Wyoming, thence along the Snake River to the Northwest, across Nevada to Sacramento, California, or southwest to Los Angeles. Suggestion for a transcontinental railroad came as early as 1832 and was formally presented to Congress in 1845. Steamboats were more immediately feasible, plying the Ohio, Mississippi, and Missouri

Rivers and reaching the head of navigation on the Missouri, Fort Benton, Montana, by 1860. The hope of a kind of Northwest Passage for shipping to the Orient via the Missouri died in the mid-nineteenth century when explorations failed to find any practical portage over the Continental Divide, nor were parallel efforts to go over the Santa Fe Trail up the Arkansas River successful in linking to the Colorado River and on to the Pacific. All these projects, culminating in transcontinental railroads in 1869, reflect an essential feature of capitalism: its need to expand. To do so, Christian America did not hesitate to wage war against Britain (1812), against Mexico (1846), and, continuously until the 1880s, against America's First Nations.

Antebellum America continued the pre-Revolutionary divergence between agrarian capitalism in the South and mercantile-industrial capitalism in the North, with land speculation arching over the two as the principal means to wealth in the United States. The South's growth is particularly interesting because history books let it be eclipsed by the North's industrialization—a good example of "Whig history," stories of the winner in political contests. Global-market enterprises from their seventeenth-century beginnings, reliant on shipping bulk commodities from deer hides to cotton, tobacco, rice, and indigo from Atlantic ports, Southern plantations required investment in land and in slaves to work the land. Immigrants who could not manage to obtain enough land to support a commercial enterprise settled on marginal uplands or migrated westward in hopes of squatting upon or purchasing better farms.

Fabled Daniel Boone exemplified the tough, manly wilderness hunter who led greenhorns and families through the Cumberland Gap in the Appalachians into rich valleys beyond. Boone came from a Quaker family of weavers in southern England who emigrated to Pennsylvania early in the eighteenth century, then farther inland to farm in North Carolina's Yadkin Valley. Daniel Boone (1734–1820) preferred hunting to farming. He and companions spent months hunting deer and beaver and harvesting wild ginseng, selling the pelts and dried ginseng to support their families. As they roamed the forests, they noted areas suited to agriculture, and could work for land speculators surveying plots with rod and chain. George Washington worked as a surveyor during the 1750s, and he, Benjamin Franklin, and Thomas Jefferson invested in companies to claim, survey, and sell western land. Boone settled his own family in Kentucky, and in 1799, in Missouri, while it was still Spanish territory. Much romanticized as a wilderness scout à lá James Fenimore Cooper's heroes, Boone was a businessman, albeit a poor one: he himself sold large tracts of land he and his employees had surveyed, and after the Revolutionary War when the United States and its states regularized property ownership, Boone was embroiled in numerous lawsuits over imprecise surveying, overlapping properties, improperly filed titles and deeds, and unpaid charges. Gilbert Imlay, a charming gentleman who, among other scandals, had a child with English political writer Mary Wollstonecraft and abandoned them, in 1785 bought ten thousand acres in Ohio on credit from Boone, promptly sold the tract, and kept the money. It was no satisfaction to Daniel Boone that Imlay, in England, published a description of the new country, his purported adventures in its wilderness, and exploits of his good companion Boone.

Emigration into the Piedmont and then across the mountains into the "Middle Ground," the eastern Midwest, was tiered: first the speculators employing men like Boone to claim and delimit huge acreages, then the actual settlers guided by agents. Boone built little colonies of cabins and operated a store and tavern in Kentucky and in West Virginia. Throughout his lifetime, he fought or negotiated with the region's First Nation, Shawnee. Settlers would retreat to small forts, waiting for truces. There were many battles, some with companies of regular troops sent by first the colonial, then the federal government, some with irregulars. Many frontiersmen in the Midwest in the eighteenth century acted like forty-niners in California in the mid-nineteenth century, indiscriminately shooting Indians like animals. One notorious incident was the wanton massacre and mutilation of an extended family of Shawnee belonging to the Mingo leader Tahgajute, called John Logan. Tahgajute was actually Iroquois. His first family was massacred, and he moved south into Shawnee territory, marrying a Shawnee woman. Then in 1774, his second family was killed when he happened to be away. Later in that year, when a truce was concluded on condition Shawnee allow Kentucky settlement, Logan dictated a letter charging that the war had been precipitated by the murders of his people, and closing with the tragic lines, "There runs not a drop of my blood in the veins of any living creature . . . Who is there to mourn for Logan? Not one."

Thomas Jefferson made "Logan's Lament" famous, the epitome of the fate of the vanishing red man. A subtext was that no one should blame the governments, state or federal, for outbreaks of war fomented by lawless vigilantes such as those who murdered Logan's family. Against condemnation of such dregs of society hanging out on the frontier, popular writing advanced a semimythical Daniel Boone (a Quaker, no less) shepherding hardworking families into the empty wilderness. The political reality was that Jefferson, more concerned with persuasive rhetoric than with truth,[2] intended to drive all Indians west of the Mississippi—gaining territory to place them there was one aim of his Louisiana Purchase, carried out, as he himself admitted, "sub silentio," without his ministers or Congress interfering. Ostensibly, Jefferson would have let the Indians become civilized citizens, but however much they adopted a farming or business way of life, they stood in the way of Jefferson's own people; Indians were competitors. A capitalist economy battles competitors. Antebellum America's capitalists waged bloody war against the continent's First Nations and Mexicans, determined to expand into their wide open spaces.

The South's agrarian capitalist expansion was driven by decrease in the fertility of their monocropped fields. Disdaining First Nations' sustainable practice of planting nitrogen-fixing beans in the same rows as nitrogen-depleting maize and pumpkins (the Iroquois's "Three Sisters"), Euro-Americans manured fields to restore fertility. A commercial plantation could not produce enough manure to maintain its large acreage; therefore, its owner had little choice but to move on to new land. In tandem with the custom of investment in land speculation, planters' need for virgin acres kept the Southern economy oriented toward ongoing westward colonization. This, ironically, kept up the market for slaves, allowing planters remaining in the East to get some profit by selling the natural increase in their slave population. Breaking uncultivated land or even hand-cultivated Indian fields was back-breaking labor best done by hapless slaves. The South's large number of rivers facilitated migrations of plantation households with their slaves, especially considering the planters wanted valley tracts. Jefferson remarked that the lack of towns in the South, compared to the North, was in part due to "our country being much intersected with navigable waters, and trade brought generally to our doors" rather than clustered in market towns.[3]

The steady push westward brought cotton planters as far as they could go, eastern Texas, by the 1840s. Farther west lay the arid southern plains, fit only for cattle. To the north were Yankees favoring an economy of family-worked farms using hired labor seasonally and spinning off its younger generations into commerce and industry, as well as westward homesteading. Southerners looked to expanding into the Caribbean and Mexico, familiar to many from visits and to some from investments in plantations, but being under foreign rule made both less attractive than America's West. During and after the Civil War, some Southern planters moved with a core of their slaves to Cuba, British Honduras, and other Caribbean regions suited to sugarcane production, particularly those planters already raising sugarcane in the United States.

Agrarian capitalism encourages experimentation with new crops and methods. Jefferson was more active an experimenter than most (generally in debt because money did not hinder him implementing his ideas), but George Washington also seriously worked at improving innovations. In this they were like their counterparts in Britain, the landed gentry who enacted the Enclosure Acts to further their more rational, scientific agriculture. Southerners used machinery (not only the cotton gin for rapidly processing cotton, but also mills for processing rice and indigo) and crops suited to lowland coastal plains that could be grown on the same plantations. Planters were eager to try such alien but commercially valuable crops, purchasing or exchanging seeds of recommended varieties. Britain's Royal Society for the Encouragement of Arts, Manufactures, and Commerce actively corresponded from London with Southerners about both plants and mechanical devices; its patronage was sought for an experimental garden in South Carolina not long after the society's founding in 1754. But cotton eclipsed any other agribusiness crop. Especially between the close of the War of 1812 and the Civil War, cotton exports constituted half the United States' export income. The global economy of the antebellum years kept cotton, and the slavery that cultivated it, dominant in the South.

Meanwhile, the North's rivers provided power for factories—"mills" using systems of shafts and belting developed from water-powered grain mills. A few were large purpose-built structures, as in Lowell, Massachusetts, financed by wealthy merchant investors; many were small, in barnlike buildings, organized by corporations of local farmers whose pooled capital diversified the local economy. Factories, large or small, drew on the "surplus" labor pool of women and children whose entry into waged labor did not disrupt the basic agricultural economy. They were paid less than a man's wage, on the grounds that they were not supporting families (whether or not a woman was, in fact, doing so), and households regarded the cash they brought in as supplementary to men's incomes from farming and artisan work. Given the poor soils of much of New England and competition between producers, women's and children's wages were often critical to maintaining a basic working-class standard of living.

Factory work introduced a mechanical discipline that Karl Marx and Friedrich Engels would recognize as alienating workers from the products of their labor. The point of factories was to increase the speed of production so that more goods were manufactured per unit of time, thus reducing the cost per unit and raising profit. Machines work faster than humans and machines can keep working around the clock. Machines do need tending, integrating humans into the production line subservient to the machine. Nineteenth-century factory workers came in at dawn and left about 12 hours later, 6 days a week. Tending machines was relentless and tedious—farm labor was physically exhausting and summer work days were long, but a person could lay down the scythe for a couple minutes without jeopardizing the production process. Not so in factories, where a moment's inattention might result in a breakdown-causing tangle. The term "wage slaves" was appropriate. As in early twenty-first-century China, antebellum northern American factories recruited thousands of young women from rural areas and housed them in barracks, demanding not only faithful labor but also chaste behavior outside of work. From the standpoint of work, the difference between these wage slaves and the legal slaves in the South was primarily that the Northern women and children could look forward to a degree of freedom when they married and created a household. There was, of course, truly a world of difference, in that free workers could not be beaten unmercifully, tortured, killed, or sold away from their loved ones.

Curiously, industrialization in the nineteenth century spurred provision of state-financed universal education. It was not so much a need for factory workers to read and write as a need to accustom workers to clock discipline. Education itself was industrialized early in the Industrial Revolution in England, notably in the Lancasterian system. Named after its founder, Joseph Lancaster, it began in 1798 in London as a means to bring literacy cheaply to poor children. Lancaster designed a large classroom rising toward the rear, with the master at a desk front and center on a platform. Windows were six feet above the floor, preventing idle looking out. Up to one thousand pupils could be accommodated with only one teacher by grouping the children according to their progress in reading and in arithmetic (separately grouped) and delegating instruction to more proficient children. Older students acted as monitors under orders from the teacher at the front, barking out words to be written on slates, then inspecting the work after each short set of words. Rigid discipline was enforced, not by beating—Lancaster was a Quaker and proud that his pupils were not beaten—but by such methods as tying the unruly child in a sack or raising him in a cage above the rows of desks. American business leaders and philanthropists thought the Lancasterian system a godsend, inculcating obedient subordination in the lower classes at one-seventeenth the cost of a conventional school (one paid teacher for one thousand pupils versus one for sixty pupils in traditional schools). Joseph Lancaster was brought to the United States in 1818 and spoke before Congress about the school he would create. In time, it became evident that the philanthropists supporting Lancasterian schools were getting what they paid for, bare literacy in resentful young workers.

Public education in Northern communities taught children to be obedient and work at routine drills imposed by middle-class supervisors. Most children left school at 12, later (early twentieth century) at 14. Except where immigrant communities brought teachers and commitment to maintaining their heritage, as did the large German settlement in Milwaukee, Wisconsin, American schools taught exclusively in English and explicitly taught patriotism. Protestant mores and belief were equated with Americanism. Even in the mid-twentieth century, all the children in a public school would sing, "Onward Christian Soldiers, Marching as to War, with the Cross of Jesus carried on before." Public schools were to be the melting pot wherein undisciplined farm kids and immigrant kids were simmered down into Americans as mass-produced and standardized as their factory outputs.

Early in the antebellum period, public education came through "Sunday Schools" organized by philanthropic groups of gentlemen in the northeast. They were not part of denominational education but were provided on Sunday to working children. A relatively liberal Protestant religion was taught as part of civic education, America being, without question, a Christian nation. Schools for the poor taught rote prayers, correct singing of hymns, orderly lines into and out of the classrooms, sitting still and quiet until called upon, and that cleanliness is next to godliness. Businessmen organizers and patrons of public schools developed in the 1830s from "Sunday Schools" and "infant schools" expected teachers to preach sanctity of private property and the moral rightness of authority wielded by the upper class over workers. There was in this a conscious effort to undercut the populism that had elected Andrew Jackson president.

REVIVALS

Against the imposition of class-based disciplines—bourgeois standards of dress, decorum, work ethic, and working-class subordination—religious revivals gave vent to emotions otherwise unseemly. Historians like to designate a mid-eighteenth-century Great Awakening as the first broadspread revival in America, and a Second Great Awakening for the first two-thirds of the nineteenth century. This fails to note the 1690s revivals in Massachusetts led by Congregationalist minister Solomon Stoddard, similar to contemporary German Pietist meetings stressing personal self-evaluation and conversion, a movement taken up in England as well. Stoddard's grandson Jonathan Edwards was a famous revival preacher in the 1730s and 1740s, and his grandson Timothy Dwight, president of Yale College, led revivals around the beginning of the nineteenth century. We can note that Americans were preoccupied with the secular matter of fomenting political revolution in the 1760s and 1770s, and with constructing a federal government in the 1780s. Saving private persons' souls took a backseat to these more urgent concerns. Once the United States was launched in the 1790s, people could again become prominent through religious evangelism. Timothy Dwight's preaching was part of an effort to continue state churches under the new republic, and when this conservative effort failed, he encouraged his students to work on building Protestant congregations and seminaries on the western frontier, then in Ohio and Kentucky. His student Lyman Beecher did so on the Ohio River at Cincinnati, where his large family included the next generation's most famous preacher, Henry Ward Beecher, and abolitionist novelist Harriet Beecher Stowe, as well as Catherine Beecher, who evangelized education for women and turned housekeeping into domestic science (explicated in the widely used manual she published). These lineages show both the tendency in "egalitarian" America for leading families to persist through generations and the differing issues that would excite them. A common denominator has been outreach to individuals, congruent with Protestantism's doctrine focusing on individual salvation through experience of conversion.

Equally American has been financial success attending revivals. George Whitefield, an English preacher who traveled around the colonies between 1738 and 1770, was depicted in one cartoon standing on a platform with a book raised in his left hand but his right hand holding a large bag labeled "Cash."[4] In 1756, he and Benjamin Franklin discussed a project to promote a colony on the Ohio for "the Publick Good" of strengthening King George's frontier. Considering the general favoring of land speculation in the West, doing well by doing good must have been in the minds of Franklin and Whitefield. Whitefield had earlier, in the 1740s, bought a plantation in Georgia to be a home for orphans—that is, White orphans—and bought slaves to work it. He had a steady income from the numerous books and pamphlets he wrote, using a very modern description of his own torments and tribulations to vivify his message of struggle toward salvation. Listeners were impressed and excited by his apparent extemporaneous, inspired speaking, unaware that he had memorized his effective texts. Whitefield died and was buried in Massachusetts, his coffin in a brick crypt attracting followers for half a century. If the lineage of Stoddard, Edwards, and Dwight carried weight in New England, Whitefield's seven lengthy crusades throughout the colonies set the pattern for celebrity evangelists.

Because so many heard Whitefield during his evangelical tours, many in the early Republic understood that rallies such as his were an effective means of preaching and swaying people toward more moral behavior. There was a religious revival in 1787 at a Presbyterian college in Virginia, triggered by a student experiencing spiritual conversion at a Methodist meeting. Although the Presbyterians would not condone emotional outbursts elicited by Methodists, the college president took up the student's enthusiasm, preaching with fervor. James McGready, a Presbyterian minister in North Carolina, attended some of these sermons and, having recently experienced spiritual rebirth after recovering from smallpox, was inspired to preach fervently to his own congregations. Moving to southern Kentucky a few years later, he attracted more and more worshippers to the summer "sacramental meetings" customary for Presbyterians. In 1800, he was assisted by several other ministers at these large gatherings, and one of the assistants brought along his brother who was a Methodist minister. McGready's preaching excited the crowd. The Methodist took advantage to go among the volatile throng, exhorting them "to let the Lord God Omnipotent reign in their hearts, and to submit to Him, and their souls should live." He "went through the house shouting and exhorting with all possible ecstacy and energy, the floor was soon covered with the slain"[5] (i.e., people who had fallen unconscious with emotion). Note the war metaphor.

Simultaneously with those of the allied Presbyterians and Methodists, Kentucky Baptists unleashed emotional rallies. Observers described the scenes as utterly chaotic, loud with cries of sinners overcome by their wickedness and of deliriously happy souls convinced of their redemption. Responsible estimates reported around ten thousand people at one meeting near Lexington, four to six thousand at others—this in what was still considered the western frontier, settled by farmers only a decade or two earlier. Of necessity, these thousands of people camped, since there were no accommodations for such multitudes in the small new villages. The revival movement exploded in August 1801, hosted by the congregation at Cane Ridge in central Kentucky. An outdoor platform shaded by a tent covering held a succession of preachers, supplementing others speaking in the local log church. As enthusiasm mounted during the week, yet more preachers began exhorting crowds by standing on logs (one was grateful to a friend who held an umbrella over his head to shield him from the Kentucky sun). Considering that listeners were packed closely in August heat, it isn't surprising that many fainted. Unbelievers attended, too, out of curiosity or to mock. Initially, Kentucky camp meetings featured a modified Calvinism, soft-pedaling Calvin's discouraging conviction that only God's mysterious gift of grace would give entry to heaven: that neither good works nor passionate prayer could save one's soul. The American version optimistically presumed that earthly ministers had opportunity to ready sinners to recognize and embrace God's offer of salvation. Revival meetings might be that moment.

Two years after the huge 1801 breakthrough meetings, some of the ministers who had preached there broke away from Calvinist Presbyterianism to found the Church of Christ, on the principle that salvation is open to everyone who seeks it. The Church of Christ was by no means the first

American denomination arising from dissatisfaction with European churches, for dissidents and Dissenters such as Quakers appeared even in the seventeenth century. What the Kentucky revival meetings introduced was a particularly American emphasis on individuals gathered en masse. In other words, preachers seemed to speak directly to each person, calling them up to the platform and then moving through the crowd, reaching out, ardently urging each individual to accept Christ and salvation—yet that individual stood in a crowd with thousands of others. Americans tout the freedom and power of the individual and affirm them in crowds. The 1801 Kentucky camp meetings came as the first generation of settlers saw themselves not so much as pioneers in a wilderness but as farmers who had cleared the wilderness and achieved statehood a decade previously. The tremendous crowds, tents, and wagons stretching for half a mile proved Kentucky was no longer a frontier. Not incidentally, American settlement had cleared more than a wilderness; it had cleared off the region's First Nations. Descriptions of camp meetings note a few Blacks (probably slaves) among the thousands of Whites, and nary an Indian.

Chaotic as the camp meetings were, they were wonderfully peaceful in the absence of drinking and fighting (offenders were outcast, as were couples taking advantage of the outdoor camping to engage in illicit sex). Love of God and Christ was proclaimed to be the rule of the day. Nevertheless, the Methodists' top bishop, Francis Asbury, recommended camp meetings to his ministers: "This is field fighting . . . The battle ax and weapon of war, it will break down walls of wickedness."[6] The war metaphor was used by another Methodist, a Maryland preacher named Benjamin Abbott, of whom it was recorded that after singing a hymn, as he began a prayer, his congregation experienced "the Lord pour[ing] out his Spirit and [slaying] them as men slain in battle. Some lay in the agonies of death, some were rejoicing in God, others were crying for mercy."[7] The Methodists' Lord was Indo-European.

JACKSONIAN AMERICA

Andrew Jackson's election in 1828 was seen as the sweeping out of the eighteenth century's genteel aristocratic leaders. Jackson's opponent, John Quincy Adams, was the son of Revolutionary War statesman and second president John Adams. The new president came from Irish immigrant parents settled on the Carolina frontier. Lacking formal education, Jackson made his career in the army, winning fame in Indian wars and commanding the Battle of New Orleans, fought two weeks after a peace treaty in Europe had concluded the War of 1812, the news not crossing the Atlantic until more weeks had past. Often pictured as a rough backwoodsman, Jackson epitomized the democratic spirit of America, land of opportunity. Opportunity knocks, looking for support. Henry Clay, congressman from Kentucky, urged an "American System" of governmental construction of roads and canals to transport goods and tariffs to protect American industries. The Battle of New Orleans had been waged to hold the huge Mississippi watershed's principal port, shipping out Midwest crops and importing slaves for the South's plantations. Tariffs would enable American manufacturers to compete in the domestic market against foreign imports, expanding both America's industrial capacity and its consumers. With adequate roads, canals, and ports, western farmers and eastern factory workers would sell to each other. President James Monroe in 1823 urged this "American System" and its corollary, recognizing Latin American republics that could enter America's expanding system. Warning European powers to keep off became the "Monroe Doctrine," arrogating to the United States the leading role, economic and political, in the Western Hemisphere. Clay, Monroe, and their colleagues pointed out that good transport routes facilitated movements of troops and armaments when enemies threaten, and they pushed for constructing a strong navy. The 1820s emphasis on building an integrated agricultural and industrial economy under federal leadership leads some historians to claim it was a "market revolution": a misnomer considering the colonies had always been capitalist and market-oriented.

Clay and his fellow congressman John Calhoun were from the western sections of Southern states, identifying with independent farmers rather than with wealthy plantation owners. The tariffs they advocated, and the national bank they promoted as means to assist investment in manufactures and western development, angered agribusiness planters who had to pay higher prices for goods they might have obtained at less cost from overseas sources. After all, ships taking cotton and indigo east across the Atlantic had to cross back for the next shipment, and loads of European products going west would overall reduce shipping costs. Crisis erupted in 1828, the year Jackson campaigned for the presidency, when South Carolina announced it would secede if everhigher tariffs were enacted. Jackson, Clay, Calhoun, and others committed to their American System mollified South Carolina by announcing a policy that would gradually lessen tariffs. The "nullification [of tariffs] crisis" indicates how capitalist development, not slavery, was the root of conflict between the North and the South: Southern agribusiness invested in land and slaves while federal policies aided industrial manufacturing and mass consumerism through selling public lands on the frontier to speculators who would bring in working families. To put it bluntly, South Carolinians were paying federal taxes, directly and indirectly, that benefitted other states.

As the nullification crisis indicates, the United States' successful weathering of the external threats centered on the War of 1812 moved the country toward internal schisms. Southern cotton production grew and grew, plantations migrating westward to new lands to keep yields profitable, so that in the antebellum period, cotton was America's largest and most valuable export—by 1860, two-thirds of her total export. Because cotton production depended on slave labor, the South drifted out of Western cultural trends during the nineteenth century. Britain and the United States had abolished the transatlantic slave trade in 1807, and Britain forbade slavery in 1833. The United States had, in 1787, set the Mason-Dixon Line (approximately the Ohio River) to divide the Southern slaveholding states from Northern states abolishing slavery. Missouri's petition to join the Union as a state in 1819 reopened the question of slavery in a nation committed to liberty. The "Missouri Compromise" of 1820 seemed to restore the 1787 balance, Missouri admitted as slaveholding but the Mason-Dixon Line extended along latitude 36° 30', with slavery prohibited in all territory north of that line. Politicians were satisfied. What they had done, obviously, was disunite the United States. The value of cotton, far above that of any other crop or American manufacture, made the South essential to American prosperity, while the North's shipping and merchandising expertise was essential to the South. Many observers of the time recognized that the South was more like the Caribbean colonies than like the US North, an observation making secession credible. By the late 1850s, a number of Southern leaders were urging that importation of slaves be reinstituted because not enough strong field hands were being bred on the American plantations.

Gradual industrialization in the North, entrenchment of slave plantations in the South; extension of the suffrage, reduction in price for public lands sold to settlers; the beginning of mass immigrations of European peasants when over a million Irish fled famine in the mid-1840s—these developments impinged on the America established by Enlightenment English gentlemen in the 1780s.

CHAPTER 8

MANIFEST DESTINY

America at mid-nineteenth century was a Protestant nation determined to dominate its continent. While slave-raised cotton was its principal export, its northern states invested in machinery and manufacturing. Their "American system"[1] focusing on mass production for mass consumption contrasted with European emphasis on fine craftsmanship for luxury markets. Toward this goal of mass production, factory owners such as Samuel Colt developed the assembly line where workers in sequence put together standardized machine-fabricated parts. Colt's guns fit nineteenth-century warfare, carried on by battalions of conscripts under professional military leadership. Discipline and obedience were imposed upon factory workers and soldiers alike, and eulogized as Christian virtues. Karl Marx, observing, was struck by the alienation of the worker from his work.

Britain's withdrawal after the War of 1812, France's withdrawal in 1763 after the Seven Years' War, and Spain's threat withdrawn by Mexico's independence in 1821 gave Americans a heady sense of unquenchable power. The New York newspaperman John O'Sullivan is credited with first popularizing the phrase "Manifest Destiny" in the July 1845 issue of the *Democratic Review*: "[I]n favor of now elevating this question of the reception of Texas into the Union . . . other nations have undertaken to intrude . . . for the avowed object of thwarting our policy and hampering our power, limiting our greatness and checking the fulfillment of our manifest destiny to overspread the continent allotted by Providence for the free development of our yearly multiplying millions."[2] Tellingly, O'Sullivan in midcentury invokes divine Providence where twenty years earlier, in 1824, John Quincy Adams had invoked Nature: "[T]he world shall be familiarized with the idea of considering our proper dominion to be the continent of North America. From the time when we became an independent people it was as much a law of nature that this should become our pretension as that the Mississippi should flow to the sea."[3] Enlightenment reasoning by patrician New Englanders like the Adams family had been overcome by fervent conviction that Americans were the true Chosen People, superseding the "ancient Israelites." Orators harped on the assertion that American expansion would carry "State after State coming into this great temple of freedom, and burning their incense upon an altar consecrated to the enjoyment of civil and religious liberty."[4] Another mid-1840s congressman made the Chosen People entailment clear, reminding his peers that if they wish to "extend the principles of civil liberty . . . they march pari passu [in step] with the migrations of the Anglo-Saxon race."[5]

This racist conviction made a crucial difference between 1840s America's two expansionist campaigns against Mexico and against British occupation of Oregon Territory. In spite of the slogan "54° 40' or Fight!," Americans could compromise on Oregon, splitting the Territory at the forty-ninth parallel, not only because pragmatically the land north of Puget Sound was not particularly wanted, but also because brother WASPs (White Anglo-Saxon Protestants) were colonizing it. Mexico, on the other hand, had been colonized by swarthy Catholics. In 1844, the *Illinois State Register* informed its readers that Mexicans were "but little removed above the negro."[6] The *Hartford Times* in 1845 urged Americans "to redeem from unhallowed hands a land, above all others favored of heaven, and hold it for the use of a people who know how to obey heaven's behests."[7] Congress heard, from one of its members, that "[t]here seems to be something in our laws and institutions, peculiarly adapted to our Anglo-Saxon-American race, under which they will thrive and prosper, but under which all others wilt and die . . . There is something mysterious about it; and, if accounted for, it can only be done on the principle that . . . they are not fitted for liberal and equal laws, and equal institutions."[8]

Mexico's resentment against US annexation of Texas, ratified by a vote of its inhabitants in July 1845, was magnified by US president Polk's encouragement of Californians to follow Texas's lead in rejecting Mexican rule. Diplomatic negotiations over the Texas issue were clouded by Polk authorizing seizure of San Francisco by American naval ships should war break out with Mexico, and ordering an American force to march, early in 1846, beyond Texas's southern boundary at the Nueces River to Matamoros on the Río Grande. When the Mexican officer commanding Matamoros challenged Americans positioned on the north bank across from the town, the American response was to blockade the river downstream to cut off the town. Two days later, on April 25, Mexican soldiers crossed the Río Grande and won a battle with the Americans. This was the "act of war" for which President Polk had been waiting. On May 13, 1846, Congress declared war.

As the campaigns progressed in 1847, American troops invading all the way to Mexico City, the slogan "Manifest Destiny" came to mean aggressive warfare. A senator expounded,

> I would not force the adoption of our form of Government upon any people by the sword. But if war is forced upon us, as this has been . . . I believe we should be recreant to our noble mission, if we refused acquiescence in the high

purposes of a wise Providence. War has its evils . . . but however inscrutable to us, it has also been made, by the Allwise Dispenser of events, the instrumentality of accomplishing the great end of human elevation and human happiness . . . It is in this view, that I subscribe to the doctrine of "manifest destiny."[9]

Public opinion, not long before hesitant to take over the degraded race to the south, was inflamed to the point that when Mexico accepted the Treaty of Guadalupe Hidalgo early in 1848, ceding California and New Mexico (present Arizona included) and accepting the Río Grande boundary with Texas, failure to insist on all of Mexico was deplored.

There are two components to America's nineteenth-century Manifest Destiny conviction. One is that the entire continent was destined to become a single nation, the United States of America. The second component was what half a century later was labeled by Rudyard Kipling as "the white man's burden." Writing for Britain's imperial conquest of India, Kipling glorified the imposition of the British raj as the duty of civilized White men to take up the burden of ruling inferior races. Astute commentators have noted that Kipling truly meant White men, male adults. Providence infused the Anglo-Saxon race with manly vigor. That manly vigor expressed itself in athletic prowess, hardheaded business success, and war. When conquest terminated a war, WASP men carried their manly vigor into dominating the races whose defeat proved the lower races' inability to govern. For Americans, the White man's burden was most prominently the task of emasculating American Indians, destroying their cultures through forbidding their languages and religions and removing their children to boarding schools. When General Grant became president in 1869, he used the manly vigor of his Civil War troops, and artillery, to once and for all conquer America's First Nations. Then he portioned out their reservations to Christian, mostly Protestant, churches to operate schools and, in many instances, to act as Indian agents. No one seems to have questioned the constitutionality of the federal government establishing religion.

MANIFEST DESTINY AND THE CIVIL WAR

Once the Mexican-American War had brought the United States its full extension across the continent, the growing imbalance between the industrializing North and export-agribusiness South came to a head. One premonition of a coming catastrophic conflict was the secession of Southern Methodists from the northern Methodist churches in 1844, followed by secession of Southern Baptists from their northern brethren in 1845. Overtly, the issue was slavery. Southern planters correctly insisted that the Constitution had embodied a compact between slave-using agribusiness states and those other states that did not depend on slave labor. Northern abolitionists' efforts to abolish slavery, and politicians' negotiations over whether new territories and states would or would not fit into the Southern bloc of slaveholding states, were seen as infringements upon that initial guarantee of Southern agribusiness practices. Most Northerners thought slavery abhorrent, pitying the poor negroes bent under the lash, their women subjected to masters' lust, children torn from parents. Still, the Founding Fathers had agreed to the compact, and no one wanted to lose America's principal export income, that from cotton.

Manifest Destiny rhetoric trumpeted liberty and freedom. Sure, it was understood to mean liberty and freedom for White men only, yet how could a reasonable man boast of his country's liberty and freedom when four million dark-skinned people were legally chattels, as totally subject to owners' whims as any donkey or dog? If Providence had chosen America to expand liberty and freedom, wasn't condoning chattel slavery straying from divine purpose? Manifest Destiny reared up in the 1840s to, from Southern leaders' standpoint, open up huge new cotton-growing lands for its important segment of the national economy. For Northerners, Manifest Destiny's overtone of divine providence made them consider whether God could have meant expansion of a regime of such inhumane exploitation, such gross denial of liberty and freedom within their blessed Republic.

Partly through the series of evangelical revivals during the Second Great Awakening that encouraged God-talk, partly through prosperity enjoyed by businessmen in the northern and middle states settled by Protestants, nineteenth-century America came to see itself as a blessed Protestant Christian nation. That is to say, America saw its roots in the Protestant Reformation. Although Martin Luther and John Calvin were seldom directly invoked, their influence was embedded in New England Puritanism and less-stringent Scot and Germanic heritages in Middle Atlantic and Midwest states. As we have seen, Luther could be bloodthirsty, and Calvin ruled with militant force. Manifest Destiny's God used war as His instrument to bring prosperity and peace.

The Civil War erupted like a volcano from pent-up fires, a firestorm killing more than 600,000 soldiers—250,000 Confederates and 360,000 from the far more populous North. As Union armies marched through the heart of the old South, their scorched-earth strategy left devastation reminiscent of the wrath of the Lord in the Old Testament. More basic was the blow to the South's economic power based on cotton. By the middle of the war, in 1863, Britain's textile mills had restabilized production by importing cotton from Asia and even Brazil. In the United States, Northern mills manufactured more wool, less cotton textiles. Loss of slave labor to the South after the war was palliated, after Reconstruction ceased in 1877, by turning Blacks into peons through sharecropping and Jim Crow laws. Four million ex-slaves in the Southern labor force kept wages low for lower-class Whites, too. Northern industrialists whose factories armed and clothed Union troops prospered. As railroads surged across the continent after the war ended, forging a transcontinental link in 1869, expanding markets pushed the Northern-dominated United States into global industrial status. God clearly was pleased by Northern Protestants' willingness to wage war against those who tried to secede from America.[10]

Northern victory in the Civil War strengthened the popular conviction that God had set humankind on a path of progress culminating in an English-speaking bourgeoisie. Americans differed from Britons in respecting the self-made capitalist industrialist or merchant prince more than aristocrats born to wealth. Postbellum rich Americans married their daughters to English lords, such as Winston Churchill's father, and kept their sons involved in business. Manifest Destiny, or Manifest Design, after the Civil War and Grant's mop-up of Indian resistance, narrowed to building industrial might. One lesson from the Civil War was that mass-produced munitions slaughtered men. Steel mills and machines made America strong. Divine Providence placed coal, iron, inexpensive bulk transport, and hordes of labor—young women and men from family farms with too many children and immigrants from impoverished Ireland, Scandinavia, and later Italy and Eastern Europe—in Protestant America.

RAMIFICATIONS OF POSTBELLUM INDUSTRIALIZATION

Industrialization changed American farming. Although the stereotype family farm included a hired man and a woman domestic, and hired threshing crews and other seasonal labor, its core labor was the owner couple. This Jeffersonian ideal yeoman and wife expected to create cash income beyond their subsistence production. They prized independence from patronage and wanted to invest to build capital. Whether homesteaders responding to land speculators or young families in settled regions, they likely had bought their farm with a mortgage and would invest in more land, stock, buildings, and machinery through further loans. American farmers saw machinery as their means to increase production and thereby income—American-made machines that raised them above brute labor and made them mechanics (i.e., skilled workers, in nineteenth-century terminology).

Federal sponsorship of homesteading came, perhaps surprisingly, nearly a century after the American Revolution. Initially, the government wanted to sell land to raise money, directly and through subsequent taxes, hence its encouragement of land speculators. Or is it that this means of revenue was encouraged by land speculators, who, after all, were the Virginia aristocracy well represented in Congress? During the 1850s, after the Old Northwest and then the eastern prairie entered the Union as states, 65 million acres of public domain were sold, most directly either to speculators or to ex-soldiers who sold their 160-acre bounty land warrant to speculators, rather than take it up themselves. Parallel to the sales of frontier land was common-law recognition, in Congress's 1841 Preemption Act, of squatters' right of occupancy if improvements had been made to the property, the principle emphasized by John Locke in justifying taking over First Nations' territories. In addition, Henry Clay's American System of subsidizing transportation development allotted millions of acres to canal, road, and railroad rights-of-way; other large tracts to reclaiming swamps; and parcels to be sold to finance public education. From these grants, thousands of farms and platted towns were carved. The bottom line was that settlers sooner or later (if squatters) paid speculators for their land.

It happened that the early 1860s were years of poor harvests in Europe but not in North America, so that demand for American wheat, carried in Union ships, escalated. Loss of cotton exports was therefore not so keenly felt, Divine Providence favoring the free states producing wheat. Cattle ranches in the Midwest were divided into wheat farms and feedlots. Ranchers moved west, regardless of the war raging in the east. Those who remained to farm dealt with labor shortages by purchasing mechanical reapers drawn by horses. Cyrus McCormick patented the reaper in 1834, five years later built a factory in Chicago to produce it, and trained salesmen to fan out across the country demonstrating it. His reaper won a gold medal in England's midcentury marvel, the Crystal Palace Exhibition in London, in 1851. The machine was a significant factor in freeing labor for industries without jeopardizing feeding that urban labor. Allowing a family with a hired man to produce a commodity to sell, it was also a factor enabling serious homesteading families to earn the money to pay for their land.

Industrialization went hand-in-glove with the trend toward mechanizing agriculture that not only spurred more factories to manufacture machinery but also promoted immigration of unskilled workers for the factories—men and women less likely to move west to farm, as American agriculture increasingly differed from the peasant practices immigrants knew. Astute policy makers pushing from the 1840s for the federal government to encourage yeoman farmers in America's western acquisitions were stymied until 1861 by Southern opposition. With the South seceded, Congress passed in 1862, at last, a Homestead Act offering 160 acres (a quarter section) to nearly anyone who filed an application, improved the land, and then filed for a title. Excluded were Confederate soldiers and American Indians.

The Homestead Act became the embodiment and fulfillment of the American ideal derived from Protestant principles of independent, self-disciplined individuals living in obedience to (supposed) universal laws. Democracy could be founded upon owners of family farms, the core of egalitarian societal relationships. A nation of farmers each secure in possession of sufficient land to provide for families would be stable, economically and politically. Physiocrats in Enlightenment France had argued that land is the only real wealth and agricultural production its only true measure. Jefferson and Franklin both lived in Paris when physiocrats—including Pierre du Pont, who would emigrate to America in 1799—participated in salons they frequented. The Homestead Act was more than an expedient promise to the hundreds of thousands enlisting in the War; it powerfully contrasted the "liberty and the pursuit of happiness" declared in Jefferson's first 1776 draft to be sacred to Americans with the Confederacy's hidebound structure of privileged and deprived classes. America's Manifest Destiny, obvious through God's favor to the Union, was to spread Protestant smallholders over the continent.

Homesteading under the Congressional Act a century after the physiocrats could not be the pastoral idyll Queen Marie Antoinette dreamed of. First

Nations had to be systematically driven off the land by the army. Miners flooded into ranges wherever someone struck gold or silver, with frontier merchants, ranchers, and freighters on their heels, much surer to make a buck than the miners were. Railroads networked, often built along routes used for millennia by First Nations travelers and traders and thereby abetting their displacement. Invention in Europe of a process for producing industrial belting from raw bison hides, 1870 or 1871, dramatically increased slaughter of bison, pulling hordes of get-rich-quick men to the plains to shoot, strip, and ship out millions of hides. During the 1870s, bison herds were exterminated in the southern half of the Great Plains, then between 1881 and 1883 in the northern plains. Without that staple food, not to mention principal trade item, Plains First Nations capitulated. Congress figured that without bison to hunt, Indians didn't need hunting territories, so regardless of promises in treaties, reservations were reduced and reduced again, opening millions more acres to White enterprises. Thus industrial demand for machinery belting killed off the American bison and beggared the peoples it had sustained in the same two decades that the federal government most actively promoted western settlement. Meanwhile, coal and iron in the Great Lakes region supported steelmaking and the valuable manufactories dependent on it, providing the United States the means to become an imperial power.

Manifest Destiny slogans continued to sell newspapers and fuel political campaigns. Without question a Protestant nation led by men of the superior Anglo-Saxon race, the United States was divinely empowered to extend its domain wherever inferior peoples languish. Having consolidated its territory from sea to shining sea, though held at bay over Canada by Great Britain and lacking popular support to overcome post-1848 Mexico, America looked for more. Cuba's rebellion against Spain, begun in 1895, beckoned for American intervention, and serious intent to build an isthmian canal linking our two oceans called for American presence in Central America. Beyond the Monroe Doctrine sphere, US traffic with Asia propelled demands for naval bases on Pacific islands. When a mine in Havana harbor exploded the US battleship Maine in February 1898, an outcry for revenge overcame the caution of older Americans who had experienced the horrors of war thirty years earlier. "The taste of Empire is in the mouth of the people even as the taste of blood in the jungle," said *The Washington Post*.[11]

War was declared in April, Spain's inept Atlantic fleet was destroyed just before the Fourth of July, and Spain quickly surrendered Cuba and, for good measure, Puerto Rico. Manifest Destiny had more to accomplish: by secret order of Assistant Secretary of the Navy Theodore Roosevelt to Commodore Dewey of the Pacific fleet, as soon as war against Spain (i.e., Cuba) was declared, Dewey took his ships into Manila Bay in the Philippines, fired upon Spain's fleet at anchor, and accepted surrender of Spanish shore fortifications. True, Filipinos were rebelling against Spain as Cubans were, and American rhetoric trumpeted the US mission to bring democracy to both, but Spanish tyranny at the far end of the Pacific was hardly the threat posed by Spanish troops ninety miles offshore in the Caribbean. The end of the nineteenth century saw the United States possessing Puerto Rico, the Philippines, Hawaii, Midway, Wake, Guam, and Samoa's best harbor, and exercising protectorate power over Panama and Nicaragua as well as Cuba. Supreme Court rulings early in the twentieth century over questions of status and rights of peoples of these islands and bases were as confusing as Justice Marshall's ingenious opinions concerning American First Nations in the 1830s. "Little brown brothers" in tropical territories were declared incapable of self-rule. Filipinos demonstrated their incapacity for enlightened government by continuing rebellion instead of gratefully bowing to US domination. William Jennings Bryan made the Democratic platform for the 1900 presidential election be a reminder that Americans affirm that governments must rest upon the consent of the governed; therefore we should not oppose the Philippine fighters for independence. Bryan and the Democrats lost the election.

The 1890s had been tumultuous. Celebrating the quadricentennial of Columbus's landing, the World Columbian Exposition opened in 1893 (its ambitious construction wasn't complete in 1892) beside Chicago's lakefront. Gleaming white buildings around a sparkling lagoon looked heavenly. All manner of American accomplishments, from heavy machinery and baroque sculptures to displays of conquered Indians, were exhibited to awestruck crowds. Then came the Panic of 1893. Railroads and banks failed, unemployment surged, strikes were put down with violence, and poor crop yields exacerbated financial stresses upon farmers and consumers alike. Three years later, crops were good, the currency issue—essentially, whether to base money supply on gold bullion reserves or on credit—had been resolved, and Eastern businessmen rallied to oppose the new populism led by Bryan, the son of the prairie. Americans need not doubt their Manifest Destiny, nor the Divine Providence that gave them power to conquer by force of arms not only the aborigines of their own continent but islands scattered over thousands of miles of ocean. Americans, like Constantine 1,600 ago, were the Anointed, Christos. *In hoc signo vinces*, battle after battle. A long-ago Jewish pacifist named Yeshua had no relevance to American Christianity.

CHAPTER 9

———·❊·———

HEGEMONY THROUGH
PHILANTHROPY

The twentieth century was an age of secularization. Science declared its freedom from matters spiritual. The United States recognized that the First Amendment to the Constitution forbids governmental support of religions. So in 1954, the phrase "under God" was added by Congress to the Pledge of Allegiance (written in 1892), and in 1956, by an act of Congress, "In God We Trust" became the United States' national motto, to appear on all her currencies.[1] For nearly forty years, Americans were rallied to oppose the Soviet Union as "godless Communists." Americans were the godly capitalists.

Tasting empire as a predator tastes blood, Americans in 1900 relied on industrial might to grasp power. Heroes of the day were the ruthless entrepreneurs—the Robber Barons—scornful of pusillanimous men hobbled by conventional business practices. Their factories, mines, and railroads were battlefields where they crushed opponents, whether competitors or workers. Men who matched their might became their comrades in arms in interlocking directorates. Andrew Carnegie (1835–1919) and John D. Rockefeller (1839–1937) were the self-made greatest captains of industry, and J. Pierpont Morgan (1837–1913), son of a banker, became banker to the world. Remorseless in pursuing business strategies, Rockefeller and Morgan were active in their churches—Baptist and Episcopalian, respectively—and Carnegie lauded Christian morality, although he was no churchgoer. Carnegie in 1889 published an essay that he titled "Wealth," which was reprinted the same year as "The Gospel of Wealth." Replacing the New Testament Gospels had not been Carnegie's aim. It was the tenor of the age that elevated his advocacy of philanthropy to the status of a gospel for industrialists and implicitly, Andrew Carnegie to the status of, if not a messiah, then the St. Paul of the new era.

Throughout the twentieth century, Indo-European militancy stirred capitalists to see building their empires as a moral duty under beneficent Providence. Carnegie wrote that his formula for philanthropy was "founded upon the present most intense individualism,"[2] explaining that the most astute businessmen would amass wealth in order to bless humanity by distributing it widely among the rest of the populace. Evolution, Carnegie believed, had produced these most gifted civilized men. Carnegie's friend Herbert Spencer advocated that the successful should ignore less fit people struggling with poverty. Carnegie instead believed the best of our race should consider themselves an oligarchy that would use its exemplary management talents to govern the rest of us. Carnegie, Rockefeller, and Morgan gave millions of dollars and other assets to fulfill the moral imperative of beneficence. Not incidentally, their huge philanthropies immortalized their names: Carnegie Foundation, Carnegie Mellon University, Carnegie Institution in Washington, DC, Carnegie Hall in New York, and hundreds of Carnegie libraries; Rockefeller University in New York, Spelman College named after Mrs. Rockefeller's Abolitionist family, the Rockefeller Foundation, and the Laura Spelman Rockefeller Memorial Foundation; the Morgan Library in New York and the Morgan gem collections in New York's American Museum of Natural History.

Figure 9.1.   Monument to Andrew Carnegie, Atlanta, Georgia
Credit: Photo by Alice Kehoe.

Rockefeller was directly inspired in 1889 by Carnegie's Gospel of Wealth, and his first major philanthropic enterprise was to turn a small Baptist college into the University of Chicago. In 1903, he launched the General Education Board to extend Baptist missionary programs beyond a sectarian focus into a fund that could support Spelman College and other schools serving larger constituencies, endorsing advice by his philanthropies advisor, former Baptist minister Frederick Gates, to eschew specifically Baptist evangelizing. Gates reminded Rockefeller, "[T]he mere commercial results of missionary effort to our own land is worth, I had almost said, a thousand-fold every year of what is spent on [foreign] missions. Our export trade is growing by leaps and bounds. Such growth would have been utterly impossible but for the commercial conquest of foreign lands under the lead of missionary endeavor. What a boon to home industry and manufacture!"[3]

The wisdom of expanding the domestic consumer pool through alleviating poverty and lack of education could hardly be missed by businessmen of such acuity. Like Benjamin Franklin, Carnegie and Rockefeller had been poor boys sent young to work, self-educated through reading books and eventually, once rich, conversing with scholars. Tellingly, the banker's son Morgan endowed elite arts and science collections rather than social-action programs attracting Carnegie's and Rockefeller's attention.

Andrew Carnegie and John D. Rockefeller illustrate the parallel streams flowing to overwhelm American democracy in the industrial age. Thanks to the immense fortunes they had amassed, they directly channeled societal forces. The two men were a strong contrast—Carnegie was short, fair, extroverted, genial, and by middle age, pudgy, whereas Rockefeller was tall, spare, and puritanical. In addition, Rockefeller was unwilling to make speeches and cultivated a quiet listening that left speakers awed by sensing, as one reporter remarked in 1905, "repressed power,"[4] although privately Rockefeller could joke. Both men were tainted by hostility to organized labor that people remembered, no matter how many millions they contributed to the public weal. Both had genius for seeing the value of mergers, constructing and managing conglomerates through which capital begot more capital. There is one striking difference: Carnegie, the evolutionist, worked hard to protest and avert war and was broken in spirit by the world war; Rockefeller, the devout Christian, apparently paid little attention to that immense horror, for nowhere in Ron Chernow's 774-page biography of him is the war mentioned.

Carnegie is certainly the more attractive figure. Born in Scotland to a handloom weaver of fine damask, 12-year-old Andrew immigrated with his parents and younger brother to the Pittsburgh area when the 1840s combination of introduction of steam-powered mechanical looms, US imposition of tariffs on linens, and economic depression impoverished the family. The boy of course immediately went to work, reading as much as he could in his meager free time by borrowing books from a Pittsburgh gentleman who opened his library to working boys. Bright and eager to get on, the small blond youth caught the notice of his employers and older coworkers, rapidly rising to partnership in new enterprises of telegraph lines, railroads, and iron bridges in western Pennsylvania. The year after the end of the Civil War, he invested in land speculation on the Kansas frontier. Pullman railroad sleeping cars were another investment, developed from his prewar involvement with patents that Pullman needed. In 1872, he organized the building of a steel mill using the new Bessemer process, intending to produce steel rails for railroads. In spite of much buying and selling of stocks in conjunction with business enterprises, Carnegie was shrewd enough to weather the Panic of 1873 without losses.

In 1900, Carnegie merged his steel company with Henry Clay Frick's coke company, and in 1901, he sold Carnegie Steel to J. Pierpont Morgan for $400,000,000 and officially retired from business, a quarter-century after he had begun the series of philanthropies that proved he did indeed believe in his Gospel of Wealth. He had also indulged his talent for writing, thirst for intellectual stimulation, enjoyment of horseback riding and carriage rides, and delight in social gatherings since the 1870s, taking parties of friends, along with his widowed mother, on months-long excursions in America and Europe. The poor immigrant from Dunfermline capped his success by purchasing Skibo Castle in the Scottish Highlands in 1897, coincidentally the year in which his much-younger wife gave him his only child, a daughter named after Carnegie's mother.

That mother linked Andrew Carnegie to her radical family in Dunfermline. Margaret Morrison Carnegie's father, a cobbler by trade (enabling Margaret to supplement her husband's earnings by binding shoes), was quite well known in the area for his socialist political activism and outspoken atheist views. Margaret's brother continued the family's antiestablishment activism, winning election as alderman in Dunfermline, and her older sister's husband, a grocer, held similar opinions, which he discussed frequently with his son and nephew on walks about the countryside and by correspondence with Andrew until his death. Distributing his wealth for the betterment of communities toward libraries, organs for churches (to provide good music for the greatest number of citizens), universities, scientific research, and peace diplomacy was quite congruent with the politics of his Morrison relatives. There was, however, a gaping disjunction between their espousal of working people's (women as well as men) wage and hours improvements, and Andrew Carnegie's indifference to his own laborers' demands.

Carnegie's modus operandi was to stay abreast of economic data and trends, plan accordingly, hire managers he could trust, and leave the daily running of his businesses to them. If they, like most businessmen, decided to increase profits by decreasing wages, then that was part of their management. Carnegie integrated components of his enterprises with mergers and sank his own capital into the latest technology, aiming to keep his mills running to produce at lowest cost. He seldom visited his plants, preferring the amenities of New York and luxurious resorts. The great scandal that tarnished his reputation was the Homestead Strike of 1892, when, for four months, union men were locked out of Carnegie Steel's foremost mill and replaced with scabs. Carnegie had told the union that because his other two mills in Carnegie Steel were nonunion, the Homestead workers would have to accept the lower wages paid at the nonunion plants. Henry Frick was in charge of Carnegie Steel, Carnegie himself traveling on extended holiday in Europe. Frick decided to hire a small army of goons from the Pinkerton Agency to break the strike. They were repulsed by the strikers and their wives and friends, both sides shooting, causing several deaths, as well as attacking with clubs. The governor of Pennsylvania refused to send militia to quell the riot, leaving it to the county sheriff. Reporters cabled stories of the outrage throughout the country and to Europe. Carnegie's lame protest that he wasn't in America didn't absolve him in the opinion of the public, which was well aware of his longstanding opposition to unions.

Rockefeller, like Carnegie, came from poverty, but his circumstances were peculiar. His father was a hustler, traveling through western New York as a "botanic physician." He married a farmer's daughter, Eliza Davison, and had her employ another young woman, pregnant with his child, as a domestic helper. This woman bore him two daughters before she left Eliza's home. Scandals about his raping a later servant and seducing women during his long episodes away from Eliza added to that unfortunate wife's travails as she worked hard to maintain their farm, only to be uprooted to move and move again. "Big Bill" Rockefeller—the man was well-built and handsome, not narrow-faced like his son who resembled Eliza—culminated his escapades by marrying, bigamously, another farmer's daughter, this one in Ontario across the border. Taking on a second wife dented Big Bill's cash, so he told his eldest son, John, to quit high school, though John was close to graduating, and seek employment at once. Experienced already in buying, selling, and bookkeeping from assisting his father when Bill was at Eliza's, John pounded the pavement in Cleveland until a firm of commission merchants hired him to do bookkeeping. The work suited him. He was not a youth who struck people as brilliant, but he was meticulous with figures and persevered. Rockefeller shared with Carnegie an appreciation for the power in numbers, an ability to collate them and perceive the true state of an economic situation.

Clerking at the commission merchants, young Rockefeller was at the office from dawn until late at night, unless it was Sunday. Sundays, he was at a Baptist mission church near the house where he and his brother William boarded. He taught Sunday School, did clerical duties for the church, janitorial duties as well, and socialized after services. Charity was, for him, a commandment and a satisfaction as early as his high school years. Four years after getting his first job, he was tithing 10 percent of his wages, giving not only to his own church but also to a Catholic orphanage and to an African American man to help him buy his wife out of slavery. He took over the role of head of household when his father left Eliza in Cleveland, choosing to live with the Ontario wife in Philadelphia.

Rockefeller left his first employment in 1858, joining two other young men as commodities traders for produce and salt. The business was crucial and lucrative during the Civil War. Rockefeller could feel justified in remaining at it instead of enlisting; he paid a substitute, as many well-to-do young men did, and contributed money for clothes and weapons for other soldiers, too. Free to watch out for his own opportunities, in 1863 he and his partner bankrolled a practical chemist—a member of his Baptist church—to take advantage of the new method of refining petroleum into kerosene for lamps. Cleveland was close enough to the oil seeps of western Pennsylvania that news of the 1859 breakthrough in reaching oil by drilling had excited the city. Drillers inundated the narrow valleys with derricks and makeshift refineries. Rockefeller, experienced in commodities trade, shrewdly chose to build a refinery just outside Cleveland at a location immediately accessible by both rail and water. By war's end, he had bought out his commodities partners and, with the chemist, reconstituted the firm as a refinery. He had also married Laura Celestia Spelman, a woman he had known since high school, daughter of a respectable businessman. Unusual for girls, Laura had studied commercial subjects in high school; valedictorian of her class, she titled her commencement address "I Can Paddle My Own Canoe." The sentiment stood her well when downturns in their father's business prompted Laura and her sister to take teaching jobs in Cleveland public schools. Brought up to be devoted to church, temperance, abolition of slavery, and civic responsibilities, Laura Spelman was the perfect mate for strongly self-disciplined, serious-minded, cool-thinking John D. Rockefeller.

The other person close to John D. was his brother William, a year younger. William was more sociable than John but, even in John's estimation, an excellent and honest businessman. He quit his job, similar to his brother's first job, as bookkeeper and partner in a produce commissions firm, to partner with John in the oil refinery. Two years later, the Rockefellers accepted another young businessman, Henry Flagler, as partner in a deal with his older stepbrother banker. Led by John D., the firm built an extraordinary company consolidating its multiple requirements, from oak barrels for oil to deals with railroads on tank-car rates. Although a substantial portion of their products was shipped abroad from New York, the firm did not neglect Cleveland's access to Midwest markets. In 1870, the partners incorporated as the Standard Oil Company (Ohio). Thirteen years later, they at last moved to New York City, the center of American business and wealth. John D. and his wife, parents of three girls and a boy, lived relatively modestly, the children taught at home by governesses to shelter them from unchristian intemperance, sloth, and profanity. Like Andrew Carnegie, John D. was constantly sensitive to economic matters but usually completed his work in the office in the morning, spending afternoons with his family and indulging his love for fine horses, especially driving four-in-hand teams. The wives of both men shared their husbands' enjoyment with horses. Both men, masters of almost incalculable wealth, controlled their horses as they did their business contacts, alert to every nuance in the interaction, cool, never blustering or shouting. Rockefeller, like Carnegie, put workaholic habits behind him once he made money, distilling the essence of big business for himself as he guided a selected team of competent associates.

Comparing the careers of Carnegie and Rockefeller, one difference was the degree of suspicion and distrust roused in the public. Carnegie was blamed for Frick's violent assault on the Homestead Steel workers and his niggardliness on wages, but the opprobrium against him pales against the anger raised against Rockefeller, the boss of Standard Oil. With Rockefeller, the problem was his—that is, Standard Oil's—monopoly on oil. The company could undersell and outbid competitors because it, or rather the set of companies in extraction, refining, cooperage, pipelines, railroads, and so on that constituted Standard Oil, had economies of scale plus complex deal-making capacity. After a research chemist he had hired developed in 1888 a means of cleansing the sulfurous stench from oil from southern Ohio, Rockefeller was more than ever committed to including scientists in his company, innovating a research-and-development segment that would become common practice in businesses in the twentieth century.

During the 1890s, Rockefeller led Standard Oil to acquire huge productive properties as new sources of oil were found. Refineries, tank cars, and distributors were expanded to service the properties. Journalists saw Standard Oil as an octopus, its tentacles squirming into everyone's pockets. All kinds of businessmen, whether paying higher rates for shipping on railroads or for oil products in regions where competition had died, were incensed as Standard Oil grew. Plenty of politicians, too, felt hurt because failed businessmen could no longer contribute campaign expenses. Outrage fueled senators' willingness to curb monopolies. In 1890, the Sherman Antitrust Act, named after Senator John Sherman (brother of Civil War general William Tecumseh Sherman), became law. Poorly worded, it didn't faze Standard Oil.

Rockefeller did not feel well during the attacks on him and Standard Oil beginning in the late 1880s. By 1891, he took time off to relax, exercise, and eat carefully at his country estate near Cleveland. He also engaged a Baptist minister, Frederick Gates, to manage his charitable giving. Gates was to Rockefeller's philanthropy as his Standard Oil companies managers were to his business concerns; they enabled him to semiretire, although, as the largest stockholder in Standard Oil, he continued to pay close attention to its prospects and advise its officers. With Gates to counsel him on major charitable projects, Rockefeller channeled his millions into building the University of Chicago and constructing foundations. These good works on a massive scale, consonant with his stupendous fortune, did not protect him from a muckraking exposé by journalist Ida Tarbell, whose articles on the trust boosted circulation of the magazine she edited and sold well in book form published in 1904. Tarbell came from the western Pennsylvania oil region and knew firsthand the wildcatting boom of early oil development, and Rockefeller's maneuvers to consolidate it. She spoke for millions of Americans when she claimed that monolithic trusts like Standard Oil act contrary to America's democratic principles. Rockefeller's decisions, in the 1890s and following decades, to create an elite university in the Midwest and to support scientific research rather than donate handsome libraries and

organs, support teachers, and pay for a fine concert hall in New York as
Carnegie did, could not win the public's approbation.

With a sternly devout Bible-reading wife as well as mother, John D.
Rockefeller should have grasped Jesus's message to incarnate divine love in
one's daily life with fellow humans. Instead, he slyly held aloof, constantly
strategizing to gain more power. In his own estimation he was highly moral
because, besides attending church and strictly avoiding ordinary sins, he did
not deliberately cheat or lie, though he might not volunteer information that
would help others. He liked ministers who preached the Social Gospel, and
expressed satisfaction that his companies did well enough during the Panic
of 1893 that their workmen did not lack accustomed wages. He did believe
that he led a Christian life meriting God's approval manifest in his astounding
accumulation of wealth. A sympathetic historian might accept Rockefeller's
conviction that he benefitted America by shifting its business model from
a multiplicity of independent and competing entrepreneurs to a rationally
constructed monolith controlling every facet of its outreach. Some historians, after the mid-twentieth century, have seen the powerful foundations he
bequeathed to be as dangerous as Ida Tarbell saw Standard Oil.

ROCKEFELLER AND CARNEGIE FOUNDATIONS' POLITICAL EFFECTS

John D. Rockefeller Sr. brought his only son, John D. Jr., into both Standard Oil and Rockefeller philanthropies. "Junior," as he was called, hewed as
strictly to Baptist conduct as his parents, and like his father, favored a more
liberal "modern" approach to understanding the Bible, rather than Fundamentalist inerrancy. Both Frederick Gates, "Senior's" manager of philanthropy, and Raymond and Harry Emerson Fosdick, Junior's advisors, were
liberal Baptists. Carnegie, semiretired in 1897 from actively leading Carnegie
Steel, hired a young Scotsman, James Bertram, to be his private secretary and
soon let Bertram handle the petitions and disbursements of philanthropy.
When Carnegie Steel merged with J. P. Morgan's trust to become US Steel,
Carnegie devoted the mornings once employed on profit-making business to
giving away his money in an equally modern organized manner. In today's
terminology, he favored seed grants and matching grants—for example,
donating library buildings to cities with the expressed purpose of goading
city governments to allocate tax monies to maintain them and their books
for the citizens. Both Rockefeller and Carnegie utilized their organizational
genius to transform philanthropy into rational, data-based—"scientific"—
managed trusts.

Carnegie incorporated the Carnegie Corporation of New York in 1911,
endowing it with 25 million dollars, equivalent to several billion dollars
today. Rockefeller sent him a well-wishing telegram, to which Carnegie
responded, "You and I are in the same boat, finding that it is harder to
administer, than to make, dollars."[5] In 1913, Carnegie set up a United Kingdom Trust in Britain to parallel the Carnegie Corporation. It was evident

to both generalissimos of industry that philanthropy on their grand scale required efficiency. Individual requests from private persons multiplied ad infinitum. Bertram, for Carnegie, and Gates, for Rockefeller, implemented the strategy of donating to institutions as means of benefitting the greatest number of persons. Bertram and Gates could then work with executives of the institutions to channel funds for maximum effect in accord with the donors' principles. Not surprisingly, they created interlocking directorates of educational, research, and funding agencies.

Overall, the Carnegie and Rockefeller foundations translated the corporate structure of industrial-capitalist America into allegedly philanthropic programs. They were run by men accustomed to the corporate business mode—women such as social-welfare leader Jane Addams were marginalized. Tellingly, in the 1920s, Herbert Hoover, an engineer par excellence, articulated the aims and expectations of the foundations' leaders to govern the United States by scientific knowledge. Huge quantities of data would be systemically gathered and statistically analyzed. From such unprecedented valid knowledge, intelligent, highly educated WASP men would deduce efficient management principles and methods for maintaining America. Their America was, of course, capitalist, taking for granted the primacy of private property.

During the 1920s, twentieth-century American public policy was forged, encouraging ownership of private homes for nuclear families, their purchase of appliances and furnishings, and planned obsolescence that would push housewives to buy again and again, keeping production and selling going strong. Hoover chaired a commission that included Christine Fredericks, who, with her husband George Fredericks, was a disciple of Frederick Taylor's time and motion studies for efficiency; she published a landmark book in 1929, *Selling Mrs. Consumer*. Presidents Coolidge and Hoover endorsed Mrs. Fredericks's Better Homes in America movement to find spiritual uplift in clean, stylish houses. Besides priming the market with mass consumerism fed by national advertising, 1920s economic policy aimed to nullify the believed deleterious dilution of American character by the millions of immigrants pulled by demand for industrial labor. Officers of the Carnegie and Rockefeller foundations, like most of their peers, worried that the Anglo-Saxon race would falter, dooming American values. Just as nineteenth-century federal Indian policy had targeted "communal" landholding in First Nations, 1920s policy targeted "communal" organizing by immigrant groups. Assimilation through settlement-house and public school education and consumer advertising should preserve American standards.

Ironically, Hoover's Research on Social Trends Committee, funded by the Rockefeller Foundation, began its ambitious project when the 1929 stock market crash initiated the Great Depression. Neither Hoover nor his advisors anticipated the breakdown it triggered. Its effect was to undermine grandiose hopes of pure scientific research revealing laws of economic behavior, and pressure social scientists to find pragmatic alleviation of the country's sufferings. There remained, nevertheless, conviction that social statics could add up to robustly grounded patterns of human behavior that could be manipulated. The 1933 Chicago Exposition emblazoned as its theme, "Science Finds—Industry Applies—Man Conforms."[6] From telling mothers that precisely mixed formula fed by a clock schedule is better for babies than breastfeeding, to correlating children's low academic performance with racial inferiority, 1930s scientists privileged measurement over observation. The Great Depression was read as a testament to politicians' ignorance of human behavior. More, not less, science would be imperative. Rockefeller and Carnegie seemed as far-sighted in discerning the promise of social science as they had been in business.

Organizing philanthropies like business corporations reflected more than tycoons' experiences. Their great foundations undertook to purge unruly and unregulated activities, as their trusts had eliminated wildcatters. The Carnegie Foundation sponsored, and the Rockefeller Foundation implemented, the Flexner Report on medical education in the United States, published in 1910. Not long before educator Abraham Flexner undertook his study, the president of the American Academy of Medicine declared, "Hygiene of the body gives a spirit of religious toleration and calm . . . hygiene of the mind gives a healthy digestion and a good income-making body and fits man for this world as well as the next."[7] Frederick Gates, the Rockefellers' philanthropy manager, was very aware that healthy workingmen were more productive than sick ones. He also was entirely convinced that scientific medicine correctly conceptualized organisms as sets of mechanically interacting parts, made sick by invading microorganisms. (He had to argue tactfully against John D. Rockefeller Sr.'s preference for homeopathic medicine, learned from his father who hustled it under his pseudonym Dr. William Levingston.) Abraham Flexner advocated a few well-funded medical schools to teach upper-class young men scientific laboratory procedures; only young men who could afford a good college education before applying should be admitted. Medical schools for Blacks and women should be closed, except for two Southern medical schools for Black men. Flexner's recommendations were highly compatible with the American Medical Association's desires to raise medicine to an elite profession commanding high salaries, secure from underbidding by women, Blacks, or men content with modest incomes.

Parallel with this move to restrict the medical profession to elite WASP men was an American Law Institute, established with a million dollars from Carnegie in 1923. The impetus purportedly was tremendous proliferation of legal cases since the 1890s, making choice of legal precedent difficult for judges. Supreme Court justices Oliver Wendell Holmes and Louis Brandeis professed no problem, but then, Holmes thought through a few basic constitutional principles, and Brandeis was a Jew. Most of their brethren in the law believed Holmes failed to see, and Brandeis epitomized, the terrible threat to the American legal profession posed by the influx of immigrants' sons, "a horde of alien races from Eastern Europe . . . accustomed to absolute government, accustomed to hate the law, and hostile above all to wealth and power."[8] Such men were "the poorly-educated, the ill-prepared, the morally weak."[9] The American Bar Association (ABA) commissioned a study like

Flexner's, anticipating recommendations that would let "the old American stock . . . avert the threatened decay of constitutionalism in this country."[10] When the report advised allowing differences in legal training in order to let "poor boys" in, and undercut corporate attorneys' power, the ABA revised the document to better match the Flexner Report, recommending two years of college before admission to law school. Once in law school, prospective lawyers should be furnished with a set of codified, clearly stated analyses of significant legal cases—a venture receiving another million dollars from Carnegie. "Legal realists," a competing school of thought advocating the view that jurisprudence is embodied in society and necessarily changes through time, could only protest and push for, at the least, citations of actual cases rather than authoritarian pronouncements of "the law."

After Carnegie's death in 1919 and Junior Rockefeller taking over responsibility for the several Rockefeller foundations around 1917, the bulk and main thrust of both tycoons' philanthropies focused on "social problems." They accepted the tenet "all social problems turn out to be problems of social control," asserted by University of Chicago sociologists Robert Park and Ernest Burgess in their canonical 1921 textbook.[11] Committees were set up to seek quantitative and experimental data—that is, "scientific" data—to develop methods of social control over labor, crime, immigration and population distribution, race relations, and international relations. Experimental psychology was a favored field, reflecting Protestant American individualism. The notorious Hawthorn Studies, manipulating workers at General Electric's Hawthorn plant, was a star example of the Rockefeller Foundation's approach; it was ultimately a scam, never actually completed but well publicized, by the shady Australian "industrial psychologist" Elton Mayo, teaching at Harvard. Mayo told businessmen that praise motivated workers better than raising wages, and, like Frederick Taylor a generation earlier, he recommended breaking up workers' camaraderie to force them to compete in productivity with each other.

"Social problems" were tied to cities (statistics show more crime occurs in cities—if one doesn't correct for population numbers, city versus rural). Logically, to reduce crime, immigrants should not be allowed to flock to cities. Through the interlocking directorates of the foundations, the Carnegie Corporation endowed in 1919 the National Research Council, created in 1916 by the National Academy of Sciences, to research "human migration." Dominated by WASP eugenicists fearful of diluting "American" blood, and reluctant to see Southern Blacks migrate north, the National Research Council's committee engaged the American Geographical Society, in 1928, to provide the scientific framework. From this came proposals for studying and possibly creating Pioneer Belts: frontiers of settlement. How neatly the perceived value of Pioneer Belts fit the Hoover commission's push for suburbs of nuclear-family homes!

Looking back today, it seems that American leaders were amazingly blind to the fascism in their ambition to control citizens. They could, if they would, see the consequences of Mussolini's contempt for democracy. Cloistering oligarchs in conference rooms apparently differentiated them from oligarchs on a podium saluted by goose-stepping brownshirts. The American gentlemen no doubt considered their Christianity sufficient distinction from Il Duce in Italy, who had renounced his mother's Catholicism for socialism. John D. Rockefeller Jr. devoted his life to directing his father's legacy into "modern" Christianity, ecumenical in its alliances in order to broaden its impact. In contrast to the Fundamentalists he deplored, Rockefeller Junior did not harangue about personal salvation. Instead, his foundations ensured that a cadre of WASP men would dominate the United States, masking their conservative capitalist agenda as enlightened science. They took it for granted that America was, and should be, a Protestant Christian nation.

CHAPTER 10

SECULARISM THREATENS

Around 1900, American Protestants split into liberal and evangelical factions. A. C. Dixon, Baptist pastor at evangelist Dwight Moody's Chicago Avenue Church from 1906 to 1911, beginning in 1905, led an attack on liberal ministers such as Henry Ward Beecher, by codifying and publishing *The Fundamentals*. From his work we get the label "Fundamentalist." Dixon fervently denounced Christians who thought improving sinners' material existence would lead them to Christ and salvation. He spoke from experience administering a million-dollar endowment to succor the poor in the Boston parish he led before coming to Chicago: "It seemed to him like common sense that if they fed the hungry, paid their rent, and gave them a good doctor and medicine, it would be good preparation for preaching the gospel to them. But when, at the end of three years, Dixon realized that soul-winning did not follow body healing, he decided to 'dispense with the whole business and get back to first principles . . . [It] is immensely easier to reach a man's body through his soul, than his soul through his body.'"[1]

Bringing sinners to Christ is a Christian's primary duty, Dixon claimed. The movement he participated in has been termed the Great Reversal, overturning the Social Gospel orientation building in the late nineteenth century. Social welfare found its home in the Progressive movement that spawned the Progressive Party in 1912, while the Rockefellers were creating their philanthropic trust to engineer America out of the social problems energizing Progressives. Protestants of Dixon's persuasion spurned do-gooders, whatever the scale of their benefices.

In early twentieth-century America, the hegemony of Protestantism was so strong that the *New York Times* reported that the 1912 Progressive Party Convention would let a delegate "speak as the spirit moves him for at least five minutes" and "give 'testimony' regarding his political conversion."[2] The delegates marched around the Chicago hall singing "Onward, Christian Soldiers" (just as, in the 1940s, all the children in my school, Woodrow Wilson Elementary in Arlington, Virginia, marched singing every Friday morning at the school assembly; so far as I know, none of the Jewish children's families objected to "Onward, Christian Soldiers"). Teddy Roosevelt himself declared to the Progressive Party, "We stand at Armageddon, and we battle for the Lord."[3] The convention closed by the delegates singing the standard Protestant "Doxology" hymn.[4]

RELIGION VERSUS LIBERALISM

Secularization affronted Fundamentalist Protestants on many fronts. "Science" is, by definition, irreligious. Given Indo-European culture's worldview of antagonistic opposition, it seemed natural to proclaim "war" between science and religion. Empirical evidence of scientists who were devoutly religious, for example, Cambridge don William Paley, could not weaken this peculiarly American ideological position. Beginning with chemist John William Draper's 1874 *History of the Conflict between Religion and Science*, the war was continued two years later by Andrew Dickson White, president of Cornell University, who elaborated his popular 1869 New York lecture "The Battle-fields of Science" into the book *The Warfare of Science*. Twenty years later, White was still at it, publishing in two volumes *A History of the Warfare of Science with Theology in Christendom*. Fundamentalists insisting on the inerrancy of the Bible would not accept that Genesis descriptions of God's creations could be anything but the literal handiwork of God laboring through six days. They pitted themselves against Darwinian evolution, banning it from school curricula and thereby making war between science and religion a reality on school boards. Periodically, the war landed in courts, from the notorious 1925 trial of teacher John Scopes in Tennessee, where Scopes was convicted and then the conviction overturned, to a series of federal trials after midcentury. Consistently, these trials determined that organic evolution is valid science and Genesis creation is Christian religion, whether or not texts promoting it use the word "God," so teaching it in tax-supported schools is unconstitutional. The alleged war between science and religion in the United States boils down to unquenchable efforts to inculcate Fundamentalist Protestant belief through public schools.

The larger picture revolves around threats to the hegemony of White Anglo-Saxon Protestants. Inerrancy of the Bible became a litmus test for obedience to traditional authorities, for those who sign agreement to that principle, as do faculty in Fundamentalist schools and members of the Creation Research Society, accept the authority of their denominational theologians to tell them which translations of the Bible are inerrant and to interpret passages therein. Characteristically of Americans, African American theologians are not among this elect.[5] Hierarchy and authority are veiled by rhetoric that emphasizes being "born again in Jesus Christ," an intensely emotional personal experience that draws attention away from preparation for it by a father figure pastor and subsequent discipleship to church leaders. Except for flamboyant Aimee Semple McPherson in the 1920s, men lead Fundamentalist Protestant megachurches. Masculinity has been integral to American

Protestantism, intrinsic in its Indo-European heritage. The twentieth century saw this powerful, ancient, cultural tradition strongest among WASPs affiliated with Fundamentalist churches. In the second half of the century, it manifested as the militant Christian Right, fighting to preserve WASPs' nineteenth-century domination.

Efforts to rationalize Christianity through science and scholarly "higher criticism" of biblical texts fit the tenor of twentieth-century mainstream American culture, in spite of Fundamentalists' opposition. That pair of practices fulfills Enlightenment values of cool, logical, systematic analyses of natural phenomena, divorced from sensuality, emotion, and a priori dogmas. Enlightenment savants thought it evident that humans had progressed from an animal-like existence to having a mastery of the natural world, for had not God given man dominion over nature? Francis Bacon, member of Elizabeth I's court and lord chancellor of Britain under James I, self-consciously inaugurated the modernist stance with his *Great Instauration* (Restoration, or Renewal), published in part in 1620. Dismissing medieval speculation, Bacon argued that truth, "the daughter of time," would duly appear through inductive reasoning from observation of the world. Feminists have castigated Bacon for saying that time itself had a "masculine birth" like Athena born from Zeus, and using metaphors of rape for men ripping veils off Nature, penetrating her and making "Nature and her children" servants to men. Bacon, of course, was Protestant, since in Elizabeth's court no Catholic might advance. His vivid prose promising power to rational analytic men made him a founding father of the modern worldview, and his method, observation followed by analysis, became the touchstone for science. "Baconian science" continues to be touted by Fundamentalists, in opposition to "postmodern" relativity and indeterminacy. Bacon's hypermasculine obsession with knowledge as power conforms nicely with the passages in Genesis where Adam names the animals and is given dominion, and it underscores the message Eve transgressed by imbibing knowledge contrary to established authority.

Twentieth-century Christian America developed diverging camps, the politically dominant liberal Protestants exemplified by the Rockefeller Foundation staffs and beneficiaries, and populist Fundamentalists limited to regional political arenas. William Jennings Bryan (1860–1925), who legally represented John Scopes's accusers in the 1925 trial, appealed to a range of conservative Christians. He ran for president of the United States in 1896, 1900, and 1908 on a populist platform, but lost to Republican candidates. Although Bryan is remembered for denouncing "Darwinism's" supposed undermining of morality, his political career was based on speaking for Western farmers suffering under tight credit and trust cartels—nineteenth-century problems. His populism had a rural base in a nation ruled by urban industrialists. Their challengers were not small farmers, but industrial unions, working men, and, after 1920, working women fighting to gain a modicum of leisure while earning enough to maintain a home.

Industrialists' belief that rational management by appointed businessmen and bureaucrats would produce a better America was quite compatible with the 1933 slogan "Science Finds—Industry Applies—Man Conforms"[6] and Rockefeller Foundation faith in professed scientists. In spite of all the millions the foundation poured into social science research over half a century, its beneficiaries failed to produce the expected scientific laws that would key in rules of control over human behavior. Franklin Roosevelt's New Deal had to deal with Depression financial catastrophes and unemployment on a scale beyond social scientists' imaginations. As the New Deal built government welfare programs and segued into unprecedented wartime government controls, it left a legacy of modern bureaucratic management invoking economist John Maynard Keynes rather than God.

John D. Rockefeller Jr.'s favorite pastor, Harry Emerson Fosdick, had published in 1922 a manifesto for politically liberal Christians. He directly attacked "the people who call themselves the Fundamentalists":

> Their apparent intention is to drive out of the evangelical churches men and women of liberal opinions. I speak of them the more freely because there are no two denominations more affected by them than the Baptist and the Presbyterian. We should not identify the Fundamentalists with the conservatives. All Fundamentalists are conservatives, but not all conservatives are Fundamentalists. The best conservatives can often give lessons to the liberals in true liberality of spirit, but the Fundamentalist program is essentially illiberal and intolerant . . . It is interesting to note where the Fundamentalists are driving in their stakes to mark out the deadline of doctrine around the church, across which no one is to pass except on terms of agreement. They insist that we must all believe in the historicity of certain special miracles, preeminently the virgin birth of our Lord; that we must believe in a special theory of inspiration—that the original documents of the Scripture, which of course we no longer possess, were inerrantly dictated to men a good deal as a man might dictate to a stenographer; that we must believe in a special theory of the Atonement—that the blood of our Lord, shed in a substitutionary death, placates an alienated Deity and makes possible welcome for the returning sinner; and that we must believe in the second coming of our Lord upon the clouds of heaven to set up a millennium here, as the only way in which God can bring history to a worthy denouement. Such are some of the stakes which are being driven to mark a deadline of doctrine around the church.[7]

Fosdick asserted that neither Paul nor John in the New Testament "even distantly allude to" the virgin birth and that a physical millennial Second Coming is an archaic notion superseded by modern theologians who, "when they say that Christ is coming, mean that, slowly it may be, but surely, His will and principles will be worked out by God's grace in human life and institutions."[8]

With liberal, secular, well-connected, modern politicians finding moral grounding in churches like Fosdick's, conservative Protestants struggled to perpetuate the Indo-European battle-ax tradition undergirding their versions of Christianity. After World War II, the United States enjoyed unprecedented prosperity, its erstwhile foreign competitors immured in rebuilding from ruins. President Lyndon Johnson launched a "Great Society" program, a "War on Poverty" instead of on infidels. His vision provoked churches teaching that humans, born stained with sin, could better strive for heavenly rather than earthly salvation.

More to the point politically, Johnson and the Supreme Court led by Chief Justice Earl Warren (1953–69) aimed to destroy America's hallowed racial segregation and disenfranchisement, which maintained its low-waged labor pool. Industrialists, agribusiness tycoons, small business owners, and independent "family" farmers all depended on Blacks, American Indians, and immigrants—including the women of these classes—for work that was heavy and dirty, or in sweatshops, or seasonal. A very large portion of America's White population felt threatened. Richard Nixon sensed that and in 1966, with a young aide named Patrick Buchanan, schemed to rebuild the Republican Party. Buchanan recalled in 2008, "What we talked about, basically, was shearing off huge segments of F.D.R.'s New Deal coalition, which L.B.J. [Lyndon Johnson] had held together: Northern Catholic ethnics and Southern Protestant conservatives." In 1969, Nixon addressed these constituencies via television: "And so tonight—to you, the great silent majority of Americans—I ask for your support."[9]

The brief 1960s flowering of the War on Poverty was aborted by the United States' imperial aggression in Vietnam. That and the Cold War against the Soviet Union were the kinds of wars the "silent majority" of Indo-Europeans considered normal. Conservatives rose from their nadir during the 1960s, invigorated to fight to keep America a Christian nation battling infidels in Asia and on college campuses. They held revivals, in person and electronically. "Make love, not war" was declared immoral—conservatives seemed not to have noticed that it might reflect Jesus's sentiment. Instead of the Social Gospel, post-1960s evangelists hammered the need to be "born again." Their emphasis was fully congruent with the modern Western concept of possessive individualism, and it connected to a new popular theme: everyone is wounded and requires healing.

Technically, the conservative Protestant movement gaining strength during the 1970s was inclined toward dispensational premillennialism; that is, that God made covenants (dispensations) with a series of nations, beginning with Israel and now with America, leading eventually to an apocalyptic final battle between Christ and the Antichrist, and the final millennium of the Kingdom of God. The elect, or saved (denominations disagree on defining these), will rise enraptured to heaven while everyone else sinks into eternal torment. Gory descriptions of this turbulent apocalypse abound in the *Left Behind* novels by Tim LaHaye, founder of San Diego Christian College, and professional writer Jerry Jenkins, a series that sold 65 million copies by spring 2008, twelve years after the first of the 18 novels appeared. LaHaye worked with Jerry Falwell in 1979 to create Falwell's Moral Majority organization, and the same year with Falwell's friend at Virginia Polytech, Henry Morris, to establish the Institute for Creation Research in southern California. Tim's wife Beverly LaHaye founded Concerned Women of America to fight acceptance of homosexuality, cohabitation without marriage, abortion, and the Equal Rights Amendment. The LaHayes' multifarious activities stress Fundamentalist dicta focused on an individual's set of beliefs. Their website, Seek God Ministries, linked to the *Left Behind* novels website, posts this central tenet: "To receive Jesus' flesh and blood means that you accept the sacrifice He made for you as the atonement of your sins. You receive the blood of Jesus by faith, by believing the gospel message. When you accept that the blood of Jesus paid the price for your sins you become reconciled to God. You will enter into Jesus and He will enter into you."[10]

Under the heading "Unity Through Compassion," Seek God cites John 3:14 (New Living Translation), explaining, "If we love other Christians, it proves that we have passed from death to eternal life." Indo-Europeans highly value *bruderbund*, band of comrades watching one another's backs in battle. "Christians are in a war, the good news is that we win," says Seek God Ministries.[11]

THE POSTWAR WAR

Vietnam confirmed to conservative Americans that the ballyhooed liberal Great Society betrayed their country. The Redeemer Nation direly needed redemption. Nixon's "silent majority" must show itself to be the Moral Majority. Jerry Falwell, leader of the titular Moral Majority, proclaimed "that Americans want to see this country come back to basics, back to values, back to biblical morality, back to sensibility, and back to patriotism . . . Our faltering [military] defenses . . . [are] permitting a godless society to emerge in America . . . A political leader, as a minister of God, is a revenger to execute wrath upon those who do evil."[12]

Balancing Vietnam's message of despair as the United States withdrew, emasculated, in 1975 was an exciting biblical miracle, the restoration of the Jews to Israel in 1948 and, particularly significant, Israel's rapid victory in the 1967 Six-Day War. The Holy Land was seized from its long centuries under infidel rule! Surely this presaged the Second Coming, the Millennium. Israel's virile, aggressive defense of its territories gave it the aura of an avenger executing wrath upon God's enemies. President Jimmy Carter, a Southern Baptist who had served in the Navy immediately after World War II, dedicated much effort to formulate a workable peace between Israel and Egypt. He was seen as wimpy in contrast to the extroverted manliness of his successor Ronald Reagan, who had spent the war years in the United States producing training films. Reagan's ersatz cowboy persona resonated with the popular 1980s "Rambo" series and other films celebrating the lone fighter with biceps pushing through his torn shirt. Raised an evangelical Protestant, Reagan, in 1983, called upon the National Association of Evangelicals to oppose Communism's "evil empire . . . the struggle between right and wrong and good and evil."[13] He himself sent Rambo-like agents to fight with reactionary movements against leftist governments, particularly in Nicaragua.

Conservative Christians' patriotic struggle to maintain US global supremacy, their fight against "the aggressive impulses of an evil empire," as Reagan urged,[14] melded with their growing struggle to maintain their traditional patriarchy. The counterculture movement of the late 1960s was above all challenging authority; authority per se; and authorities in schools, cities, and households. Women were emancipated in 1964 by the Civil Rights Act. They literally began to wear the pants, heretofore unthinkable for women in business locales or respectable dining and entertainment venues. (Actresses Marlene Dietrich and Katherine Hepburn enhanced their glamour by flaunting trouser costumes. Glamour is more than beauty; it is dangerous enchantment.) With girls and women now legally entitled to work and live on a par with boys and men, with young women in jeans nearly indistinguishable from long-haired young men, with young women rebelling against being sent to make the coffee, it looked like an end to families. That would mean an end to the nation! The backlash was powerful, reaction equal to the action.

Reagan tall on his horse was an icon[15] from America's mythic frontier democracy. Below him was his petite, pretty wife, looking up with adoring eyes. Both, of course, were professional actors. Reagan was a self-made millionaire, and the couple were church-going Christians; together they personified the ideal American family for the millions horrified by countercultural drugs and promiscuity. That hang-loose ethic was the epitome of secularization, totally amoral so far as conservatives could see—although flower-children communes somewhat resembled Jesus's radically egalitarian, peace-loving group of disciples. Reagan's rhetoric folded the godless, undisciplined hippie culture into the godless Soviet aggressor, the evil empire of the Antichrist rampant on the other side of the globe and pushing up like dragons' teeth among us in American meadows.

It's a chicken-and-egg question whether Reagan's political rhetoric encouraged the militant Christian Right to move onto the mainstream stage, or the growing strength of Christian Right organizations stimulated Reagan's speechwriters to curry favor with them. Reagan's echt-Calvinist policies, such as trickle-down economics and a strong military, fit Christian Right principles derived, like Calvin's own cultural principles, from the Indo-European ideology of the *bruderbund* warrior aristocracy. Always embattled, they display the elaborate weaponry—Star Wars missiles, for example—signaling their high social status. Now the country's leaders were men in suits, marshalling their followers by mounting the television dais. They exhorted them to be guerrillas fighting Satan in surrogate wars and by electing like-minded state and congressional representatives. Claiming that America had capitulated to secular godlessness, evangelical organizations proliferated: Jerry Falwell's Moral Majority and Liberty College, Beverly LaHaye's Concerned Women of America, Phyllis Schafly's Eagle Forum, Pat Robertson and Ralph Reed's Christian Coalition of America, and James Dobson's Focus on the Family.

The apex of conservative promotion was the 1994 Contract with America promulgated by Republican Party staffers. Said to have been drawn from the 1980 Republican campaign,[16] the contract was a platform announced six weeks before congressional elections midway through Bill Clinton's first presidential term. Whether the contract was crucial or not, Republicans won a majority in Congress that November. Coauthor Newt Gingrich became Speaker of the House, and Tom DeLay became House majority whip. Contract promises included reducing the size of federal government; making its transactions more transparent to the public; cutting taxes; "getting tough on crime" by building more prisons, enlarging police forces, and supporting the death penalty; sharply limiting welfare (the Personal Responsibility Act); and forbidding US troops to serve under United Nations command while cutting US payments to the United Nations Heady with newfound electoral success, Republicans led by Gingrich demanded President Clinton be impeached for perjury when he denied having sex with intern Monica Lewinsky (fellatio, he tried to insist, isn't "having sex"). The triviality of the charge, coupled with the way its pursuit was impeding the work of Congress, disillusioned many citizens, beginning the downslide of the Christian Right.

At its height in the 1980s and 1990s, the militant Christian Right championed "family values," signifying monogamous heterosexual legal marriage with a breadwinning father, a caregiving mother, and obedient children. "Family values" excluded homosexual persons from marriage and, in some jurisdictions, from adopting children—that is, from creating families. At the extreme of conservatism, Bob Jones University (Greenville, South Carolina) forbade interracial dating and marriage until 2000, holding that God had made distinct races, thus "mixing" races defied God. For most evangelicals, miscegenation was tacitly incompatible with "traditional families." So are "matrifocal" families headed by women. In 1965, the US Department of Labor issued the Moynihan Report, "The Negro Family: The Case for National Action," attributing the parlous state of ghetto Blacks to "disintegration" of families, specifically absent fathers. Racism, through overt discrimination and through poor schooling, hindered Black men from gaining steady employment, and policies on welfare payments, needed because of consequent unemployment, usually would not permit women to collect if a man was living in the home without contributing to its finances. Instead of seeing absences of fathers to be the result of government policies, direct and indirect in failure to forbid racist discrimination, liberals as well as conservatives bemoaned Blacks' moral dereliction. Liberals gradually realized that matrifocal ghetto families are the product of high unemployment, but conservatives continue to exacerbate the situation by campaigning for more arrests of drug dealers (low-level street dealing is a way for young Black men to earn money), and more prisons, incarcerating the unemployed rather than mounting massive programs to provide jobs. The US Department of Justice reported, "At current levels of incarceration newborn black males in this country have a greater than a 1 in 4 chance of going to prison during their lifetimes, while Hispanic males have a 1 in 6 chance, and white males have a 1 in 23 chance of serving time."[17] There is glaring disjunction between these figures and honoring family values.

"Family values" politics largely ignores embattled Black families. It cannot ignore its apparent subordination of women. LaHaye and Schafly purport to find no disrespect to women in Christian Right pronouncements against women pastors, but among evangelicals, as among Roman Catholics, there are movements to ordain women. The Southern Baptist Convention passed a resolution in 1984 against ordination of women, and formally adopted in 2000 the statement that scripture limits the office of pastor to men.[18] Its Baptist General Conference declares that scripture gives God's plan for the following:

- the father as spiritual leader, provider, giving of himself in love for his wife and children as Christ gave Himself for the church (Eph. 5:21; 6:4; Col. 3:19–21)
- the mother as partner, companion, and helper to the father, submitting to the leadership of her husband, loving him and her children (Col. 3:18; Eph. 5:22; Prov. 31; Titus 2:4)
- the children as obedient to the parents, respectful of their elders, and attentive to the instructions of God and parents (Col. 3:21; Eph. 6:1–3; Luke 2:51–52; Lev. 19:32)[19]

Responding in 1987 to the growing feminist movements among evangelicals, the newly organized Council on Biblical Manhood and Womanhood affirmed, "Adam's headship in marriage was established by God before the Fall, and was not a result of sin (Gen 2:16–18, 21–24, 3:1–13; 1 Cor 11:7–9)."[20] When Sarah Palin, governor of Alaska, accepted the Republican nomination for vice president in August 2008, the council's website posted a series discussing whether her governorship and candidacy is contrary to scripture; the writer concluded that a woman taking secular governmental offices is not offensive, but expressed concern that Palin might neglect her husband's and children's needs—it would be better if she were "a sage-like woman in her sixties with no children at home."[21] In this reading of scripture, the church and family are the places where patriarchal gender roles must be maintained.

Divorcing secular from religious spheres as the Council on Biblical Manhood and Womanhood does is a move to contain and overcome secularism. Implicitly, it gives higher value to church and family than to secular activities in that it places them under direct relevance to scripture, and secular institutions farther from scriptural guidance. This did not preclude efforts to reverse secularism. Perceived dissolution of American moral standards in the 1960s spread of counterculture behavior spurred Francis Schaeffer (1912–84), a prominent evangelical theologian, to set out a dichotomy between secular and scripturally guided conduct: "The basic [premise] was that there really are such things as absolutes . . . in the area of Being (or knowledge), and in the area of morals . . . Absolutes imply antithesis . . . right and wrong, . . . true and false."[22]

Schaeffer went on to explicate, in a 1976 book *How Should We Then Live?*, "God himself had told mankind to have dominion over nature" (Genesis 1:28)—a direct slap at countercultural, back-to-nature movements—and, obviously even more imperative, dominion over our daily lives, which implies control of the society enveloping us.[23] In line with Fundamentalist expectation of an imminent Second Coming of Christ, Schaeffer warned, "I don't think we have a lot of time. The hour is very late, but I don't think it is too late in this country. This is not a day of retreat and despair. In America it is still possible to turn things around. But we don't have forever."[24]

Such a sense of crisis underlay Jimmy Carter's presidency. Carter felt the tension, but his strong feelings toward pacific solutions placed him on the liberal side of Fundamentalists. Disappointed in their hopes for a forceful political ally, Fundamentalist leaders took it upon themselves to restore Christian dominion to the United States. They were certainly correct in asserting that America had been a Christian nation, whatever the intent of the deist founding fathers. That it should be a Christian nation is another issue. Bolstered by their upbringing in the still overtly Christian nation of the interwar period, Carter's liberalism goaded these leaders to organize.

Francis Schaeffer introduced the term "co-belligerency" to describe a coalition of conservatives fighting for particular issues, even though they might challenge each other on other issues.[25] In the coalition were Pat Robertson of the 700 Club radio and television broadcast empire; D. James Kennedy of Coral Ridge Ministries; James Dobson of Focus on the Family; Tim and Beverly LaHaye; Charles Colson (Nixon's aide, who became an evangelist after being in prison for his role in Watergate); and Jerry Falwell, who founded Moral Majority in 1979. Paul Weyrich, a Republican activist enjoying support by Joseph Coors of the brewery fortune, organized prayer breakfasts for Washington politicians, lobbyists, and evangelical leaders, in addition to developing the Heritage Foundation. "Secular humanism"—an opprobrious term introduced by Francis Schaeffer—would be thwarted.

CHAPTER 11

ASSAULT ON THE
SECULAR NATION

The death of Francis Schaeffer in 1984 was a pivot for the Christian Right in America. Schaeffer had been speaking from his pastoral retreat L'Abri (The Shelter) in Switzerland when he advised, as he titled his book, "How Should We Then Live." The generation of active evangelical leaders in the 1980s would not retreat into rural shelters.

Jerry Falwell's Moral Majority, founded in 1979, was the most prominent of the plethora of Fundamentalist organizations. It damned abortion and homosexuality as sins, opposed the Equal Rights Amendment to the Constitution, and warned against the Strategic Arms Limitation Treaty. Falwell's "pro-life" principles did not extend to an end to the death penalty. He and his co-belligerents in the Christian Coalition, Pat Robertson and Ralph Reed, called upon Christians to stage public rallies, lobby candidates and elected representatives and officials, and vote to overturn what they perceived to be liberal betrayals of God's ordained order. Clearly, this was the God of the Old Testament. Jesus's call to follow him, to abandon parents and siblings,[1] his radical open friendship with women, and his praise for Martha who sat listening to him rather than working in the kitchen with her sister (Luke 10:39–41), all demonstrate Jesus's rejection of patriarchal "family values." Above all, Jesus did not appeal to nationalist sentiments even though he lived in a recently conquered kingdom. The militant Christian Right, on the contrary, demands that the United States be a patriarchal Christian nation.

General George Patton is a hero to the Christian Right. Fundamentalist pastor Steve Hickey tells his congregation that "you do not win a war hunkering down. Patton said, 'The only way you can win a war is to attack and keep on attacking, and after you have done that, keep attacking some more.'"[2] Hickey continues his battlefield call: "God is restoring the governmental office of apostle in His warring End-time church. He is wrapping up His plans and purposes on earth. He desires to see His church awaken and arise, fully restored to their appointed office so they can effectively subdue the earth, reclaim the land, free the captives, and release the spoils plundered by the enemies of God."[3] Pastor Hickey, working from his Harvest Church in Sioux Falls, South Dakota, founded the Regional Apostolic Mobilization "as a vehicle to establish the kingdom of God on the Northern Plains," according to his book's back cover; on the front is a photo of three bighorn rams—he will RAM God's kingdom through.

Rams: in scripture, Genesis 22:13 tells of a ram caught in a thicket where Abraham was about to sacrifice his son Isaac. God forbade the human sacrifice, so Abraham, noticing the hapless animal behind him, slaughtered and offered it instead. Pastor Hickey is not thinking of this scriptural ram, nor of the Lamb, Christ, whom Christians usually identify as the fulfillment of Abraham's sacrifice.[4] His is the Germanic word *ramm*, meaning "to strike, batter, drive by hard blows,"[5] as did General Patton.

Away back in the Battle-Ax Culture period, Indo-European warriors rammed their weapons at their battle opponents. Through the millennia, the battle-ax or battle-hammer symbolized the Indo-European ideal hero, from India's Indra with his club (*vajra*) to the Germanic Thor with his hammer. Thor—Donar in Germanic—personifies thunder (compare modern German *Donner*, "thunder"). He hurls his hammer—that is, thunderbolts; until early modern times, Europeans commonly believed that prehistoric stone celts were Thor's thunderbolts fallen to earth. As Thunder, Thor was the most physically powerful, most actively masculine, of the Germanic gods. Thunder occurring with wind and rain, Thor and his hard hammer are associated with earthly fertility, consecrating marriages and also funerals (Thor can resurrect the dead).[6] Thor drives a chariot pulled by—yes!—two male goats whom he resurrects from their bones after slaughtering them for a feast. Thor's chariot beasts indicate he is the Germanic equivalent of the Indian *Rig-Veda's* god Pusan, who similarly drives a chariot pulled by goats and is beseeched for

Figure 11.1.   Thor with his hammer and crossed spears

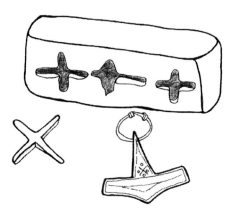

Figure 11.2. Silversmith's mold, medieval Scandinavia, producing both crosses and Thor's hammer amulets

Credit: Drawings by April Bernath: Thor after bronze figurine in grave, Ekhamman, Uppland, Sweden; mold and amulets in National Museum of Denmark, after illustration in John Lindow, 2001, Handbook of Norse Mythology, ABC-CLIO, Santa Barbara, CA.

fertility.[7] Bones of goats and sheep are so alike that even specialists cannot distinguish early domesticated species. A zoologist might identify the bones of Thor's chariot beasts as rams. Norse did have a ram linked with a warrior god, Heimdall, guardian of the gates of heaven who will blow his mighty horn when the end of our world comes; extant sources are not clear as to whether Heimdall may have been conceptualized as a ram, or if his horn was a ram's horn, or if he was accompanied by a ram.

Linking America's militant Christian Right to pagan Thor is more than speculation. A cult devoted to Thor developed during the late tenth century CE as the Germanic peoples of Scandinavia and northern Europe were being proselytized for Christianity. Amulets of Thor's hammer became popular, with casting molds prepared so that either the hammer or a Christian cross could be selected.[8]

He held his battle-hammer with both hands on a crosspiece, thus early medieval crucifix pendants could resemble the god's hammer, especially if, as on a piece from Sweden, the cross is human-shaped and has Thor's fierce blazing eyes.[9] Thor's goats are depicted on medieval German churches. Thor's day—Thursday—was preferred for weddings in Germany until the end of the medieval period. Proselytizers equated Thor slaying the terrible Midgard serpent, a fight that cost the life of the exhausted god, with Christ slaying Leviathan and then dying.[10] (Christ as divine incarnation is eternal; therefore, he could battle the Old Testament Leviathan, regardless of his short earthly incarnation as the man Jesus.) Thor, ever ready to do battle, enfolded

Christ as institutionalized Christianity enveloped medieval Germanic peoples. Although scholars have assumed that the "Thor cult" represents last-ditch resistance of proselytized pagans, the evidence can instead be interpreted as persistence of belief in Thor. Discussing the contestation in medieval Scandinavia between pagans and Christian missionaries, an Oxford professor remarks on an episode in the Kristni and the Njáls Sagas: "It shows . . . how Christians regarded Thór; he might sink to the level of a demon, but no one could say he did not exist."[11]

Thor is described as "the rampart of divine society . . . it is enough for the frightened Æsir [gods] to pronounce his name to make him rise up, menacingly, in an angry state, móðr, which makes him resemble his monstrous adversaries. Nothing then restrains him, not even legal scruples."[12] Here is the militant Indo-European champion, defending the gods with berserkr power. Popular culture puts him into comics and movies with Superman, Captain Marvel, Batman, Spiderman, the Terminator . . . and Popeye the Sailor Man. Theologian Robert Jewett recognized this iconic figure, terming him "Captain America":

> [He] never seems to seek or enjoy the accolades of the community, and in the classical tales, he never rides off with the beautiful girl. In the taking-courage episode before the final confrontation with the Bad Guy, he decides to be faithful to himself and what he believes right, without regard to the inevitably cowardly attitude of the crowd. Having so resolved, he becomes curiously immune to criticism if he happens to break one of the ideals or laws in the battle. This is where Popeye's can of spinach fits in. His initial desire is to be passive, but when he receives the clear call to battle he must faithfully but regretfully obey. He then becomes a channel of divine justice and whatever he does to win the battle is tolerated. Spinach symbolizes quite effectively the unpleasant obligation to redeem the community through violence as well as the implicit promise of strength so that victory is inevitable. Just as in the book of Revelation, to be faithful causes one to suffer, but it also qualifies one to be the victor in an apocalyptic battle in which no holds are barred. On this basis the stereotype combines such seemingly contradictory elements as a perfectly clean and basically passive hero, committed to lawful obedience, carrying out his highest form of faithfulness by violating cleanliness, law, and passivity.[13]

The iconic figures are Indo-European warriors. They exemplify what classics scholar Georges Dumézil labeled the "second-function" warrior: neither morally upright, intellectual, "first-function" priests and judges nor commoner, "third-function" producers and merchants. Together, the components of the three functions make up a structure of checks and balances, notably in the United States, where the Supreme Court balances the executive president/commander-in-chief and the democratically representative Congress.

Throughout Indo-European societies, tripartite structure divides members into three "estates" (Lords Spiritual, Lords Temporal, Commons in Britain; aristocracy, freemen, serfs; or upper, middle, working classes), ideally respecting each other's contributions. Dumézil emphasized that, in the real world, those in second-function positions characteristically try to usurp powers properly reserved to the other two classes. Second-function individuals, in mythology and real life, are tempted by their lust for power to override legal strictures. A good example was Richard Nixon, and in the climatic October 1973 weekend when he struggled to fire Archibald Cox, special prosecutor investigating the Watergate scandal, the ancient Indo-European tripartite structure of checks and balances triumphed over the second-function usurping executive. It is noteworthy that many well-known evangelists who exercise executive abilities building multimillion-dollar organizations behave like second-function leaders, violating moral and often financial laws. Jim Bakker, Jimmy Swaggart, Billy James Hargis, Garner Ted Armstrong, Kent Hovind, Ted Haggard, Newt Gingrich, and Tony Alamo are contemporary examples. Francis Schaeffer's son and designated heir, Frank, turned against his father after making widely used films based on "How Should We Then Live?" Frank's book revealed Francis to have been quite the second-function warrior, not a saint.

Christian warriors were galvanized in the mid-1960s by a concatenation of liberal movements, from Lyndon Johnson's "Great Society" War on Poverty and the 1964 Civil Rights Act to hippie counterculture. Although Johnson's program fit Christian Social Gospel goals, its federal government location colored it secular, an expansion of big government into what had been municipal and state administrations; furthermore, it looked socialist to conservative citizens. The Civil Rights Act slammed the hierarchy comfortably enjoyed by White Protestant men, their authority grounded in their Bible reading. Daily, their sensibilities were offended by the sight of long-haired young men and young women in jeans or granny dresses, looseness of clothing the visible sign of sexuality unloosed and work ethic lost. Barry Goldwater's 1964 campaign for the presidency rallied conservatives, but they lost the election. Billy Graham was the most prominent evangelist, his well-run organization holding enormous revival rallies, yet he was a diplomat rather than a warrior, intimate golfing companion and counselor to every president from Truman to the Bushes.

According to a study published by Baylor University Press,[14] Francis Schaeffer better assuaged the anxieties of American Protestant young people, at least from middle-class families. He collated scriptural verse with art history, tracing Christian understanding through the ages via paintings, and insisted his reasoning leading to professing Fundamentalist Protestantism was philosophically logical. Glossing the appeal to middle-class college youth, Schaeffer extolled the spiritual euphoria that comes from giving oneself to God. L'Abri was almost a commune, young people sleeping here and there, the dining table crammed with them listening intently to their bearded guru discoursing for hours. Intellectual philosopher he considered himself to be, nevertheless teaching a simple dichotomy easy to grasp, between God and secular humans, right and evil. He used martial language, too: "Christians must realize that there is a difference between being a cobelligerent and an ally . . . The church of the Lord Jesus Christ is different."[15]

Jerry Falwell declared, "Jesus was not a pacifist. He was not a sissy"[16] (somewhat a non sequitur). Pete Peters, pastor of La Porte Church of Christ (La Porte, Colorado), trumpeted, "[P]hony churches and preachers of our day have caused our warrior types to feel archaic, unneeded, and less than Christian . . . America's decline and weakening can be attributed to the switch from a (strong, logical, masculine) Bible-based Christianity to a (weak, emotional, illogical, feminine) non-Biblical Judeo-Christianity."[17] In one sentence, pastor Peters constructed a Manichean dichotomy:

Strong	Weak
Logical	Illogical
Masculine	Feminine
Bible-based	Non-Bible-based
Christians	Jews

And in line with the Christian set, he fights against gun control: "KNOW YOU NEED YOUR GUN TO PROTECT YOURSELF AGAINST GOVERN-MENT."[18] Even Rick Warren, pastor of Saddleback Church, a megachurch in California—so moderate an evangelical that Barack Obama chose him to give the invocation at his January 20, 2009, inauguration—wrote in his bestselling *The Purpose-Driven Life*, "Don't ever try to argue with the Devil . . . You can't bluff Satan with logic or your opinion, but you can use the weapon that makes him tremble—the truth of God. This is why memorizing Scripture is absolutely essential to defeating temptation . . . If you don't have any Bible verses memorized, you've got no bullets in your gun!"[19]

Actor John Wayne personified the militant Right's ideal. Ronald Reagan eulogized, "Everything about him—his stature, his style, his convictions— conveyed enduring strength," and he quoted fellow actor Elizabeth Taylor: "He gave the whole world the image of what an American should be."[20] This gunslinging hero lived on the frontier, fighting alone to save pusil-lanimous townspeople from evildoers. A big guy, strong—Thor, too, lived on the frontier of Asgard, came when he was summoned to battle attackers feared by the other gods. Sometimes a John Wayne character brandished his rifle like a hammer to bash the foe. The essential continuity between pre-Christian Germanic ideology and medieval enfolding of Germanic deities within Christian images, between ancient and contemporary Indo-European societies, calls for this second-function warrior to save common folk. He is a man of action, not an intellectual (unlike Francis Schaeffer, who never became an icon). He is as rock, firm in his convictions as rifle-toting actor John Wayne.

THE CHRISTIAN RIGHT ORGANIZES

At the end of the 1970s, a sufficient number of Christians had organized for political action that meetings were held to construct cobelligerancy. The movement was predominantly Fundamentalist Protestant, although key leaders—Paul Weyrich and Phyllis Schafly—were Catholic, and one, Howard Phillips, was Jewish. Reflecting the political geography of the United States, Virginia hosted the two leading political organizations, Pat Robertson's Christian Coalition and Falwell's Moral Majority, the former because northern Virginia is part of the Washington, DC, focus of government, and the latter stemming from the strong Bible Belt Fundamentalism of southern Virginia. The greater Washington area brings together lobbyists working for the National Rifle Association, strategists in the Heritage Foundation and Free Congress Foundation (both founded by Weyrich), Republican Party staffers, and conservative members of Congress. A 1979 meeting between Jerry Falwell, Paul Weyrich, Richard Viguerie, Howard Phillips, Ed McAteer, and Robert Billings of the National Christian Action Council produced the name "Moral Majority" (attributed to Weyrich) and launched Falwell into national politics.

The Christian Action Council had begun in 1975 with Dr. C. Everett Koop (later to be Reagan's Surgeon General), theologian Harold O. J. Brown, Francis Schaeffer, and Billy Graham, aiming to pressure Congress to restrict abortions—that is, it was meant to constrain the 1973 *Roe v. Wade* Supreme Court decision that abortion was a private matter, not within the purview of government. Relevant also was the expiration in 1979 of the effort to have states ratify the Equal Rights Amendment (ERA) drafted to protect women's rights. Phyllis Schafly had led the campaign against the constitutional amendment through her Eagle Forum, also known as Stop-ERA, mobilizing conservative women by declaring that the ERA would force homemakers into wage work. Schafly herself, though mother of six, is a Harvard Law School graduate seemingly seldom at home. Fifteen years of radical legislation, from the Civil Rights Act through *Roe v. Wade* and the Equal Rights Amendment, pulled militants together to assault "secular humanism."

The Moral Majority flamed and then sputtered in the 1980s. It was insufficiently focused to hold advocates. Tellingly, the most successful militant Right organization is called Focus on the Family. Dr. James Dobson, credentialed as a child psychologist, published in 1970 a parenting guide called *Dare to Discipline*. Selling more than a million copies in a decade, it was followed by an extraordinary revelation of the militant Christian Right's obsession with domination and violence, *The Strong-Willed Child*. In this book, a small girl playfully pretends she will cross a line her father has just instructed her to stay within. Dobson declares, "The entire human race is afflicted with the same tendency toward willful defiance that this three-year-old exhibited. Her behavior in the gym is not so different from the folly of Adam and Eve in the Garden of Eden." After considering whether this little child might be simply irresponsible, Dobson concludes,

Responsible behavior is a noble objective for our children, but let's admit that the heavier task is shaping the child's will! A spanking is to be reserved for use in response to willful defiance, whenever it occurs. Period! . . . Should a spanking hurt? Yes, or else it will have no influence . . . Two or three stinging strokes on the legs or bottom with a switch are usually sufficient to emphasize the point, "You must obey me."

By learning to yield to the loving authority (leadership) of his parents, a child learns to submit to other forms of authority . . . Without respect for leadership, there is anarchy, chaos, and confusion . . . a child learns to yield to the authority of God by first learning to submit (rather than bargain) to the leadership of his parents . . . We are not typically kind and loving and generous and yielded to God. Our tendency is toward selfishness and stubbornness and sin . . . Jesus Christ . . . alone can "cleanse" [the child] of rebellion.[21]

Here is Captain America speaking, beginning gently, transmogrifying into fervently embattled salvific passion. Democracy, as a principle, is dangerous secular humanism. It must be stingingly beaten down.

Dobson obtained a bully pulpit through his child-rearing advice, purportedly nonpolitical. His books brought him speaking engagements and a radio program, enabling him to resign his position at Children's Hospital of Los Angeles in 1977 and devote his energies to expanding his influence. His Family News Service radio programs air on hundreds of stations across the country, amplified by videos on parenting, his monthly magazine, and online Citizen-link. Since 1991, Focus on the Family has occupied a large campus in Colorado Springs, Colorado, where more than a thousand employees labor, a large number in answering questions and pleas for help pouring in from listeners. During the 1980s, Dobson served on a Reagan National Advisory Council on juvenile justice and delinquency and was a familiar of Reagan's domestic policy advisor, Gary Bauer, himself an evangelical. After Reagan, Dobson had fewer direct contacts with the White House, instead carefully presenting himself as nonpolitical, a doctor concerned with the health of American families. Behind this, he continued to ally with cobelligerents in the assault on secular America.

Love and concern for one's children is an instinct—strengthened through natural selection over millions of years—that humans must work out within the societies in which they live. Dobson teaches that the nuclear heterosexual family led by the husband-father is the means to raise a nation of soldiers of Christ, submitting to the authority of pastors as they fulfill the Great Commission to dominate the earth. Women may work outside the home (like many of his employees in Colorado Springs), but they must recognize that God endowed men with leadership; wives should counsel their husbands without forgetting that it is women's grace to be, finally, submissive, or as John Eldredge puts it, "captivating." Eldredge, another militant evangelical man, runs Ransomed Heart Ministries, also in Colorado Springs, selling his Wild at Heart to men: "Every man was once a boy. And every little boy has dreams, big dreams: dreams of being the hero, of beating the bad guys, of doing daring feats and rescuing the damsel in distress. Every little girl has dreams, too: of being rescued by her prince and swept up into a great adventure, knowing that she is the beauty." The complementing Eldredge book for women is *Captivating*.[22]

Echoing Francis Schaeffer's insistence on black-and-white dichotomies, Dobson cannot tolerate homosexuality. Abortion, which could reduce the population of evangelicals, is forbidden, while the morality of legal execution (the death penalty) is not questioned. Focus on the Family sanctifies patriarchal authority, exercising its power through brutalizing children while women look on. Dr. Dobson quotes scripture without acknowledging Jesus of Nazareth's radical call: "I am come to set a man at variance against his father, and the daughter against her mother . . . He that loveth father or mother more than me is not worthy of me" (Matthew 10:35, 37). If Matthew's Jesus was Christ, then Focus on the Family is unchristian.

AND ON THE FAR RIGHT

Jerry Falwell in Lynchburg, Virginia, was close to the rock-bottom Fundamentalism of Young Earth creationists, believers in the literal words of approved Protestant Bibles (King James and New American Standard translations). Near Lynchburg, Virginia Polytechnic State University in Blacksburg had hired Henry M. Morris as professor of civil engineering. Morris studied hydraulic engineering to better understand the magnitude and effects of Noah's flood. He taught that Christians should understand these four foundational events:

1. Special creation of all things in six days
2. The curse upon all things, by which the entire cosmos was brought into a state of gradual deterioration ["entropy"]
3. The universal Flood, which drastically changed the rates of most earth processes
4. The dispersion at Babel, which resulted from the sudden proliferation of languages and other cultural distinctives[23]

It was at Babel, Morris declared, that "the entire monstrous complex . . . Pantheism, polytheism, astrology, idolatry, mysteries, spiritism, materialism . . . was revealed to Nimrod . . . by demonic influences, perhaps by Satan himself."[24] Morris's stark denouncement literally demonized secular humanism. Jerry Falwell and other pastors in the region befriended Morris as Falwell built up his own church in Blacksburg. By 1969, Virginia Polytechnic asked Dr. Morris to resign.

At that time, Falwell was energetically establishing Lynchburg Baptist College (now Liberty University) to train evangelical pastors, teachers, and others devoted to the Great Commission to aggressively win the world to Fundamentalist Protestantism. Another Baptist, Tim LaHaye, held similar ambitions for a college, Christian Heritage, in southern California. LaHaye persuaded Dr. Morris to relocate to San Diego, to serve as academic vice president of Christian Heritage College and director of the affiliated Institute for Creation Research, a faculty for promoting "scientific creationism." Alongside supporting the Institute and the college, Tim LaHaye led a growing congregation and with his wife Beverly, founder of Concerned Women of America, worked toward political outreach. Neither Lynchburg Baptist nor Christian Heritage were as stringently fundamentalist as Bob Jones University (founded in 1927). Insofar as Bob Jones represents a separatist position, a parallel universe to secular America, keeping its students busy on campus and discouraging mixing with more lax Christians; Lynchburg Baptist, Christian Heritage, and the newer Patrick Henry College (opened in 2000 in northern Virginia) prepare students to work in the secular world. They will evangelize, but not necessarily as church leaders. Nevertheless, Patrick Henry students must profess, "Satan exists as a personal, malevolent being who acts as tempter and accuser, for whom Hell, the place of eternal punishment, was prepared, where all who die outside of Christ shall be confined in conscious torment for eternity."[25]

Given that these and other Fundamentalist Christian colleges require students and faculty to accept the classic Five Fundamentals—biblical inerrancy, virgin birth and deity of Christ Jesus, his crucifixion as atonement for humans' sins, his bodily resurrection after death, and authenticity of his miracles—they tend to assert the first tenet, biblical inerrancy, to be the essential key to the other four, and thereby to salvation. Therefore, the militant Christian Right campaigns to substitute Genesis for secular sciences' accounts of evolution of the universe, earth, and organisms. Fundamentalist theologians and pastors had, for a century, since Robert Chambers's *Vestiges* in 1844, and Darwin's *Origin of Species* in 1859, dismissed universal organic evolution as speculative and contrary to the Word of God, until the US reaction to the Soviet Union's 1957 launch of Sputnik spawned 1960s programs to improve American science education. To fight godless Russia, Americans had to be better scientists.

Patriots that they were, evangelicals rose to the call by founding the Creation Research Society in 1963, and by 1969, with Henry Morris's move to southern California, Creation Science, Inc., was set up there to publish textbooks presenting Genesis as science. Morris is said to have introduced the label "scientific creationism" as a course title in 1970 for Christian Heritage College, and the next year he published an article in *Creation Research Society Quarterly* recommending a "two-model pedagogy," one model being accepted organic evolution and geology, and the other—oppositional dualism again—an array of data purportedly validating Genesis. For example, indeed, the favorite example, is that the Grand Canyon is said to have been carved by the tremendous outflow of Noah's Flood. Furthermore, stratigraphy showing fishes and amphibians in the lowest strata and mammals near the top does not indicate evolution through time, but the natural habitat of fishes below water, and the intelligent, if futile, effort of mammals to climb higher than the rising flood. The one principle of historical sciences that scientific creationists could not manage in their model is the rule that data from the past should be explicable through processes observed in the present. Creation scientists are obliged to assert that some ancient events were God's miracles.

Throughout the United States, Fundamentalist school board members and state legislators attempted to mandate scientific creationists' two-model version of earth and organic history, and/or ban the word "evolution" from mainstream textbooks. Because major textbook publishers depend on book choices made by Texas and California, where curricula are selected at the state level and Fundamentalists are significant voters, from the 1970s on, "evolution" was often a missing link in K–12 biology textbooks, more or less described only with euphemisms. Periodically, a teacher or parent brought a First Amendment lawsuit against imposition of a Christian religious position into public education. Periodically, a lawsuit would reach a federal court that invariably ruled in favor of the plaintiffs, holding that creation science/ scientific creationism and, more recently, "intelligent design" (creation by a Godlike intelligence) are religion, not science, and so cannot be taught in public schools under the aegis of science. Undeterred, Fundamentalists insist that it is scientific to take sections of Genesis and match them to observed material. They assert they are using a method of doing science promoted as "hypothetico-deductive" by philosopher Carl Hempel in the mid-twentieth century. George Gaylord Simpson, a leading mid-twentieth-century paleontologist, assailed Hempel's method as inapplicable to historical sciences.[26]

If creation science is science, then it ought to have a place in natural history museums. Mainstream museums consistently politely refuse requests to include "the other model." Jerry Falwell had a creationist museum built in 1984 on the Liberty College campus, Henry Morris had one from the beginning of the Institute for Creation Research in California. Topping these is Answers in Genesis's Creation Museum in Kentucky, opened in 2007. Adhering to a literal "young-earth" reading of Genesis—that is, a day in Genesis is 24 hours, thus the earth and organisms were created in six actual days in 4004 BCE—Answers in Genesis's museum spared no expense to show visitors how six thousand years ago before the Flood, humans heard dinosaurs roar. The two-model pedagogy is illustrated by a diorama of paleontologists excavating a dinosaur, one man to be saved by his belief in Genesis, the other lost through his atheism. One exhibit starkly denounces believers who don't understand that we live in a Francis-Schaeffer world of "absolutes." Compromises such as accepting an "old-earth" position that days in Genesis might have really been geological ages are literally damning. The museum sells a book designed to furnish students with questions to challenge secular teachers. It seems unlikely that the Creation Museum will convert a freethinker; instead, it will probably reinforce already-committed Fundamentalists, and it can be a godsend to Christian schools and homeschooled children of believers.

Higher education for such young people can include graduate degrees in the sciences from colleges accredited by the Transnational Association of

Christian Colleges and Schools (TRACS), begun in 1979 through Henry Morris to give standing to the Institute for Creation Research, whose graduate degree biology and geology programs were deemed unacceptable by the secular accrediting agency. TRACS became a federally recognized accreditation agency in 1991, thanks to President George H. W. Bush's secretary of education Lamar Alexander, subsequently a senator from Tennessee. To be accredited by TRACS, a school must profess the following:

> *The Bible.* The unique divine inspiration of all the canonical books of the Old and New Testaments as originally given, so that they are infallibly and uniquely authoritative and free from error of any sort in all matters with which they deal, scientific, historical, moral, and theological.
>
> *Biblical Creation.* Special creation of the existing space-time universe and all its basic systems and kinds of organisms in the six literal days of the creation week.
>
> *Historicity.* The full historicity and perspicuity of the biblical record of primeval history, including the literal existence of Adam and Eve as the progenitors of all people, the literal fall and resultant divine curse on the creation, the worldwide cataclysmic deluge, and the origin of nations and languages at the tower of Babel.
>
> *Satan.* The existence of a personal, malevolent being called Satan who acts as tempter and accuser, for whom the place of eternal punishment was prepared, where all who die outside of Christ shall be confined in conscious torment for eternity.[27]

With Henry Morris on the board of TRACS, his Institute of Creation Research (ICR) and LaHaye's Christian Heritage College were granted accreditation.

ICR moved in 2007 to Dallas, Texas, considered a more practical central location by Morris's sons John and Henry Morris III. Texas does not recognize TRACS as a legitimate higher-education accrediting organization. ICR explained on its website, "Pursuant to California and Federal law, ICRGS currently offers an M.S. in Science Education, mostly online, to qualified students who are not Texas residents. ICR is currently examining its legal options regarding how it can best serve the educational 'gaps' of Texas residents."[28] ICR is quite explicit on its website that it offers, as it states, a "unique" Masters in Science Education online program, because it

- teaches science from a creationist perspective;
- grounds the learner in a biblically based program in the sciences with science and teaching science as the focus;
- educates the learner to discern the biblical perspective in science and science teaching;
- provides the learners (science teachers) a chance to network with other science teachers so they can develop a network of Christian educators who support creation science (research shows that students in interactive online programs know each other better than those in face-to-face classes);

- assists the learner in developing creation apologetics in his or her science classroom; and
- teaches the learner how to develop curriculum, instructional strategies, and classroom activities related to creation science.[29]

Massed opposition from Nobel science laureates in Texas universities and medical colleges, Texas Academy of Sciences, American Institute for Biological Sciences, the Biological Sciences Curriculum Study nonprofit corporation, and hundreds of individual scientists and educators made it clear that Texas would not, as the Austin *American-Statesman* newspaper put it in 2008, allow "the wars over the teaching of both evolution and intelligent design that have splintered Kansas for the past nine years."[30]

"Splintering" was the aim of the coalitions of Christian Right pastors to wedge (a favorite word) into public education, on the one hand establishing Christian colleges shielding Christian youth from secular seductions and on the other hand taking advantage of public ignorance of scientific criteria to embed Fundamentalist precepts in public discourse. The desired, and partially achieved, result was to solidify the popular stereotype of conflict between science and religion, set up so that, inevitably, science had to be satanic because religion is on the side of God. Surveys by the Barna Research Group, a sociologically respectable Christian organization, found that in 2007, approximately 43 percent of US adults may be classified as evangelicals by Fundamentalist criteria, and this percentage rose from 35 percent surveyed in 1991. Some of the criteria are that Satan really exists, that "the Bible is accurate in all that it teaches," and that "God . . . created the universe and still rules it today."[31] Barna surveys report that only 26 percent of evangelicals are college graduates. It found in 2004 that half of American evangelicals had "accepted Jesus Christ as their savior" before they were 13 years old, two-thirds by age 18, and 13 percent by age 21. In 1999, 26 percent of evangelicals identified themselves as "part of the Religious Right." One-third of born-again Christian adults professed belief in moral absolutes, contrasted with 16 percent of non-born-again adults.[32] These figures indicate that thirty years of coalitions had increased the proportion of Americans in the Christian Right from one-third to two-fifths, an assault on secularism weaker than prayed for but nonetheless politically significant.

CHAPTER 12

INTERLOCKING DIRECTORATES

BUSINESS AND POLITICS

Presbyterian theologian C. S. Calian heard men in his congregation remark, "I read the *Wall Street Journal* and my Bible together daily." From his questioning, he wrote *The Gospel According to the Wall Street Journal*, concluding, "The *Journal* always sees illusion and realism in terms of vested interest."[1] Far from a straight chronicle of business, the *Wall Street Journal* was, for the entire twentieth century, controlled by the wealthy, conservative Bancroft family. Editorials in the newspaper accepted "the Judaeo-Christian view of man, created in the image of God but marred by original sin."[2] Midcentury editor William H. Grimes wrote in 1951, and the newspaper reprinted in 1972, "Our comments and interpretations are made from a definite point of view . . . We believe in the individual, in his wisdom and his decency. We oppose all infringements on individual rights, whether they stem from attempts at private monopoly, labor union monopoly or from an overgrowing government."[3] Being marred by original sin apparently wouldn't detract from individuals' wisdom and decency.

Waldo Beach, a professor in Duke University's Divinity School, perceived a dichotomy between Sunday and mundane ethics among professedly Christian businesspeople:

> In the Men's Bible class, or in church, [the businessman] will profess, ardently and honestly, his allegiance to the great Christian virtues of universal love and brotherhood, of a trustful reliance on the providence of God, of sacrificial service to the cause of Christ, of humble contrition and infinite forgiveness . . . But back at the office on Monday morning, he . . . is now back in the world of real life, where a different game is played and other rules called for. It would be impossible for him, as an insurance company executive, to run his office by the rule of absolute forgiveness. In the business world in general, he knows, a forethoughtless trust like that of the birds of the air would not look impressive

to auditors or stockholders. In the realm of politics, local and international, contrition and self-sacrifice are impossible to practice, for politics is a rough-and-tumble business, no holds barred. Therefore the rules of good citizenship on earth in the political game are different, regrettably, from the rules of citizenship in heaven. Universal love, inclusive of friend and enemy, like and unlike, is indeed a beautiful and noble principle. But no nation which applies such an ethic in its foreign policy could hope to survive.[4]

This may be *realpolitik*, but it's hardly Jesus's teaching.

The militant Christian Right coalition's assault on secularism in America did not target a lack of Christian ethics in business. Businesspeople fight competitors, fight to increase profits. At one extreme is Bob Jones University, which sent out a team of debaters in 1974 that I heard in Milwaukee. Their reiterated message was that Satan is real; he can be anywhere, in any guise—he can be your spouse, your parent, your child, your neighbor, your business associates. In other words, you are alone except you accept Jesus Christ as spirit companion. Enlarging on this frightening warning, the Bob Jones team said that this world is red in tooth and claw, a battleground where, because any business transaction may be trafficking with Satan, we cannot hold to ethical principles, for by that we will lose the battle—Satan doesn't play by ethics. Christian ethics lie in heaven. (It was hearing this Bob Jones message that provoked me to research the paradox of professed Christians advocating abandoning ethics.)

Bob Jones University's creed, published on its website, reiterates the word "blood":

University Creed

Atonement

I believe in His vicarious atonement for the sins of mankind by the shedding of His blood on the cross.

Jesus Christ . . . literally took our place and suffered our penalty.

But he was wounded for our transgressions, he was bruised for our iniquities: the chastisement of our peace was upon him; and with his stripes we are healed. *Isaiah 53:5* . . .

Who his own self bare our sins in his own body on the tree, that we, being dead to sins, should live unto righteousness: by whose stripes ye were healed. *1 Peter 2:24*

. . . Christ's shed blood, then, paid the price (atoned) for our sin . . .

And almost all things are by the law purged with blood; and without shedding of blood is no remission. *Hebrews 9:22* . . .

But if we walk in the light, as he is in the light, we have fellowship one with another, and the blood of Jesus Christ his Son cleanseth us from all sin. *1 John 1:7*

Through this payment, the wrath of God at our sin was appeased, or propitiated.

Herein is love, not that we loved God, but that he loved us, and sent his Son [to be] the propitiation for our sins. *1 John 4:10*

> Being justified freely by his grace through the redemption that is in Christ Jesus: Whom God hath set forth to be a propitiation through faith in his blood, to declare his righteousness for the remission of sins that are past, through the forbearance of God. *Romans 3:24–25.*[5]

Compare this preoccupation with blood with the Nicene Creed, professed in most Christian churches since 325 CE, where the word "blood" does not appear, only "[Jesus] was crucified also for us under Pontius Pilate. He suffered and was buried" (1662 Anglican Book of Common Prayer).[6] Bob Jones University's "Statement of Christian Education" claims, "Our defining beliefs are the shared core of the great historical creedal statements of Protestant Christianity" and then states that its Fundamentalist founders "drew battle lines and committed themselves to an aggressive separatist theological stance. Hence, our anti-ecumenicism."[7]

Pat Robertson's Regent University, within easy driving distance of our nation's seat of power in Washington, DC, does not post a creed. Originally called CBN University for Christian Broadcasting Network, Robertson's cable television enterprise, Regent was renamed to acknowledge its service to God; the university reflects Robertson's proclivity for engaging with secular politics. Son of a conservative Senator from Virginia, Pat Robertson studied law at Yale before choosing to obtain an MA in divinity and ordination as a Southern Baptist minister. His mission with Regent University is to train evangelical Christians to work in and with government. Its business programs are administered as the School of Global Leadership and Entrepreneurship. There,

> we seek to assist in the transformation of current and future leaders by guiding them through a rigorous immersion in the study of secular and sacred knowledge so they may discover the deeper Truths of scripture . . . we believe that inspired innovation is granted through Divine transformation . . . [students] experience God-inspired revelations and applications throughout their studies. Each faculty member is a devoted follower of Jesus Christ. For those engaged in business, management or leadership of an organization, the school provides a unique perspective in innovation, excellence and the impact of biblical principles in today's world.[8]

The school's vision is "to provide Christian leadership in transforming society by affirming and teaching principles . . . described in the Holy Scriptures, embodied in the person of Jesus Christ, and enabled through the power of the Holy Spirit. *Soli Deo Gloria.*"[9]

Against the battering-ram, battle-ax calls to action from pastors such as Pete Peters, Steve Hickey, and the Bob Jones faculty, less overtly militant pastors like Pat Robertson and Rick Warren reiterate that they, as evangelical Christians, should be servants—servant to God, of course; in earthy matters, a team in cobelligerency, in coalition with other Fundamentalist organizations of comparable sophistication. As servants to God, working under His direction to fulfill His Great Commission, they feel humble but inspired. Regent University's story of its founding teaches this:

> Regent's vision began in August 1975 at Disneyland's Grande Hotel just outside Los Angeles, California. M. G. "Pat" Robertson, Founder and President of the then fifteen year old Christian Broadcasting Network, bowed his head to give thanks for a lunch of cantaloupe and cottage cheese. He was seeking God about the decision to purchase a few acres of land in Virginia Beach, Virginia to build larger facilities for his rapidly expanding television ministry. The WYAH studio building located in Portsmouth, Virginia, and headquarters for the Christian Broadcasting Network, was taxed beyond its limits. "As I bowed my head," Pat recalls, "I sensed the Lord speak to me. Buy all 143 acres and build an international communications center and school for my glory to take the message of Jesus Christ to the world. Little did I know then what God was about to do" . . . Pat opened his eyes and looked up from the table. God said, "Build it." He had learned over the past fifteen years to take God at His Word. Step by step, God ordered the events and unfolded His plan. Pat purchased all 143 acres of prime commercial property.[10]

Instead of posing as John Wayne, Robertson and Warren appeal to laypeople's anxiety over canons of adequacy:

> Have you ever felt that your calling is not as "spiritual" as someone else's? Has a friend or a leader in the church ever implied that if you were really "on fire for the Lord" you would drop your current profession and enter what is commonly referred to as "full-time ministry"? Have you wrestled with why God would give you skills and abilities in the field of business if that is not a valid use of your time?
>
> In fact, this has now become a burgeoning movement of the Spirit. Today, it is loosely called the "business as mission" or the "Kingdom business" movement, but these are not new ideas. They are freshly packaged in a way that fits the global marketplace. Because God desires to use the whole body of Christ to advance the Kingdom around the world, He has opened up several options to gifted business professionals.[11]

Rick Warren explains, "At Saddleback Church, we have a group of CEOs and business owners who are trying to make as much as they can so they can give as much as they can to further the kingdom of God. I encourage you to talk with your pastor and begin a Kingdom Builders' group in your church."[12]

CEOs

Rick Warren has remarkable talent for talking with everyone and anyone, from Barack Obama to seminars of Southern Baptist pastors, and the twenty thousand members of his Saddleback Church. He dresses in California casual Hawaiian shirts and sandals. His messages are highly focused and clear. Besides teaching a "Purpose-Driven Life" and instructing on building "Purpose-Driven Churches"—the titles of the bestselling books that made him a multimillionaire able to "reverse tithe" (he gives 90 percent of his income, from the books and spin-offs, to his church)—he preaches his PEACE Plan for saving the world:

P = Plant churches or (a revision of the original) promote reconciliation
E = Equip servant leaders
A = Assist the poor (This is to be worldwide)
C = Care for the sick (This became controversial because Warren and his wife Kay specifically call for caring for people who are HIV-positive or have AIDS, a disease linked by many conservative Christians to homosexual or promiscuous sexuality)
E = Educate the next generation

According to Warren, he is calling for a return to nineteenth-century evangelism incorporating the Social Gospel, "deeds not creeds," he says, to combat the five great evils of today's world: "spiritual emptiness, corrupt leadership, poverty, disease, and illiteracy."[13]

Although Warren considers himself a Southern Baptist, many members of the denomination consider him heretical, not only for espousing the social gospel, but also for introducing contemporary rock-style "praise music" in place of customary hymn singing and for talking about listeners' problems with marriage and daily life rather than, as one disgruntled older congregant put it, "preach[ing] on somebody going to hell."[14] Above all, Warren preaches on how to increase church membership. His staff runs workshops for pastors. They are taught to work at attracting and keeping young adults with guitar and rock music, expensive audio and visual systems to enhance sermons with images on screens, casual dress, "human interest" stories, and recreational activities, in addition to a variety of Sunday School and adult classes and discussion and support groups.

Megachurches, such as Warren's Saddleback Church or the older Crystal Cathedral of Robert Schuller in Garden Grove, California, take as a given the power of positive thinking, reminding us that this insight dates back, as a phrase, to Norman Vincent Peale's 1952 bestseller. Schuller explicitly links his "possibility thinking" to Peale's positivism, with two of Schuller's books including introductions by Peale.[15] Peale popularized the use of human-interest anecdotes and celebrity testimonials, both integral to Schuller's preaching and books. Three generations of highly popular American evangelicals thus have downplayed, or even repudiated (in Schuller's case) the negative message of sin and damnation so central to Christian denominations. Their appeal is obvious. So is the abundance on the Internet of denunciations of their positivist, life-affirming preaching—Rick Warren is even fingered as the Antichrist.[16]

Warren continues another of Peale's practices, addressing and affiliating with business leaders. In the 1930s Depression, Peale joined the founder of IBM, Thomas J. Watson, James Cash Penney the founder of J. C. Penney stores, and the highly popular radio host Arthur Godfrey in an organization to assist business executives to find employment. Sociologist Michael Lindsay quotes Douglas Holladay: "Christian ministers say to business leaders, 'If you will fund our ministry, we'll never ask you any questions again about what you're doing' . . . Basically we don't want business people to be engaged in ministry"[17] Pondering that, Holladay resigned his pastor post to enter business, convinced that by mixing with business leaders as one of them, he could more effectively fulfill the Great Commission, according to Matthew 28:19–20 and Mark 16:15: "Go into the whole world and preach the gospel to every creature . . . make disciples of every nation." Lindsay discovered, through interviewing a hundred business executives, that many were more comfortable interacting with their own kind than with, for example, ordinary members of congregations. Church committees hemming and hawing over trivia, admitting confusion upon presentation with spreadsheets, are likely to frustrate business CEOs. This is why evangelicals host conferences at expensive resorts so that wealthy, powerful executives will feel at ease in accustomed surroundings and be receptive to funding and leadership requests. Lindsay uses Robert Wuthnow's term "parachurch"[18] for the networks of business leaders meeting in brief, focused conferences but maintaining communication electronically. Importantly, he notes that these executives may profess commitment to evangelical Christianity yet may not belong to any congregation. They confided to Lindsay that pastors did not address their problems. Socializing with their peers and participating in efficiently run meetings to promote big-time philanthropic ventures, these CEOs believed they were using their God-given talent in God's mission; anything on a lesser scale, with common folk in local congregations, would be a waste of that talent.

Megachurches appeal to evangelical businesspeople because they are structured like large corporations, the senior pastor a CEO delegating sectors of the operation to his staff, and they share the ethos of capitalism, with growth, expansion, and increasing income the signs of success. America's mantra, "bigger, better," resonates throughout megachurches: "Lakewood Church, which recently leased the Compaq Center, former home of the NBA's Houston Rockets, has a four-record deal and spends $12 million annually on television airtime . . . 25,060 attendance, pastor Joel Osteen."[19] Megachurches meeting in athletic stadiums and evangelical businesses, such as James Dobson's Colorado campus of acres of employees, embody the Great Commission, visibly reaching out over thousands. *Forbes*, the business magazine, ran a series of articles under the lead "Christian Capitalism," highlighting the enormous sums realized by megachurches and Christian ventures. Christian publishing supplies not only thousands of local bookstores and online sellers but also Wal-Mart, Target, and Sears stores. Wal-Mart alone is reported to take in more than one billion dollars annually from its sales of "Christian" books, videos, music CDs, and merchandise spin-offs such as toys modeled on Christian cartoon characters.[20] A small paperback titled *Prayer of Jabez* (1 Chronicles 4:9–10), justifying prayer for financial success, sold more than 11 million copies, profiting its Christian publisher by eight million dollars.[21] Christian music, and especially Christian rock bands and singers, is now mainstream, playing in major popular-music venues and, in the case of Danny Gokey, leader of the praise team at a Milwaukee evangelical church, making it to the final competition on the television show *American Idol* in March 2009.[22] Christian movies earn millions by showing in theaters and in churches; the films of the LaHaye-Jenkins *Left Behind* bestsellers faithfully embed the Fundamentalist eschatology in plenty of violence and gunplay, requested by the Christian fans.[23] Fraud by "Christian" financial brokers went big-time, too, with operators such as Clyde D. Hood of Mattoon, Illinois, promising a "51-fold return in 275 days" on hundred-dollar investments. According to the account in *Forbes* magazine, Hood asked for prayers as well as money "in this battle against Satan and his disciples" obstructing the promised quick payoffs. Satan won when Hood was convicted of fraud and money laundering.[24]

The global recession that began in 2008 provoked belt-tightening even in the megachurches, plus soul-searching among evangelicals. Charles Colson, jailed and born again in Jesus after his employer Richard Nixon was forced to resign the presidency, asserted in *Christianity Today* that "God is in control during the financial crisis. God often uses adversity for his greatest blessings and the markets are his."[25] Al Mohler, president of Southern Baptist Theological Seminary in Louisville, Kentucky, posted "Economics 101," reposted on *Christianity Today*'s website:

> No one has explained basic economics as well as Adam Smith did in his 1776 classic, *The Wealth of Nations* . . . an economy is based upon the transfer of goods and services from one individual to another. Each partner in the transaction must believe that this transfer is in his or her own best interest or the transfer is not voluntary. Both parties seek to gain something from the transfer. Since no one person can meet all of his or her own needs alone, a vast economic system quickly takes shape. Individuals trade goods and services through the exchange of currency or another agreed-upon form of value.
>
> At every stage, the transfer is made because those involved desire and intend to achieve a gain. The legal entity of a corporation allows individuals to band together in a common economic cause with certain legal protections. A stock market allows individual investors to buy an interest in a company, thus allowing the corporation to use their capital in hopes of future gain. The market works because all concerned hope to gain through the process . . .
>
> The Bible clearly teaches that the worker is worthy of his hire and that rewards should follow labor, thrift, and investment . . . Given the nature of this fallen world and the reality of human sinfulness, we should expect that greed will be a constant temptation. Greed will entice the rich to oppress the poor, partners in transactions to lie to one another, and investors to take irrational risks. All of these are evident in this current crisis . . . trust is the most essential commodity of all when it comes to economic transactions . . . Prudence would indicate that the less government intervention, the better. Adam Smith was confident that a "hidden hand" within the economy would rectify excesses and punish bad actors. I think he is basically right . . . Everything we are, everything we do, and everything we own truly belongs to God and is to be at the disposal

of Kingdom purposes. This world is not our home and our treasure is not found here.[26]

A month earlier, when the crisis hit in September 2008, a *Christianity Today* headline reported, "In Crisis, Wall Street Turns to Prayer":

> On Monday, Christians on Wall Street set up special prayer meetings for the week. First came the special prayer conference calls on Monday and Tuesday nights. Then, starting Wednesday, extraordinary prayer meetings were scheduled at Merrill Lynch, Goldman Sachs, JPMorgan Chase, Citigroup, Morgan Stanley, Deloitte, and elsewhere. Pastors began planning to gather for a sidewalk prayer meeting outside of the stock exchange.
>
> Mac Pier of the New York Leadership Center started getting calls from friends who were losing their jobs. "Of course, I prayed with them that God would give them the spiritual and financial resources they need." Pier says that the Wall Streeters who called him were stunned . . . [A Lehman employee said] "I have never seen grown men cry like that."[27]

MILITANT CHRISTIAN ENTREPRENEURS

Rousas John Rushdoony (1916–2001) was a Presbyterian minister who insisted all human knowledge comes from God, and the Bible is God's textbook, or manual, for human behavior. It follows that the Bible supersedes the US Constitution, although Rushdoony believed that the Constitutional Convention intended to construct a limited state that would protect Christians' efforts to live by biblical precepts; the industrial Union's victory over the agrarian Confederacy in 1865 weakened the Puritan decentralized government he considered America's godly heritage. Beginning in the 1950s, Rushdoony published a series of books setting forth his conviction that Christians should "reconstruct" America to once again use the Bible as the sole guide for society. He particularly excoriated American public schools, in his view the principal culprit inculcating secular humanism and obedience to ungodly socialistic government. Christians should pull their children out of public schools, instead using homeschooling or Christian schools—hence some of his followers call their effort the "Exodus Mandate" and use photos of World War II Dunkirk retreat to illustrate their mandate.[28]

In 1971, Rushdoony's daughter Sharon married Gary North, who had been a summer intern working for her father in 1963; and in 1973, after North completed a PhD in (economic) history at the University of California–Riverside, Rushdoony hired his son-in-law at the Chalcedon Foundation, his institute for promoting his ideas. Both Rushdoony and North considered themselves libertarians, since they believed in minimal government and laissez-faire economic policy, but they disagreed on activism: Rushdoony was a separatist, and North wanted to engage in Washington politics. North worked for Texas congressman Ron Paul in 1976 (Paul ran for president as an independent in 2008), then in 1979 moved to Tyler, Texas—no income tax in that state, he notes[29]—to run his Institute for Christian Economics (ICE). Through North's indefatigable writing (more than fifty books, regular newsletters, lectures), ICE became the principal source for Christian Reconstructionism.

North states,

> There are a lot of definitions of the kingdom of God. Mine is simultaneously the simplest and the broadest: the civilization of God. It is the creation—the entire area under the King of Heaven's lawful dominion. It is the area that fell under Satan's reign in history as a result of Adam's rebellion. When man fell, he brought the whole world under God's curse (Genesis 3:17–19). The curse extended as far as the reign of sin did. This meant everything under man's dominion. This is what it still means. The laws of the kingdom of God extend just as far as sin does. This means every area of life. God owns the whole world: "The earth is the LORD'S, and the fulness thereof the world, and they that dwell therein" (Psalm 24:1). Jesus Christ, as God's Son and therefore legal heir, owns the whole earth. He has leased it out to His people to develop progressively over time, just as Adam was supposed to have served as a faithful leaseholder before his fall, bringing the world under dominion (Genesis 1:26–28) [thus, "Dominion theology"]. Because of Jesus' triumph over Satan at Calvary, God is now bringing under judgment every area of life. How? Through the preaching of the gospel, His two-edged sword of judgment (Revelation 19:15).

Reform and Restoration

> The kingdom of God is the arena of God's redemption. Jesus Christ redeems the whole world—that is, He bought it back. He did this by paying the ultimate price for man's sin: His death on the cross. The whole earth has now been judicially redeemed. It has been given "a new lease on life." The lease that Satan gained from Adam has been revoked. The Second Adam (Jesus Christ) holds lawful title. The world has not been fully restored in history, nor can it be; sin still has its effects, and will until the day of final judgment. But progressively over time, it is possible for the gospel to have its restorative effects. Through the empowering of God's Holy Spirit, redeemed people are able to extend the principles of healing to all areas under their jurisdiction in life: church, family, and State. All Christians admit that God's principles can be used to reform the individual. They also understand that if this is the case, then the family can be reformed according to God's Word. Next, the church is capable of restoration. But then they stop. Mention the State, and they say, "No; nothing can be done to restore the State. The State is inherently, permanently satanic. It is a waste of time to work to heal the State." The Christian Reconstructionist asks: Why not? They never tell you why not. They never point to a passage in the Bible that tells you why the church and family can be healed by God's Word and Spirit, but the State can't be. Today, it is the unique message of Christian Reconstruction that civil government, like family government and church government, is under the Bible-revealed law of God and therefore is capable in principle of being reformed according to God's law. This means that God has given to the Christian community as a whole enormous responsibility throughout history.

This God-given responsibility is far greater than merely preaching a gospel of exclusively personal salvation. The gospel we preach must apply to every area of life that has been fouled by sin and its effects. The church and individual Christian evangelists must preach the biblical gospel of comprehensive redemption, not just personal 'soul-winning.' Wherever sin reigns, there the gospel must be at work, transforming and restoring.[30]

What could be more straightforward or easier for a businessman to understand? There is a bit more to Christian Reconstruction than simple logic:

It is time to sign up for a religious war that will last for the rest of your life. If we do our work faithfully, maybe we will start seeing some major victories before we get very far into the next millennium. I think we will. I smell victory. I think the enemy, for the first time in a century, has begun to smell defeat. They are trying to speed up their timetable because their dream of a one-world order is unravelling. Technology is now against them: decentralization. Newsletters are multiplying: alternative information sources. The World Wide Web is beyond anyone's control. The public schools are disintegrating . . . We have the Bible, the U.S. Constitution, and an understanding of freedom. Freedom works. It produces abundance. Socialism produces poverty. It exists only because Western capitalists and governments have subsidized it with taxpayers' money . . . At the very least, we ought to adopt this as our political minimum, our non-negotiable demand: "My hand out of your wallet; your hand out of my wallet; no handouts from the government; and handcuffs for the thieves."[31]

Again, this is straight out of the Bible, the Ten Commandments: Thou shalt not steal. Or as Gary North puts it, "We are about to see the inescapable curse on every society that says, 'Thou shalt not steal, except by majority vote.' "[32]

Beyond his pure economics phrasing, North holds that John Calvin correctly understood that humans live under a covenant with God—a contract. Calvin's Geneva is Gary North's model for Christian Reconstruction. If US citizens glory in living in a nation under law, Gary North promises a whole world under law, bound by a contract spelling out what men must do, "a God-given assignment to conquer in His name (Gen. 1:28; 9:1-7)."[33] North, like most Fundamentalists, does not use inclusive language because his English-language Bible doesn't. I have quoted extensively from North because he most unequivocally links the American businessman's outlook with militancy. He appeals to the American businessperson who wishes to be Christian, not only by explaining their contractual relationship to God/Jesus and its obligation to practice capitalist expansion, but also by abjuring physical rebellion: "Rather than an appeal to armed revolution, American Christians initially need to use the existing legal order—which was originally Christian in origin—to recapture these institutions or else (e.g., tax-supported education) abolish them."[34] Stirring talk, no bloodshed. And no taxes.

Gary North's fierce talk is rhetoric common among evangelicals. D. James Kennedy (1930–2007), charismatic pastor of megachurch Coral Ridge Ministries in Fort Lauderdale, Florida, wrote in *Reconstruction: Biblical*

Guidelines for a Nation in Peril (1982), "Judged by every Biblical and historical precedent, America is plunging toward the brink . . . Among [the] evils are: liberalism in theology, relativism in ethics, humanism in education, socialism in economics, statism in political policy, corruption in government, immorality in entertainment and the arts, dishonesty in mass communications, defeatism in the rear guard action against crime, retrenchment in international relations and, the most ghastly of all, a policy of mass murder of pre-born humans . . . My Christian fellow Americans, let us arise and rebuild the ruins left by decades of godless leadership and policies."[35] How shall we reconstruct a godly world?

> God has placed within this earth all manner of resources which we are to take and fashion . . . only by work can you enter into that kingdom that God has ordained for you . . . Work . . . ennobles the spirit . . . to humbly realize that however well we might have succeeded in the eyes of men, in the eyes of God we are mortally flawed and have fallen short. Therefore, we trust in nothing other than the death and life of Jesus Christ . . . thereby, we may know that we have eternal life. Biblically-guided work is essential to the reconstruction of America.[36]

Embedded in this noble talk are concrete policy guidelines for robber-baron enrichment: "Calvin agreed that the state had no right to undertake schemes of redistribution of wealth in order to achieve an economic equality. The legislative taking of wealth under the guise of legality is no less stealing than if it be done by robbers and thieves . . . The worst thing that could happen to any nation would be the total equalization of its wealth . . . The Bible . . . makes this statement: 'If any would not work, neither should he eat.'"[37] Kennedy does not discuss Matthew 22:39, in which Jesus states that the second great commandment, after loving God, is, "You shall love your neighbor as yourself." Matthew reported (Matthew19:21) that Jesus told a wealthy young man, "If you want to be complete, go and sell what you have and donate it to the needy, and you will have treasure in heaven; then come and follow Me," as his disciples did (Matthew 19:27).

CAPITALISM AND THE MILITANT CHRISTIAN RIGHT

Late in life, Thomas Jefferson translated the Gospels, using his own capacity for higher criticism to winnow the likely actual words of Jesus of Nazareth from posthumous additions and distortions.[38] Jefferson promoted agrarian capitalism, speculating in land, as did most men of his class. His political opponent Alexander Hamilton publicly inveighed against Jefferson's Deism as part of Hamilton's prolonged fight for a stronger central government and support for commercial interests.[39] These opposed positions epitomize the division between the slave-economy South and industrial North that crashed into the Civil War and subordinated the South to Northern capitalist economic power. Militant evangelists, interestingly, are generally Southerners.[40]

States' rights, subject of so much struggle in the last quarter of the eighteenth century and again in the mid-nineteenth, are incongruously melded into individuals' rights and denouncement of government power in evangelists' discourse.

Evangelists on the political Right fervently believe that free-market capitalism is the only economic principle compatible with religious freedom—for them!—and Bible-centered living. We might cynically observe that no other system would so richly reward men from modest beginnings. Cynicism aside, the Right's conviction that capitalism is the one and only divinely blessed system comes straight from its Calvinist precept of the Genesis (1:28) commandment that humans must "be fruitful and multiply." Some of us, surely including Thomas Jefferson, see this as simply encouragement to procreate our kind. Evangelicals on the Right interpret "multiply" to mean "mass production," "mass marketing," capital gains, multiplication of consumer outlets. Was Genesis foretelling Starbucks on every street corner?

Proliferating Starbucks selling an unnecessary, innutritious product at exorbitant prices may be a triumph of American market-era capitalism. Its extraordinary multiplication could be a metaphor for evangelism. Right-wing American evangelists, like Starbucks, want every street to be full of warmed, energized people "filled with the Spirit," as with a grande latte. Capitalists seek profits by expanding market share while reducing expenditures, often through economies of scale, just as megachurches aggressively market themselves and benefit from economies of scale such as preaching to ten thousand congregants in a remodeled professional athletic stadium. Perhaps the parallel between expansionist capitalism and evangelicalism makes capitalism peculiarly compatible with, and attractive to, conservative evangelicals. Stanford University marketing guru Steven Blank borrows from them to speak of businesspeople positioning their product in the market as "earlyvangelists" (early evangelists) whose "mission" is "to turn a small cadre of early evangelists into a mass market, *yet to have the customers in that mass market believe they are still a small and elite group.*"[41]

Individualism is another parallel between market capitalism and evangelicalism. Market capitalism is highly rational in that it relies on organized spreadsheets, measurements and statistics, flowcharts, managerial plans, and other tools taught in schools of business. All of these manipulate units; groups are aggregates of units rather than collectives. Evangelicals are aggregates of individuals who have been "born again" into a one-to-one personal individual relationship with Jesus Christ. They may flock together in churches, but each one must have experienced their own one-to-one when taking Christ Jesus into their heart. Thus evangelicals decry the Social Gospel and socialism alike for providing material succor to designated groups instead of going one-on-one persuading individuals to pray for succor (in the case of televangelists, to tithe to be prayed for). The private experience of conversion, the holding of a direct link with Christ, is obtaining a kind of private property—Macpherson's "possessive individualism."

There is, of course, Weber's and Tawney's thesis that capitalism and Protestantism are causally related (discussed in Chapter 5). Anthropologists E. Paul Durrenberger and Dimitra Doukas draw a distinction between the "gospel of work" and the "gospel of wealth," the latter attributed to Andrew Carnegie. Fieldwork in New York's Mohawk Valley and in eastern Pennsylvania's coal region revealed that, even in these economically depressed Rust Belt areas, working-class people value skills and hard work fulfilling household needs. They contrast their visibly productive labor with the unearned wealth of the moneyed class, specifically those who get money by investing money—capitalists. Durrenberger and Doukas did not find religious denomination affiliation to be significant; instead, they found that class separation between WASPs and "white ethnics" resulted in the two classes using different churches and cemeteries as well as different schools and leisure places. Working-class families worked hard to produce food by gardening, fishing, and hunting; to maintain houses and machinery; to provide services such as hairdressing and small grocery stores; and to earn money in public-sector jobs, often part-time. Many took food stamps and other public assistance. They told the anthropologists that, along with hard work, they valued "neighborliness." That is, they believed in helping others in their community without regard for compensation. Neighborliness undergirds the informal economy of bartering services and off-the-record sales in yards and flea markets. For these people, "dominion" and "subdue" are foreign words reeking of exploitation and oppression, the conditions their labor unions fought, bloodily, a century before.[42] The anthropologists' on-the-ground study takes evangelicals' debates into another dimension, where "capitalism" is not in opposition to "socialism" but to "neighborliness."

Capitalism as untrammeled business profit making fits into the militant Christian Right's campaign against "statism," the intrusion (as they see it) of government into people's lives. Their postulation of a black-and-white opposition between Bible-centered and humanist rules of law rails against any regulation from secular agencies; their ideal is Calvin's Geneva ruled by a theologian and an ecclesiastical consistory advising a lay council. A free market would produce—or, in their belief, has already produced—the greatest good for the greatest number by not curbing or channeling people's desires for goods and services. That "the greatest number" does not encompass everyone, leaving an impoverished underclass, is an unfortunate effect of free markets—and anyway, Jesus said the poor are always with you (Matthew 26:11). Freedom, freedom to follow Bible teachings in one's life, is the principle claimed by the Christian Right. Be born again in Christ Jesus, and He will prompt one to right actions. Seek godly pastors to counsel one when that voice is muffled. Every person's goal must be eternal life, for the alternative is eternal damnation. Those who have a talent for business should exercise that God-given talent, and laissez-faire free-market capitalism has proven for five centuries to be the closest to the heavenly kingdom that we can manage on earth, given that we humans are born in sin. If some CEOs of huge corporations manipulate the books, that is unavoidable, considering even the most committed Christians can be misled by Satan. Battling temptation, a businessperson must be a warrior. Capitalism is competition. Free markets are arenas where rivals fight for profits. Rightwing Christian businesspersons wield electronic weapons in place of battle-axes. Rust Belt working people see there's no place for neighborliness in that world.

POSTSCRIPT

The Internet, in its lavish bounty, offers a website for opponents of a Christian America: BARF, Biblical America Resistence Front, describes itself as "Biblical America: the social movement that seeks to use the Bible as the sole basis of all governance and social interaction . . . BARF: a resource for all who work to monitor and counter the Biblical America movement."[43]

CHAPTER 13

FORTIFYING THE HOME FRONT

The hearts and minds of America's children are the prize for the militant Christian Right. Their godly capitalist state unburdened by taxes or welfare will not be installed within the lifetimes of today's leaders—only a bloody revolution, such as Fidel Castro led, could truly overturn a government, and they are not about to jeopardize themselves and their families. Instead, the militant Christian Right promotes Christian schooling in homes and in Christian schools. Along with Christian popular music, films, and general reading, Christian schooling segregates the Right's young from its bugaboo, secular humanism. When they reach adulthood, they are trained to go out, a mighty force to subvert that godless government and institute Bible-centered law.

A very basic proclamation of the Christian schooling principle is this, by the American Association of Christian Schools:

Statement of Faith

We believe that the Bible, both the Old and New Testaments, was verbally inspired of God, and is inerrant and is our only rule in matters of faith and practice. We believe in creation, not evolution; that man was created by the direct act of God and in the image of God. We believe that Adam and Eve, in yielding to the temptation of Satan, became fallen creatures. We believe that all men are born in sin. We believe in the Incarnation, the Virgin Birth, and the Deity of our Lord and Saviour, Jesus Christ. We believe in the vicarious and substitutional Atonement for the sins of mankind by the shedding of His blood on the cross. We believe in the resurrection of His body from the tomb, His ascension to Heaven, and that He is now our Advocate. We believe that He is personally coming again. We believe in His power to save men from sin. We believe in the necessity of the New Birth, and that this New Birth is through the regeneration of the Holy Spirit. We believe that salvation is by grace through faith, plus nothing minus nothing, in the atoning blood of our Lord and Saviour, Jesus Christ.

We believe that this Statement of Faith is basic for Christian fellowship and that all born-again men and women who sincerely accept it and are separated from the world of apostasy and sin can, and should live together in peace, and that it is their Christian duty to promote harmony among the Believers.

We further believe in the Biblical doctrine of ecclesiastical separation, and therefore believe that churches and Christian schools should not be associated with, members of, or in accord with organizations or movements such as the World Council of Churches, the National Council of Churches, the Modern Charismatic Movement, or the Ecumenical Movement.[1]

Christian schools often cite Deuteronomy 11:18–21:

Fix these words of mine in your hearts and minds; tie them as symbols on your hands and bind them on your foreheads. Teach them to your children, talking about them when you sit at home and when you walk along the road, when you lie down and when you get up. Write them on the doorframes of your houses and on your gates, so that your days and the days of your children may be many in the land that the LORD swore to give your forefathers, as many as the days that the heavens are above the earth.[2]

"Where is the separatist organization, on a national level, that will champion our cause?," cried Dr. Al Janney in 1972 (according to Christian Schools International website). To answer, the American Association of Christian Schools was organized in Dallas, Texas, in November 1972. Its paired programs provide educational materials and services to member schools (claiming 170,000 students in 2009), and legal services to "protect member schools from government entanglement."[3] Entangled in the Christian schools' promotion of "religious freedom" and "freedom of association" is dedication to "free-market economy." Peter Sprigg, vice president for policy at the Family Research Council, warns that any legislation that forbids discrimination against hiring homosexuals is an infringement of a free-market economy; furthermore, "[t]he more open homosexuals become, the more people with traditional values will be forced into the closet."[4] The American Association of Christian Schools lists pending legislation, such as the Employer Non-Discrimination Act, with the comment, "Please encourage your Representative to OPPOSE this legislation."[5] Its agenda of "religious liberty, family values, and pro-life issues" mirrors that of other militant Christian Right organizations, well beyond academic schooling. The large national Christian schools associations have, since the late 1960s, paralleled the militant Right's campaigns, engaging in open opposition to secular education.

Parents who fear exposing their children to secular ideas and, worse, homosexuals, have an option even safer than sending the little ones off to a Christian school: homeschooling. Once an option principally for missionaries' children in foreign lands and children on remote ranches or research stations, homeschooling has spread exponentially since the 1980s. The Home School Legal Defense Association, claiming that well over a million American children are homeschooled, asserts, "Remember, our children are dying souls entrusted to our care!"[6]

Homeschooling advocates from Christian organizations assume that a mother will remain at home, caring for and schooling her children—Christian groups are not thinking of wealthy families hiring tutors and governesses to school their children at home. Fathers are to guide and counsel their children. A leader of the Christian homeschooling movement, Michael Farris, wrote half-a-dozen books for homeschooling parents. The blurb for one of his books indicates that fathers are not expected to be the principal in-home teacher: "As a husband, home schooling father of ten children, Chairman & General Counsel for HSLDA, [Chancellor of Patrick Henry College] and frequent conference speaker, Mike understands the pressures of juggling the demands of family and career."[7] Homeschooling by Christian parents ostensibly promotes raising a child imbued with Christian faith and morality, but it also reinforces the conservative ideal of a breadwinner father and stay-at-home mother.

Farris's multiple roles encapsulate the aims of right-wing evangelical homeschooling: raising a churchgoing Christian family with sharp gender roles and working to overwhelm secular America with legislation favoring conservative evangelical positions. The Home School Legal Defense Association states on its website that its "board of directors founded Patrick Henry College . . . [but] the College's board of trustees is completely separate and distinct from HSLDA's," yet "Michael Farris is chancellor of the College, and is General Counsel of HSLDAS."[8] Patrick Henry College is to produce legions of Michael Farrises, devoted to maintaining a Christian home while vigorously pursuing litigation and legislation to impose their intolerance and laissez-faire free-market economy upon the United States.

Segregated Christian education, whether taught in a home or in a Christian school, boasts that it is Bible-centered. Take a look at Christian Schools International's curriculum for grade one in its *Walking with God and His People* series:

SUMMARY

Unit 1: 1 John (7 lessons)
Unit 2: Creation, Fall, Noah, and Babel (6 lessons)
Unit 3: Abraham (9 lessons)
Unit 4: Isaac and Jacob (6 lessons)
Unit 5: Joseph (12 lessons)
Unit 6: Moses and Israel (12 lessons)
Unit 7: Settling the Land (15 lessons)
Unit 8: Judges: Othniel, Gideon, Samson, and Ruth (10 lessons)
Unit 9: Samuel and Saul (9 lessons)
Unit 10: David (10 lessons)
Unit 11: King Solomon (5 lessons)
Unit 12: Psalms and Proverbs (7 lessons)
Unit 13: Divided Kingdom (9 lessons)

Unit 14: Exile: Daniel and Esther (7 lessons)
Unit 15: Return from Exile (6 lessons)
Unit 16: Christmas (7 lessons)
Unit 17: Easter (10 lessons)

Flexible Christmas, Easter and Epistle units are provided.[9]

Yes, this is for six-year-old first-graders.

"Students need a challenging, comprehensive academic curriculum built on a foundation of biblical absolutes," says the website of Discover Christian Schools. "Education is not focused on possibilities but on certainties found in God's Word . . . The best preparation for effective service is to be well grounded in one's mind before direct engagement of the culture."[10]

Tree of Life, a Christian homeschooling curriculum source, explains, "man has always sought after the Truth. What makes the pursuit of Truth so difficult is that the Fall of man, precipitated in part by the Father of Lies, Satan, has resulted in our loss of perfection. We are now a deeply flawed creation—totally depraved in fact; that is, every inclination is toward sin. This has made man's pursuit of Truth perilous and, as is his nature, has devised a veritable obstacle course on which to run this race."[11] And Discover Christian Schools bluntly states, "Christian schools have the same type of kids non-Christian schools have. Sinners."[12]

History courses in right-wing Christian education tend to emphasize heroes. Children are to be inspired to emulate heroic leaders, and pragmatically, teaching about heroes personifies chronologies and events, making history a series of stories. "While the faithful saints leave a lasting heritage for those following, the scoundrels of history remind us of the curse introduced into the world because of sin. And yet, these vessels of wrath were prepared before time began, alongside the vessels of mercy, for God's glory. In these series of lectures, we discover some of the great blessings of lives lived for God and the great tragedy of those attempting to deny God His glory."[13] Although Christian curricula urge teachers, whether mothers or employed in schools, to engage children's interest through narrative, dramatizing heroes' deeds, and craft projects, their lesson plans include considerable use of workbooks, flash cards, rote memorization, and frequent quizzes on memorized items—practices that instill discipline and obedience.

Arlin and Beka Horton, running one of the oldest and largest Christian curricula providers from Pensacola Christian College, follow this approach to history:

American history is usually presented as a series of conflicts—rich vs. poor, black vs. white, North vs. South, labor vs. management, male vs. female, etc.

Our A Beka Book texts reject the Marxist/Hegelian conflict theory of history in favor of a truthful portrayal of peoples, lands, religions, ideals, heroes, triumphs, and setbacks. The result has been positive, uplifting history texts that give students an historical perspective and instill within them an intelligent pride for their own country and a desire to help it back to its traditional values.

We present government as ordained by God for the maintenance of law and order, not as a cure-all for the problems of humanity. We present free-enterprise economics without apology and point out the dangers of Communism, socialism, and liberalism to the well-being of people across the globe. In short, A Beka Book offers you a Christian and conservative approach to the study of what man has done with the time God has given.[14]

Christian curricula producers advertise their independence from secular influences. A Beka Book assures parents,

Our skilled researchers and writers do not paraphrase progressive education textbooks and add Biblical principles; they do primary research in every subject and look at the subject from God's point of view. Of course, the most original source is always the Word of God, the only foundation for true scholarship in any area of human endeavor. Thus our publications are built upon the firm foundation of Scriptural truth and are written by dedicated and talented Christian scholars who are well grounded in the practical aspects of classroom teaching. For excellence for your Christian school, you can trust A Beka Book.[15]

Crossroads Christian School (CCS), headquartered in Crestview, Florida, assists homeschoolers' online access to the major curriculum approaches popular in Christian schools. They advise,

CCS believes that parents should be given the ability to choose their teaching methods. Some parents prefer to use all textbooks such as ABEKA [A Beka Book] or BJU [Bob Jones University]. Others prefer using workbooks such as School of Tomorrow [A.C.E.] or Alpha Omega. Many families enjoy unit studies such as Prairie Primer, Amanda Bennett, Far Above Rubies, Learning Adventures, Life in America, etc. And literature-based programs, such as FIAR and Sonlight, are becoming rapidly popular. The Charlotte Mason approach is also popular and effective. We will work with parents as much as possible. Parents have the freedom to use the teaching method that works best for their family. This includes textbooks, work texts, unit studies, Charlotte Mason approach, Principle approach, Classical approach, relaxed schooling, unschooling, eclectic schooling, etc.[16]

To help homeschooled children feel less isolated, Crossroads created class rings with the symbol of the Cross, sold through Wal-Mart.

Classical is perhaps the most conservative of the Christian curricula. It seriously teaches Latin and calls its program the Latin Trivium: Latin, Logic, and Rhetoric. Its basic text is Aristotle's *Rhetoric* and *Poetics* (Edward Corbett editions). Justifying its narrow curriculum is its motto, "Multum, non Multa" ("much, not many"). Latin will "provide a fundamental framework for early Christian history" as well as a pre-Enlightenment education: "Not only are children thus equipped able to appreciate the noblest ideas that

Western civilization has developed, they are also armed to defend their faith and freedom in a culture that attacks them with ideas and words that are contrary to God's Word."[17]

Veritas Press in Lancaster, Pennsylvania, is another curricula source hewing to "Classical" education. Its owners say, "After reading *Recovering the Lost Tools of Learning* by Douglas Wilson we decided to start a Christian Classical School. Following the consideration of many history texts we were convinced that we wanted to teach history chronologically, integrating biblically recorded history with events not recorded in history. So we created a history card program that integrated the best books available on the topics discussed in the cards." Among Veritas's many texts is *Classically Cursive Attributes of God*, by B. J. Jordan, which promises that "[t]hird graders can work on their cursive writing utilizing the Shorter Catechism and passages focusing on the attributes of God as their copy work."[18]

REVISIONIST HISTORY

Pastor Douglas Wilson of Moscow, Idaho, a leader in Christian schooling, teaches,

> If we want to understand the culture wars of the twentieth and twenty-first centuries, we must come to grips with the culture wars of the nineteenth century. In order to do this, it is necessary to get clear on the nature of American slavery, which was not what its abolitionist opponents claimed for it. If it had been, it is hard to see how the biblical instructions could have been applicable—for example, I would not cite I Timothy 6:1–4 to a person trying to escape from a Nazi death camp. "Obey the existing authorities!" But if antebellum slavery was the normal kind of sinful situation that Christians have had to deal with regularly down through history (e.g., one comparable to what Paul, Philemon, and Onesimus had to address), then the instructions in I Timothy 6 make perfect sense. We need to learn that the antebellum situation was one of Normal Sin, not one of Apocalyptic Evil.
>
> That our nation did not remove slavery in the way it ought to have been removed helps to explain many of our nation's problems in dealing with contemporary social evils. Those evils include abortion-on-demand, radical feminism, and rampant sodomy . . . We have done this under the "protections" of the Constitution. When in our history did we take the wrong turn that allowed the Constitution to be abused in this grotesque fashion? Christians need to learn to argue that the events resulting in the cataclysm of 1861–1865 had something to do with it, which I believe is incontrovertible.[19]

Wilson claims that, in Rome, "scriptural instructions [I Tim. 6:2; Phil. 10–19], carefully followed, resulted, over time, in a peaceful elimination of Roman slavery," and could have eventually eliminated slavery in the United States without a war.[20] (In the epistle to Timothy, Paul advises slaves to respect and honor their masters, and in the epistle to Philemon, he sends

Onesimus to him "no longer as a slave, but better than a slave" under Paul's protection.)

Gary North (in this context, ironically surnamed) summarized, "The South abandoned the state's rights legacy when it concluded after 1865 that the state has the right to educate children at taxpayer expense. That surrender was vastly more significant in securing the defeat of the Southern tradition than General Lee's symbolic transfer of his sword to General Grant at Appomattox Court House. Grant allowed Lee to keep his sword. The South was not allowed to keep its tradition."[21] The horror was that "[f]or a century, the South's public school curriculum has been written by humanists in northern universities and published in New York City. Reconstruction failed officially in 1877; the South's public school monopoly—'Made in New York'—triumphed almost completely over the next century."[22] North praises Mel and Norma Gabler, a Texas couple who levered Texas's market power over school textbooks into censorship on the national level. Texas has a board of citizens decide which texts will be approved for its schools, making the state the largest single market for K–12 textbooks. Major publishers cannot afford to lose that market. Beginning in 1961, the Gablers spoke to the board, to politicians, and to PTAs and churches, attacking evolution as unsupported theory and finding numerous small errors of fact in history texts. Their lack of academic credentials—Mel had one year of college, Norma none—seemed of no consequence to them: their website states,

> Q. Who are the analysts chosen to go over the textbooks in question, and what qualifications have they?
> A. This credential mongering is an ad hominem tactic to dodge inconvenient criticism. If points raised are valid, what matters the source?
> Where the Gablers were coming from is up front on their website, their organization is "an original contribution to the Christian conservative intellectual renaissance."[23]

Militant Christian right-wing revisionist history is not confined to the South; witness Pastor Douglas Wilson's home base in Idaho (Moscow! that must be galling), but it focuses on the South and has more followers in the South. According to their interpretation, the War between the States was a war between Christians and apostates. Technically, they say, it was over states' rights versus federalism; states' rights logically permit a state to secede; rapacious commercial interests in the North would not allow that, because they needed the South's resources, products, and consumer markets. Slavery, they say, was a trumped-up issue really confined to a small number of more-or-less mad abolitionists. Southerners preserved the godly, Bible-based, family living on its land, obeying its virile honorable male head. They were Calvinists, accepting predestination, signifying that God had destined some to be White men of honor, others—women and Blacks—to be weak vessels requiring men's protection and guidance. Destroying the Confederate army of godly Christian men, the North scourged the America forged by the Founding Fathers.

In 1994, in Tuscaloosa, Alabama, 27 people organized the Southern League to work toward secession from the United States. Upon a legal challenge from the Southern League of Professional Baseball Clubs, Inc., the group changed its name to the League of the South. Two founding members published "The New Dixie Manifesto" in 1995 (in the *Washington Post*), calling for secession by 15 states—4 more than the original Confederacy. The league demanded "home rule" in terms of states' rights and local control, especially over schools, so that racial segregation could be reinstituted. It openly advocated that the Confederacy should be a Christian nation, claiming that the Confederate flag featured a cross and should be flown as a symbol of a God-fearing people. Part of the founding group, signing themselves the Fifteen Ministers, published "The Moral Defense of the Confederate Flag: A Special Message for Southern Christians" in the league's *Southern Partisan* magazine.[24]

Southern Partisan's editor, Christopher Sullivan, served as the Sons of Confederate Veterans commander-in-chief. Hardly surprising is it that he explains that St. Andrew was one of Jesus's disciples and that the X of the flag is really a St. Andrew's cross. "Andrew" is the Anglicized Andreia, a Greek name meaning "manhood" or "valor," very appropriate for the self-styled paragons of manhood carrying the Confederate flag. The magazine is the flagship of the League of the South, denouncing books and films that denigrate "Southern culture" and such misguided foolishness as the legislatures of Virginia and North Carolina apologizing for slavery.[25] Later, it posted an address by Paul Gottfried, given in Raleigh, North Carolina on that state's Confederate Flag Day, March 3, observed since 1988. Gottfried complained that Northerners compare slavery in the South to the Nazi Holocaust, but "[a]t the very least, reason would require us to acknowledge that Southern slave owners were vitally concerned about preserving their human chattel, even if they sometimes failed to show them Christian charity and concern. Unlike the Nazis, these slave-owners were not out to exterminate a race of people."[26] A response posted on March 28, 2008, by Peter Henderson noted, "All things considered blacks have been surprisingly willing to see the virtues

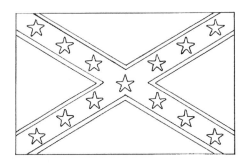

Figure 13.1. Confederate flag
Credit: Drawing by April Bernath.

of the south. For example, many have expressed sympathy with the view that the battle flag stands for something other than slavery."[27]

Strange to say, this can be substantiated. Jack Glazier, professor of anthropology at Oberlin College, observed an African American man participating in a Civil War reenactment at the Jefferson Davis Memorial in Fairview, Kentucky, Davis's birthplace. The man identified himself as a Black Confederate, wearing a Confederate uniform and carrying a Confederate battle flag. He told Professor Glazier that he represented the "loyal slave," and when Glazier expressed doubt, he told him, "You've been talking to a Yankee."[28] At Fairview's 2008 commemoration of Davis's birthday, which happened to be the bicentennial of his birth, a film was shown about Robert E. Lee, who, with his fellow Confederate general Stonewall (Thomas) Jackson, is celebrated as not only a hero but the very epitome of manhood. Jefferson Davis and John C. Calhoun are revered as strict constitutionalists manfully battling corrupting Northerners to save states' rights. The Sons of Confederate Veterans and the League of the South, with overlapping membership, promote the idea that these men represent the flower of Southern chivalry, landed aristocrats valiantly upholding the God-given hierarchy of which they were the apex. United Daughters of the Confederacy, sister to the Sons, is proud of its earlier member Dolly Lamar who tirelessly campaigned against woman suffrage. Historian Edward Sebesta points out that a solid bloc of Southern states rejected the Nineteenth Amendment giving women the vote (enough states passed it to make it law).[29] The neo-Confederates, as they style themselves, would restore a regime led by well-born Anglo men, where women and a laboring class had no legal rights and schools accepted the inerrancy of Protestant Fundamentalism.

EVOLUTION

Most notorious of the Christian Right's principles is its adamant opposition to accepting Darwinian organic evolution. On their website, the Gablers list "[s]cientific weaknesses in evolutionary theories" first among their "areas of concern." Other concerns include "[p]rinciples and benefits of free enterprise," as well as the "[o]riginal intent of the U.S. Constitution" and "[p]honics-based reading instruction."[30] (Phonics instruction is contrasted with "whole-word" recognition instruction, which emphasizes striving for meaning. Phonics conform better to the rote memorization favored by Christian schooling.) The fundamental error of evolutionists, according to the Christian Right, is failure to accept human depravity—"original sin."

Notions of progress were developed by eighteenth-century humanist philosophers and were a principle of Auguste Comte's Positivist evolutionist philosophy and Herbert Spencer's Synthetic Philosophy, but not Darwin's biological principle of natural selection. As scientific work based on observation of natural phenomena, Darwin's studies are necessarily atheistic—that is, without reference to any possibility of a god's actions. Darwinian evolution became the great paradigm of twentieth-century biology. Special creation of species by God is contradicted by Darwinian evolution, therefore narrow literal reading of Genesis seems incompatible with contemporary biology. In line with Francis Schaeffer's demand for either/or absolutes so popular with the Christian Right, conservatives cannot accept the position of mainline denominations[31] that God instituted organic evolution with the intent and knowledge that it would, in time, produce humans ("theistic evolution"). The Vatican decreed this interpretation in several papal encyclicals on evolution, notably by Pius XII in 1950, tentatively, and more forcefully by John Paul II in 1996. John Paul was influenced by his principal advisor on doctrine, Cardinal Ratzinger, who succeeded him as Pope Benedict XVI. Ratzinger accepted the argument of German theologian Karl Rahner, SJ, that the incarnation of Christ was the culmination of God communicating himself through organic evolution. Notwithstanding this evolution of understanding within the Roman Catholic and major Protestant churches, the militant Christian Right demonizes Darwin and contemporary biology.

Biologists mostly shake their heads over the Right's apparent obtuseness in regard to a beautifully simple and powerful description of an almost infinitude of observational data. They see that the Right generally accepts microevolution (within species), so why not evolution on larger scales? The answer is not that evolution has no place for God—theistic evolutionists accommodate God—but that it has no place for depravity. If humans are not born tainted by sin, if humans, like other organisms, have merely bred for greater chance of survival and reproduction, then there is no need for Christ the Redeemer. Pragmatically, if humans are not threatened by eternal damnation, they might ignore churches. Jesus of Nazareth may have preached love (and poverty), but Christianity is built on fear.

Evangelicals are up front about the critical importance of biblical inerrancy: if the Bible is not necessarily true, then perhaps its promise of redemption may be false. That doubt is Satan's seduction. The horrible outcome of general doubt about the absolute truth of the Bible would be millions of souls lost forever. A Christian who loves his fellow men should not stand idly by while Satan works the crowd. Depravity ensuing from Adam's sin demands Christian evangelism. And what was Adam's sin? Tasting the fruit of knowledge on his own. God had to banish the humans he had created from the garden of paradise, but mercifully he revealed salvation through the words of scripture.[32] Darwin, like Adam, tasted the fruit of knowledge on his own, by his own researches, with no recourse to the Word of God.

Evolution is particularly seductive and dangerous:

> A non-Christian school teaches that evolution is true. This is especially fascinating to young boys because of their love of dinosaurs. This teaching rejects the truth of a Creator and often creates an environment that ridicules a child who may question evolution as fact . . . Undermining the Creator and confusing the child has the effect of casting doubt and disbelief in the first 11 chapters of the Bible. Because the remainder of the Bible stands on the foundational

truths of the book of Genesis, casting doubt on the first 11 chapters under-
mines the validity of the entire Bible (2 Timothy 3:16).[33]

"Science" in non-Christian schools is said to be "[n]aturalism—everything
comes from matter, time, and chance," whereas in the Christian school, "science" teaches that "God is the Creator and Sustainer of all things; science
involves knowing God through knowing His world."[34]

A whole suite of sciences comes under the issue of evolution for the militant Christian Right. Geology interpreted to encompass millions of years
must be challenged as contrary to Genesis. Geological formations supposed
to result from persistent minute erosion should instead be seen as evidence
of the world deluge described in the story of Noah. Current concerns over
environment degradation and global warming must be combated, because as
the Gablers stated, "[e]nvironmental 'science' textbooks . . . environmental-
ism expands government control over private property. It scapegoats certain
groups (capitalists, Christians) and is quasi-pagan (Gaia worship). These are
elements of fascism." Textbooks should instead teach that "[u]se of more
natural resources creates new technology, which turns useless raw materials into usable resources."[35] The Gablers praised the A Beka Christian high
school history text for "explaining that nature-worship, animism, and super-
stition kept the Indians from taming the wilderness like the Europeans did."[36]
A Beka Book clearly defines that "[s]cience is the study of God's order, provision, and reasonableness as revealed in His physical creation."[37]

ORDER AND DISCIPLINE

Divine Providence (according to the Mel Gablers website) intervened to win
the day for the Christian Right when "[a]t the final SBOE [Texas State Board
of Education] vote, one member was absent, another abstained. Thus the
seven textbook reformers won, exorcising this festering malaise, because in
math as in sex ed and non-phonics reading, destructivists minimize traditional algorithms/standard rules and encourage students to invent their own
dysfunctional alternatives."[38]

Math in a Christian school is taught as "[a] reflection of the mind of an
orderly God who has made us in His image to understand His world . . .
Education is not focused on possibilities but on certainties found in God's
Word."[39] A Beka Book praises mathematics most highly:

> Mathematics is the language God used in His creation of the universe, and thus
> it is logical, orderly, beautiful, and very practical in science and in daily life.
>
> No subject matter better reflects the glory of God than mathematics. To
> study mathematics is to study God's thoughts after Him, for He is the great
> Engineer and Architect of the universe.
>
> Unlike the "modern math" theorists, who believe that mathematics is a crea-
> tion of man and thus arbitrary and relative, we believe that the laws of math-
> ematics are a creation of God and thus absolute. All of the laws of mathematics

are God's laws . . . Man's task is to search out and make use of the laws of the universe, both scientific and mathematical.

A Beka Book provides attractive, legible, workable traditional mathematics texts that are not burdened with modern theories such as set theory . . . Besides training students in the basic skills that they will need all their lives, the A Beka Book traditional mathematics books teach students to believe in the absolutes of the universe, to work diligently to get right answers, and to see the facts of mathematics as part of the truth and order that God has built into the real universe.[40]

Another of the most widely used Christian curricula is that of ACE, Accelerated Christian Education, calling itself the School for Tomorrow. Its philosophy cites the Bible, of course: "The proper way to teach a child is described in . . . Isaiah 28:10, which tells us, 'For precept must be upon precept, precept upon precept; line upon line, line upon line; here a little, and there a little.' "[41] Curricula are sold in 12-workbook packages by grade, kindergarten through eighth grade, and by subject for high school, packages ranging in price (in 2012) from $369 for the set of first grade subjects when bought with answer keys, to $180.94 for the basic twelfth grade four subjects, social studies (civics and economics) to be ordered additionally. ACE emphasizes that its curricula are individualized for each child by diagnostic testing to determine which workbook packages are needed, and the series of lessons, quizzes, and mastery tests by which children progress at their own pace. Homeschooling parents may select materials according to their own preferences for their children but are urged to begin with the $19.95 Parent Orientation Guide kit. Orderliness is important. The following list gives some of the "Basic Laws of Learning":

- [The child's] learning must be controlled, and he must be motivated.
- His learning must be measurable.
- His learning must be rewarded.[42]

"Control" is the critical word here. For all their rhetoric about freedom and liberty, the militant Christian Right wants control. Their "freedom" calls to mind Germany's Nazi slogan *"Arbeit Macht Frei"* ("Work Makes One Free"), set over the gate to Auschwtiz death camp. Over and over they reiterate the premise of absolutes, they abhor nuances. Theologian Harry Blamires, in his book *The Christian Mind*, devotes a chapter to "Acceptance of Authority," insisting,

One has to reassert christianly [sic] the principle of authority. First, God's authority; then the authority of his revelation, his commandments, and his Church . . . Certainly the Church has preserved the concept of a loving god, a merciful God, a compassionate God. But have Christians generally themselves any vivid sense of God's power and his dominion? . . . It cannot be denied that this is the God we are supposed to worship—not just a companionable God who is to be sidled up to and nestled against, but an awesome God before whom the worshipper prostrates himself, a wrathful God whose raised right arm can shake the universe.[43]

Thor, again.

Blamires goes on to explain that modern society fails to realize that the Father is not a Dagwood Bumstead bumbler but "power-laden authority . . . The father was the loving provider and defender whose hand was open in liberality and raised in protection: he was also, at the very same time, the awesome ruler to whom implicit obedience was due."[44] "Implicit obedience" must be inculcated. Implicit obedience is therefore the heart of the militant Right's curricula. It is inculcated in Christian schools by orderliness in movement as children line up at doors, march through corridors, take their seats upon signal and remain in them, raising their hands (or in some schools, little flags color coded for answer or request) to be recognized in an orderly fashion. Implicit obedience is drilled by attention to workbook exercises, quizzes, and mastery tests. Where a secular classroom may encourage exploration of resources in "discovery learning," the Christian school sets up "carefully planned demonstrations that can be performed with a minimum of equipment."[45]

Blogs written from home by conservative Christian mothers are windows into the preponderance of drilling in their method of educating. "Grace Indelible's" blog links to "A Chosen Child" blogs by Kim, adoptive mother of a 14-year-old boy who, from the attached photo, looks part African American. His father says, on a comment posted to "Anne's" post on the website about strict discipline,

> Our son is very strong-willed [James Dobson's book *The Strong-Willed Child* made this label popular] but also has additional issues caused by the fact that his birth mother participated in recreational drug use while he was in utero. He has been diagnosed with bipolar disorder, sensory integration disorder, fetal alcohol effects, oppositional defiant disorder, and "a grab bag of other emotional and psychological disorders and disturbances."
>
> The church we attended when he was kindergarten aged said the things you have mentioned here. We were even advised to act like we had completely lost our minds while applying corporal punishment with a belt in order to scare him into future compliance.[46]

The boy is in a special-education class, but even with a one-on-one personal aide, he cannot always cope with the demands of school (Kim doesn't say whether it is a Christian school). Kim posted on April 9, 2009, "David is in trouble at school again! He has a three-day suspension . . . I think I know why he's having such a problem. He isn't listening. I gave him several easy chores with one- or two-step directives to complete. However, I found that either the steps were not followed in the order I gave them or they were skipped altogether . . . his mind shuts off after he gets the general concept . . .

He then gets upset and angry when the adult tells him he hasn't gotten it right." How does Kim deal with the unhappy boy?

> Last week I shared how David was having to write sentences in order to get him to listen better. His listening has gotten a bit better, but his behavior is still not up to what it should be.
>
> Even though this is spring break we can't let this area slide and let him just have fun so I have changed what he is to write. Last week it was directions, but this week I began him at Proverbs 1:2. He must listen then write down what I say. I am quoting just a section of the verse, but at the end of the passage he must read back to me what he wrote. This has caused him some concern as he can't always read what he wrote. If it is wrong he must rewrite the verse.
>
> Since so much of Proverbs deals with the wise versus the foolish man I thought that would be the perfect place to begin. As we are going along I am explaining what the verse means so that he also gets the concept.
>
> It is not the spring break that I had envisioned.[47]

Kim titles this blog entry "The Foolish Little Man." It is Proverbs 1:7 that speaks of "foolish men" who "despise wisdom and instruction." David does not seem to merit that condemnation.

Another conservative Christian mother blogs with a link to a website called "White Washed Feminists," alluding to feminists who remain committed to their churches while carefully questioning patriarchal structure and principles. Parenting is much discussed, with several contributors warning against the Dobson strict discipline advice advocated by, among others, authors Michael and Debi Pearl. "Anne," who posts on her "Homeschool blog," described her efforts to follow the Pearls' *To Train Up a Child*:

> My experiences with the Pearls started when Piper was a year old. I was pregnant again, with Bridget, and having a hard time with discipline. In every way that Reagan had been easy, Piper was hard. A strong word would cause Reagan to cease bad behavior while that same word would cause Piper to scream at me. She made me feel embarrassed . . . The Pearls spoke with such authority, that I simply accepted that they were authoritative, and began implementing their methods . . . I used a ruler or a wooden spoon for Reagan, and a pencil or the spoon handle for Piper (as I was unable to find the kind of switch they spoke of in their books, and read that this was an acceptable alternative). The Pearls taught that the switch was appropriate for training and discipline, so I used them for both. I implemented them completely, taking all that they taught to heart. Much to my surprise, it didn't work.
>
> I was stunned. How could God's way not work for me? The Pearl's book was peppered with scripture, surely their way must be correct! . . . I increased our switching, and worked at 100% consistency, which is what the Pearl's said was needed to receive total obedience. But it still wasn't working . . . [M]y kids' . . . continued lack of total obedience only made my failure more obvious. I increased the switching, certain that must be where my problem was. Then fear set in. The harder I became, the more Piper rebelled. Our relationship had turned adversarial. I had to win . . . I had failed as a mother and I had failed

to be a Berean testing everything the Pearls said against scripture. After heavy prayer, I found myself humbled before the God who forgives, and who shows grace and mercy to his children.

Anne found books by Fundamentalist "grace-based discipline" advocates, "put down the switches," talked with her children, emphasized good consequences from "good choices" she offered, and reports they are now the loving and cooperating team she desires.[48]

"Normalmiddle," posting a comment to Anne's blog "Selling Fear," said, "I wanted good, godly, obedient kids and a happy family. I let the culture-war fear overcome me, and before I knew it, was long down the path towards a patriocentric lifestyle . . . out of my fear of rebellious, unsaved, ungrateful kids."[49] White Washed Feminists[50] are disturbed by the popularity of Doug Phillips's Vision Forum, selling books under the categories "Beautiful Girlhood" and "The All-American Boy's Adventure Catalog." The former promises that, "[a]mid a culture brimming with mixed messages, shallow and self-serving ideals, and depraved 'role-models,' may you and your precious daughters find the following pages to be a refreshing and edifying oasis of innocence."[51] Regarding the latter, "[t]he courageous boy is on a mission from God to take dominion over the earth. This is why he loves to learn, to investigate, to master disciplines, and to search out the mysteries of creation. His basic textbook for life is the Holy Scriptures . . . motivating him to demonstrate an unflinching loyalty."[52] The site sells toys for boys: an amphibious remote-control tank; a replica Confederate officer's sword; an 1850 US Staff officer's sword; cowboy spurs, hat, and chaps; and a marshmallow blaster gun. For girls, the site sells dolls, doll dresses, a "Sacajawea book and doll dress" and "American Indian tunic" (Sacajawea is described as devoted to serving her men), and a tea set on a tea trolley.

Vision Forum posts these lines from a homeschooled girl's "graduation speech": "I am delighted to be at home under my father's authority, serving him and Mama and our family, and in doing so preparing to someday serve a husband and children. I have learned from God's word and Daddy and Mama that there is no better or more fulfilling role for a woman than to be a keeper at home as God created her to be."[53] This is patriocentrism. That last line refers to the counsel that Christian young women should not be in college, sleeping in unsupervised dormitories and exposed to depraved (their word) courses.

One Christian school educator urges parents to ensure their children will receive

a Christ-centered worldview. From as early as kindergarten, Christian schools are teaching and modeling a Godly perspective regarding every aspect of their education, from math to physical education class. Incidentally, if Christ is not the center of PE class, what does competition look like? If Christ is not the center of History class, where does God fit into the history of mankind? Does He, or doesn't He? These are just two of dozens of perspectives that children are taught every day for 30 hours a week. Do the math! 30 hours a week times 36 weeks of school equals 1,080 hours in the classroom in a school year. Now multiply that by 13 years. It equals 14,040 hours that children are absorbing worldviews.[54]

Doing this math reveals how stringently the narrow absolutist worldview can be inculcated by Christian schooling. Nearly two million American children are homeschooled,[55] the majority by professing Christian parents; add to these another million-plus attending Protestant Christian schools, and the number of Americans segregated from the secular world, drilled to obedience to absolutist authorities, becomes significant for the country's future. Their goal of a Bible-ruled United States can only be termed fascist.

True to their long, Indo-European tradition, these Christian children often are taught that they are, or should be, "warriors." Cherokee Christian Schools calls its students "Warriors," its newsletter is "The Monthly Warrior," its podcast is "WarriorCast," and its logo on the top of its website is really cool: a knight with lance and shield on a spirited horse rocks when one's mouse pointer touches it, and children's voices shout a war cry. Its "Prayer Warriors meet every Thursday morning from 8:30am–9:30am over coffee and breakfast goodies, do a brief devotion, and pray for our teachers and staff." The school states, "The goal of a Premier School must also be to graduate Biblical Worldview 'Warriors' for the Lord who live out their faith in the marketplace of ideas, their families, and their callings . . . Cherokee Christian Schools will become the place that you choose to equip your child to become a warrior for Christ in every way."[56]

The Southern Baptist Association of Christian Schools in Windermere, Florida, uses capital letters to communicate their aggressive message:

> Approximately 600 Christian schools are supported and operated by Southern Baptist churches and state conventions. WHAT IF . . . the nation's largest Protestant denomination aggressively supported Christian education as a new strategy for church growth and discipleship for children and parents? . . . Baptist schools were recognized as a powerfully community outreach and were listed in the same breath with other missions and evangelistic efforts? . . . there were thousands of Baptist schools of excellence all across America, teaching Biblical truth all week long to millions of American children? THEN . . . young people would stay in our churches to invigorate them as Kingdom warriors. TURN THE "WHAT IFS" INTO REALITY AND WE CAN CHANGE OUR WORLD FOR CHRIST IN ONE GENERATION![57]

DEPRAVITY IS THE FOUNDATION

Michelle Power, a teacher at Cherokee Christian Schools, described her philosophy: "I also want my students to learn that they are not able to be perfect. They are meant to strive for their best, but to realize that their best may not always be perfection. I have had many students in the classroom that find this hard to accept. We are sinful creatures and as much as we want to be perfect we are not."[58] For these conservative Christians, human depravity is the foundation of human life. Secular humanism's intolerable error is to disbelieve that we all bear God's curse upon Adam. Genesis (3:16–19) says only that God decreed that men must toil for their subsistence, women will suffer pain in giving birth, and humans must die and decay. Not until Christianity was institutionalized, two centuries and more after Jesus, was the curse interpreted to signify that humans are innately sinful—that is, depraved. The Catholic Church instigated mandatory confession of sins before communicants could take the Eucharist and be sanctified; Protestants eschew private confession to a priest but similarly impute sin to every human. Thus James Dobson could recommend regular whipping for even small children, because they too bear sin. Christian teachers must lead children to recognize sin in themselves, to fear its consequences will be eternal painful damnation, then to relieve the anxiety they have induced by promising salvation through Jesus the scapegoat.

Christian schools profess great love for the children entrusted to them, yet paradoxically overwhelm children with the image of God as wrathful Lord. True, the Old Testament presents God as a warlord, taking care of his followers so long as they are faithful. In the New Testament, that warlord generously sent his people a Lamb to be given up as sacrifice. Indo-Europeans as well as Semites sacrificed, including human sacrifices; Norse sacrificed humans to Odin, hanging the person and piercing him with a spear,[59] like the Roman soldier piercing the hanging Jesus. Teaching children that they must be warriors fighting for their Lord's kingdom lies millennia deep in Indo-European tradition. Militant Christians add to the inculcation of obedience to authority—the wrathful Lord and his stewards—an anxiety over hardly perceived sins lurking like tapeworms in the gut. Gnawed by fear, children yearning for salvation will joyfully enroll in God's legion. They are the troops who will fight by means of politics in Congress, legislatures, the judiciary, school boards, and missions to extirpate from America all but their Indo-European battle-ax cultural tradition.

CHAPTER 14

EVOLVING TRADITION, RESILIENT BACKLASH

A warrior culture can enthrall millions for millennia, even today in America. Barack Obama recognized its power when he chose Rick Warren to give the invocation at his 2009 inauguration. Warren, megachurch preacher and bestselling self-help author, reinforced Obama's centrist position. Casually dressed and overweight, Warren is the picture of the average American man at the beginning of the twenty-first century. Waving his chubby arms, he exhorts his fellow preachers attending to his motivational messages, "think about the exponential explosion of ministry when millions upon millions of small groups in millions upon millions of churches organize in such a way that each person can do their part in attacking the five global giants . . . spiritual darkness, lack of servant leaders around the world, poverty, disease, [and] ignorance . . . Billions of people have never even heard the name of Jesus Christ. Three thousand distinct people groups around our world wouldn't even know the name of Jesus if they heard it."[1] Rick Warren has grandiose goals, and believes that a conventional suit hobbles servants of the Lord. The militant Christian Right of the generations after Jerry Falwell, Pat Robertson, and James Dobson are carrying out their Great Commission far beyond the proprieties adhered to by their elders.

ON THE BLURRY EDGE

Franklin Graham soberly carries on his father Billy's evangelical business; Frank Schaeffer left and excoriated his father, Francis; James Dobson's son Ryan skateboarded into a new ministry targeting his pals. "Skateboarding Rules," Ryan Dobson posted on his website, and instead of competing with his father on daytime radio broadcasts, he podcasts.

Ryan Dobson, born in 1970, attended Biola University in La Mirada, near Los Angeles, a school claiming, on its website, that "the resurrection is one of the best-attested facts of classical antiquity. He [Biola Professor Hazen] said that the case is so good, that you can take the 'bare bones' facts provided by the scholars who are unbelievers and skeptics and when you weigh them carefully, a resurrection is the best explanation for those facts."[2] Biola hosts the annual Science Fair for the Southern California region of Association of Christian Schools International (ACSI). Its dean of sciences explained, "The ACSI science fair is unique from other science fairs in that students are also challenged to identify and integrate Biblical truth in their projects."[3] Within this viewpoint, Ryan pursued a BA in communication studies, wrote books titled *Be Intolerant, 2 Die 4,* and *Wrecked,* and then was ordained in 2007. He married, was divorced (a painful event for his "Focus on the Family" father), and married again. Taking a break from troubles, young Dobson went fly fishing in the mountains: "It is one of the most perfect settings I've ever been in. Then it hit me. Why was this scene created? God knew I'd think it was cool."[4]

Hot to be cool. From the multimillion-selling *Left Behind* novels and their movies, through Christian rock and heavy-metal bands and hip-hop and rap, surfboards, skateboards, and motorcycles, young Christians are pulled into the militant Right. Those who resist being suits at Regent University or Patrick Henry College can soak up sun, shirtless, at Christian music festivals. They can display their Christian tattoos. They should not fornicate, but this abstention fits very well the Indo-European warrior tradition adjuring men to conserve that body fluid essential to masculine strength and power.

Hypermasculinity exudes from these cool dudes evangelizing to skaters, surfers, bikers, and National Rifle Association supporters. Men-only retreats and Promise Keeper rallies in football stadiums underscore the militant Right's insistence on patriarchal separation between men and women. Both retreats and rallies feature pastors speaking as if man-to-man, sharing with the men in the crowd the emotions and burdens of being a man. It goes without saying that the militant Right will have few women leaders beyond those such as Beverly LaHaye, heading women's groups—Phyllis Schafly alone spoke on a par with men leaders. Fundamentalist pastors quote Paul (1 Corinthians 14:34–35): "Let your women keep silence in the churches: for it is not permitted unto them to speak; but they are commanded to be under obedience, as also saith the law. And if they will learn any thing, let them ask their husbands at home: for it is a shame for women to speak in the church."[5] Pastors' sons take up the ministry, daughters remain silent.

Dr. R. C. Sproul Jr., another of these sons of well-known pastors, created his own literally pastoral pastorate in the mountains of southwestern Virginia. The logo of his Highlands Study Center shows a sword slashed across a book, presumably the Bible, circled by olive branches rising from a rope. His website tells how "[f]inding the church awash in worldliness, we set about helping Christians live more simple, separate, and deliberate lives for the glory of God and the building of His kingdom." Rhett W. commented, "Not your ordinary emasculated Christian ministry!" Owen W. added, "A place to get sound Biblical teaching from real men serving the real God."[6] The patriarchy R. C. Sproul Jr. preached turned on him for disobeying its rules, specifically giving communion to children too young to understand it, contrary to the Westminster Presbytery's Book of Church Order, and starting new mission churches without authority from the Presbytery. A couple of the real men in the congregation protested Sproul Jr.'s ways, for which he ordered the congregation to shun them. Carrying the conflict to the Presbytery's General Assembly, the dissenters revealed that Sproul had used the Reformed Presbyterian Church's tax ID number for his own enterprises without the church's permission, construable as identity theft under Virginia and federal laws. For this crime and rebellion, the General Assembly on January 26, 2006, deposed Sproul Jr. and three men associated with him in his ministry.[7] Nothing daunted Sproul Jr., who is still running his "covenantal, agrarian" community at this writing, six years later, and publishing its newsletter, advising that "[r]eading trains the mind to engage in spiritual warfare. We hope you'll stay with us as we labor to take every thought captive."[8]

Meanwhile, an ingenuous remark by Sproul Jr. that the good ol' boys and their families are just "prairie muffins,"[9] gave Carmon, the good Christian woman who runs Buried Treasure bookshop from her home, the inspiration to post the Prairie Muffin Manifesto:

3) Prairie Muffins are aware that God is in control of their ability to conceive and bear children, and they are content to allow Him to bless them as He chooses in this area . . .

17) Prairie Muffins place their husbands' needs and desires above other obligations, arranging their schedules and responsibilities so that they do not neglect the one who provides for and protects them and their children . . .

18) Prairie Muffins are fiercely submissive to God and to their husbands . . .

19) Prairie Muffins appreciate godly role models, such as Anne Bradstreet, Elizabeth Prentiss and Elisabeth Elliot. They do not idolize Laura Ingalls Wilder (Little House on the Prairie) or Louisa May Alcott (Little Women); while they may enjoy aspects of home life presented in their books, PMs understand that the latent humanism and feminism in these stories and in the lives of these women is not worthy of emulation . . .

11) Prairie Muffins own aprons and they know how to use them . . .

32) Though we abhor the idea of women being involved in the military and fighting battles which men are commanded to fight, Prairie Muffins recognize that there is a real battle in which they are on the front lines: the battle of the seed of the woman against the seed of the serpent. In this most-important conflict, we gratefully serve King Jesus in the capacity He has given us, waving our wooden spoons and rallying our children to stand alongside us in the battle, training them to be mighty warriors in the defense and furthering of God's kingdom.[10]

And so on for a total of 51 clauses.

WARRIORS

Onward, Christian soldiers!

Fight 4 Christ unabashedly promotes boxing. God bless them, they say on their website; they promise, "We donate a portion from EVERY order [of goods] to Christian churches and organizations."[11] (Which churches and organizations they do not specify.) Their pictured stable of fighters leaves no doubt that a Christian can be a formidable man. John Eldredge, promoter of the *Wild at Heart* books from his Ransomed Heart Ministries (Chapter 11), would have to recognize that these men found their passion. There is a disquieting echo here, with these men in "combat sports," of Eldredge's "boot camps":

> Its Boot Camp week here at Ransomed Heart. 450 men from all over the world are heading to Colorado for a profound encounter with God. We just finished packing the U Haul we take up to Crooked Creek Ranch with all our stuff in it. Work crew guys are flying in today. Part of our team will head up this afternoon to the camp, the rest tomorrow morning. There is excitement in the air.
>
> This is a Boot Camp week, and man, can we tell. All sorts of warfare flying around here. Physical stuff like internal bleeding and chest pains. Sleeplessness. Emotional stuff like marital tension, and all sorts of agreements being "suggested" by the enemy. Oppressive "fog."
>
> Its like he comes, probing the perimeter, looking for some way in.
>
> The reason for boatloads of assault is that these weekends are some of the most profound, healing, freeing, life-changing weekends these men will ever in their lives experience. No joke. Its a big deal. It will change hundreds of lives forever. When you rescue a man, the reverberations of that are almost limitless. You rescue a marriage, and a family. You rescue his children, and generations after them.[12]

Fighting, Warfare

Twice in the twentieth century, Christian Germans rallied to fight en masse to aggrandize German power. Disturbed by his homeland's martial spirit, German scholar Klaus Theweleit studied records and novels of German soldiers, particularly the Freikorps groups of soldiers who refused to give up their weapons after their fatherland's surrender in 1918. Some retreated to farms or worked as foresters, keeping alive the military culture that would fuel Nazi expansion. Others formed gangs plotting Germany's resurrection, assassinating political leaders such as Jewish industrialist Walter Rathenau, and murdering each other in competition for leadership. Theweleit is horrified by Freikorps's lust for blood: "When blood whirled through the brain and pulsed through the veins as before a longed-for night of love, but far hotter and crazier . . . The baptism of fire! The air was so charged then with an overwhelming presence of men that every breath was intoxicating, that they could have cried without knowing why. Oh, hearts-of-men, that are capable of feeling this!"[13] With that undertone of homoeroticism, the

Freikorps violently asserted homophobia. While these *Männerbund* brother-hoods indulged in orgies of whippings and beatings, even on women deemed untrustworthy, their wives waited patiently at home.

The Freikorps paralleled the US Ku Klux Klan in that both originated with demobilized soldiers (the KKK with Confederates after the Civil War). Both flourished after World War I as secret brotherhoods yearning for romanticized agrarian societies where White men such as them would domi-nate. The Freikorps, as members or former members of the German army (where the Iron Cross was the highest military decoration) used crosses, and the Klan burned crosses at their rallies.

Christians' Cross, of course, was the Roman imperium's instrument for execution by torture. Thus, logically, it is a suitable symbol for White men's violent campaigns for domination.

Germans fantasized themselves to be the Aryan master race. Kaiser Wil-helm II, monarch during World War I, had copies of the pseudoscientific racist book by expatriate Englishman Houston Stewart Chamberlain, *Die Grundlagen des Neunzehnten Jahrhunderts* (Foundations of the Nineteenth Century), 1899, distributed throughout Germany to schools, libraries, and army officers. Chamberlain asserted that Aryans were the highest-evolved human race, and Teutons the highest and most virile of Aryans. Later, to be a hero to Adolf Hitler, who would attend his funeral, Chamberlain described an epic struggle between tall, blond, manly Teutons and the despicable con-niving Jewish race. No Jew having ever done anything admirable, Chamber-lain was sure that Jesus Christ was son of a Roman soldier, and St. Paul and King David were of more Aryan than Jewish parentage. Martin Luther he could "picture fifteen hundred years ago, on horseback, swinging his battle-axe to protect his beloved northern home."[14]

Americans—that is, White Anglo-Saxon Protestant Americans—were more than simply the master race to Pastor Peter Peters, of Scriptures for America, an "outreach ministry of the LaPorte [Colorado] Church of Christ . . . dedi-cated to proclaiming the true Gospel of Christ Jesus throughout the earth,

Figure 14.1. Nazi Iron Cross
Nazi Iron Cross medal.
Credit: Drawing by April Bernath.

and to revealing to Americans and the Western Nations their true Biblical Identity." This Christian Identity, as the loose movement is termed, proclaims nothing less than that WASPs are the only people truly covenanted with God:

> God was saying [Genesis 17:19] His covenant was not going to be with Ishmael or with any of the children of his concubines but with a son to be called Isaac. (From Isaac's sons we get the term "Saxons.") . . .
>
> "Jerusalem will be inhabited without walls because of the multitude of men and cattle within it." Zechariah 2:4.
>
> In the New American Standard Bible, the words "without walls" has a side note beside it and the definition says "like unwalled villages." First of all, Jerusalem is going to consist of unwalled cities because of the multitude of men and the cattle within it. There are more cattle in Keith County, Nebraska, than there is in the entire state of the Israelis. A county in what is called the "Great America Desert" which our people allowed to bloom. Many of the prophesies that they try to tell you happened in that other land really happened right here in this land. We made the desert bloom. On July 4, 1776, a nation was born in one day and it is all in keeping with prophesy.[15]

Peters published a newsletter, "The Dragon Slayer," and in 2009, he released a DVD exposing the dastardly satanic "sorcery behind the layout of Washington DC, our Nation's Capitol [sic]." The DVD ($19.95) will reveal "Mighty Weapons" to prevail against this evil.[16] One is to

POUND & PULVERIZE with IMPRECATORY PRAYER POWER

> SPECIAL PRAYER #3—THE GATLING GUN PRAYER: Pray for the return of our Lord and the establishment of his governing kingdom upon earth.
>
> Jesus gave us the example of what a perfect prayer should be as he instructed his disciples in Matthew 6:9–13 [the "Our Father" prayer].
>
> Notice that these short and to the point issues can be prayed as a spiritual Gatling gun that fires powerful bullets in rapid succession. This is a powerful and well known prayer which is often prayed from memory without recognizing its awesome petition for our Lord's return.

To gain full strength, Peters begged God to "stir us to raging warfare against those who have hidden in their secret designs of evil sorcery. Awaken us to the wicked deceptions that have been placed upon our people and our nation. Forgive us for being so gullible and stir heated anger within us. Give us the courage to rise up and wage spiritual war in fiery judgment. Preserve your own and destroy our sneaky enemy among us."[17] Continuing to provide us with mighty weapons, Peters unveiled on his website,

> [T]he Pistol Prayer, pray it at the exact beginning (top) of each hour when you are awake. (Try to remember and do this at the top of each hour: if you forget, then at least sometime in the hour.) When you do it at the top of the hour, you

will feel the added power due to others in the body of Christ praying it at the same time.

Now the Rifle Prayer is to be prayed in synchronicity as well, at 7:00 pm Mtn. time Monday through Fridays, and it will be aired on the SFA Worldwide Broadcasting Network at that time as well. We have also added a new dimension to the Rifle

Prayer by putting it in song, to the tune of "A Mighty Fortress". Remember that many of the Psalms were prayers put to song. (Go to our website to hear it, and it is available on CD as well.) Prayer put to music is a powerful weapon for the tearing down of strongholds. Add faith to the music with the prayer, and the synchronicity, and it will override their magical sorcery stronghold, just like Moses' miracles overrode the magicians in Egypt. We covered this as well in the documentary debut on Sunday March 15, 2009, and it is archived at our website, www.scripturesforamerica.org. Keep firing the Pistol and Rifle Prayers for all of 2009![18]

If this seems mad in more than one sense, try some other web links. Ronald Weinland believes he is pastor of God's only true church on earth, and appointed to be the end-time prophet, the first prophet in 1,900 years. Late in 2008, Pastor and Mrs. Weinland went to their prophesied post for the end-time: "This is a very sobering time for my wife and me as we are in the city [Jerusalem] that God prophetically describes as Sodom (spiritually). We are in a hotel room a block away from where we can look down upon one of the higher points of the old city and specifically at the Jaffa Gate. It is in this area where the two witnesses will be killed and three and one-half days later, Jesus Christ will begin His return to this earth as King of kings."[19] Who are those two God-chosen final witnesses? None other than Ronald and Laura Weinland! Sobering, indeed.

An Anthropological Perspective

It is astounding that people who profess a profound, intimate relationship with Jesus should want to label themselves "warriors." The simple explanation is that Christianity was imposed by royal fiat upon most Europeans, and for these militants, it persisted as a superficial gloss upon native Indo-European religion. This historical view suggests that the major Christian churches' emphasis upon obedience to authority was integral to these national conversions—*cuius regio, eius religio* (whom the king, his the religion). When shrines to Indo-European deities and local spirits were replaced, by order of authorities, with churches and chapels in the same holy locations, the literal superficiality of Christianity was manifest. Indra the Dragon-Slayer was now to be called St. George, or the Christ—picturing Christ spearing a writhing dragon was popular.

The image lives on, appropriated by scriptures for America's "Christian outreach ministry professing to teach Anglo-Saxon, Germanic, and kindred peoples of the world their true Biblical identity."[20]

Figure 14.2.   St. George, with his cross on his shield, spearing a dragon
Credit: Drawing by April Bernath.

The militant Christian Right perpetuates itself by instilling fear. Its most fundamental premise, one so familiar in America that it is taken as a fear natural to humans, is that everyone has a soul in danger of eternal damnation. That fear is so unnatural that it takes great effort to instill it and to maintain it—Dr. Dobson's method of regularly whipping young children will do it, as will strong regimentation in a Christian school and unceasing reiteration in Christian workbooks, readers, music, and videos. That fear seems really incongruous in contemporary America, where no one need starve or freeze or be attacked by wild beasts. Popular media feed the premise that man is innately violent, the premise embedded in Indo-European culture.

Humans are not innately violent. We come from millions of years of natural selection for cooperation. Our infants are born entirely helpless and must be nurtured for years. We instinctively feel kindly toward round-faced, big-eyed, plump little ones, an instinct profitably used by Disney and artists drawing big-headed, round-faced, big-eyed children to lure moviegoers and buyers. No one simply looking at a baby sees it stained with sin. Militants are fighting, first of all, against those millions of years of natural selection when only babies whose families nurtured them survived to reproduce. Nurturing within the family was supported by cooperation between families. Groups of families contested territory—violence was never unknown—but daily life was mostly experienced within neighborly villages. To counter that commonplace experience takes a lot of effort.

Jesus of Nazareth taught a radical vision of brotherhood, every person equal in a community valuing spirituality over wealth and power. He used the threat of losing God's favor to impel people into his ministry. In a Roman world of harsh punishments including crucifixion, bloody entertainments, and military readiness, Jesus's tortured death and his urging people to be anxious over their souls' entry to heaven gained prominence. Jesus crucified embodied people's horrible consciousness of violence in their lives, whether in cities or in countryside ravaged by plunderers. His vision of heaven for saved souls appealed to the thousands fearing the very real terrors of the overexpanded, vulnerable Roman Empire. That very old notion of transferring evils onto a goat and driving it out of the community carried on with a new twist, a man taking on all humans' sins and carrying them through death, out of society. Sufferers were promised final bliss by this redemptive act. A religion assuaging people's suffering in a cruel empire replaced Jesus's radical challenge to reform Judea.

Then Constantine, the Germanic contender for Rome's throne, marched toward battle and saw familiar symbols, likely a battle-ax and crossed swords, in a cosmic vision with the words *In Hoc Signo Vinces* ("By this sign, you will conquer"). A canny bishop proffered an extraordinary interpretation of the sign: not the traditional symbols of battle success, but far more, the letters signaling Anointed. Constantine was destined to be emperor! More than simply victory in the upcoming fight was foretold in the sky. With the fulfillment of the vision's promise, Christianity became Roman. It became a hierarchy of power.

North of the *limes* of Rome, indigenous Germanic ideology continued even after nominal conversions of populations to official Christianity. Rome's legacy was a hierarchy of authority topped by the Anointed; popes are literally anointed to perpetuate the lineage. As we saw in Chapter 4, Protestants protested the authority of the Roman Church, not the concept of authority per se. Within Protestant states, there was tension between authority embedded in bureaucracy, and the older tradition of the *männerbund*, the band of fighters loyal to their leader and eager to do battle. Twentieth-century Germany particularly harbored this tension, with the Freikorps after World War I followed by Nazi enthusiasm for the Aryan myth—Hitler selecting tall blond men to bond in elite army corps and to beget the master race in *Lebensborn* maternity homes. Nazi Germany is the nightmare militant Christian Right, an excrescence upon Christian Western societies. Perhaps it seems exaggerated, even unfair, to link Nazi Germany and the American militant Christian Right through their shared ancient Indo-European Germanic ideology. There's no way a beer-hall putsch could happen in America. Still, Timothy McVeigh was a Christian who in 1995 blew up a public building, killing 168 people, of whom 19 were small children. He had registered as a Republican and joined the National Rifle Association. He had found friends who shared his passion for guns, quotes from Patrick Henry about liberty, and view that he was good and the government was evil; one friend assisted him in destroying the Murrah Building.[21] Militant Christian warriors can wreak havoc in America.

"The Natural Direction of Life Is Degeneration, Not Evolution," proclaims Dr. John Morris, president of the Institute for Creation Research and son of its founder, Henry Morris. "Time is short. The death of a once great culture looms . . . Justices see our Constitution as 'evolving to fit the needs of a maturing society' . . . One of the very strongest arguments against evolution has always been the tendency for every system, living or dead, individual or societal, moral or mundane, to wear out, deteriorate, or die. As is common to all experience, nothing, absolutely nothing, gets better on its own."[22] The militant Christian Right lives in culturally induced fear and trembling, told that our everyday observations of a good world, good people are false and dangerously misleading. It is the worldview of a hapless Bronze Age villager, amid thatched homes and granaries crackling with flames, looking at the upraised arm of a helmeted warrior bringing that battle-ax down.

Jesus of Nazareth would have felt himself that villager. Militant Christian Right leaders picture themselves wielding the battle-ax. America is transmogrified into a dragon with Satan's horns, the quintessential alien. The dragon has many heads—secularism, evolution, pacifism, feminism, gay marriage, sex education—and it refuses to die. America remains a battleground. The warriors teach their children in their Christian schools to shout war cries.[23] Relentlessly indoctrinated, even in cursive handwriting workbooks, the children learn to deny seeing goodness in the world or in humans. They learn that their greatest, perhaps only, real joy will be their private, individual, inward-focused emotion that their Savior has entered their heart. They can release some of the tension drummed into them by engaging in sports and praise-worship, and when they are adult, they can obtain pleasure in the marriage bed. Even as parents, they will battle Satan, whipping their little children to ensure they will fear and obey authority.

The culture of the militant Christian Right in the United States is integrated and bounded. Insisting on dual absolutes, godly and satanic, and a single criterion to be godly—namely, accepting Christ as an intimate personal savior—that culture is a complete cradle-to-grave package of child-rearing, schooling, political affiliation, books, entertainment, and social group. Positions may not be logical—how can capital punishment be accepted and aborting mere embryos damned?—but they are maintained predictably black-and-white. Members can be confident that the Bible they read (in English) is inerrant, they will be saved in heaven, their pastors are likely inspired, their role as man or woman decreed. Nothing to question. They are called to be Christian warriors.

Called, or conscripted? To a secular eye, the militant Christian Right engages in jihad, as fanatic as any Muslim war. As much as any Muslim in a tribal village, militant Christian evangelists have been immersed in their faith community, taught to abhor and struggle against everyone else. We humans are gregarious mammals, and that instinct for bonding with our community makes it easy for people to accept what is taught by parents and the adults our parents respect. Instinct for community makes it difficult to listen with an open mind to outsiders, particularly those who have been labeled as opponents. There will always be some defections from the militant Right, some people who read the Gospels and realize Jesus of Nazareth was a pacifist, a feminist, a radical socialist; but there will be millions who hold on to the essentially pagan Christianity Constantine established.

Indo-European battle-ax cultural tradition is a rewarding way of life. In the guise of competitive free-market capitalism where businessmen make a killing, wield the ax against surplus employees and benefits they aren't forced to confer, this ancient worldview of *bellum omnium contra omnes,* war as the natural condition, can yield riches. Four millennia ago, the battle-ax warriors carried plunder from the field; today their descendants take multimillion-dollar bonuses. Trophy wives are theirs, too. Fighting is a man's way. Patriarchy makes every man a lord, an earthly reflection of God the Father. It makes women captivating.

Politics go in cycles. Conservative governments reluctant to tax the rich get nations into deficits, then liberals pull them out, only to lose to conservative challenges and promises. After the turbulent 1960s trashing, that Battle-Ax Culture pulling us into the black hole of Vietnam, citizens were attracted to Ronald Reagan's homey all-American visage and his touting "family values." Economic prosperity makes citizens feel good. Bush senior rode the wave, lost to the apparently centrist Clinton, then maneuvered his alcoholic son into the presidency. Pure disaster, in the form of disastrous Middle East wars and economic bust, gave Barack Obama the opportunity he sought. The militant Christian Right has been loud and visible, riding its warhorses against abortion and homosexuals, but the Great Recession of the twenty-first century makes it difficult to feed those warhorses.

On May 19, 2009, newspapers reported that the Pentagon dropped its Bush-era practice of placing a Bible quote every day on the cover sheet of its Intelligence Update sent to the White House.[24] The fight against secular America lost on that front. It didn't die, and its momentum from more than four millennia carries it on. Militant Christianity swings its battle-ax against Satan's minions tolerating diversity. It is indeed easy to see its battlefield eternally present in human societies. An anthropological view across time and geography shows that is only a particular cultural tradition. Humankind is not locked into a fight between evil and good; the Jewish prophet Jesus from Nazareth said, it is reported, "Blessed are the gentle, for they shall inherit the earth."[25]

CHAPTER 15

CONCLUSION

THE CULTURE OF MILITANT CHRISTIANITY

Anthropology can penetrate the conventions of American society, revealing its segments and their ideologies. The American militant Christian Right is a segment that sees itself as a nation, not merely a religion. Its cultural principle of oppositional dualism constantly constructs boundaries, making it a good case study, relatively clearly delineated, for anthropological analysis of a large, contemporary "imagined community" (as Benedict Anderson cogently defines "nation").[1] Here, I have followed the thread of its worldview and ethos, back and back, unbroken, to our earliest documents of Indo-European beliefs and their archaeological manifestations in the Bronze Age Battle-Ax Culture. The study expands as that ethos of *bellum omnium contra omnes* dominated nominally Christian institutions, producing the Crusades; fissioning "the church" and then the Protestant movements; and welding capitalist economics to imperial ambitions, not least in the United States. Today's Christian Right mythologizes American history, a textbook example of Malinowski's insight into myth as social charter.

An anthropological analysis that finds Indo-European culture to have persisted for four thousand years, adapting to three continents' environments without losing its fundamental premises, discomfits many scholars accustomed to narrower research niches. Overriding disciplinary domains is a hallmark of anthropology; we commit to a holistic approach, weighing pertinence of data but ruling out nothing ad hoc. The anthropologist must become conversant with both scientific and humanistic fields as one's research uncovers, or analysis discerns, topics ordinarily covered by other disciplines. My own research into "scientific creationism," begun to answer students' confusion over an alleged conflict between science and religion, led into the origins of institutional Christianity, then to Constantine and his Germanic heritage, and then to its Indo-European roots and early archaeological traces; in the other direction, it led to the function of biblical inerrancy for Fundamentalist groups, to evangelicalism and its myth charter in the "Great Commission," to the "Wall Street Gospel" linking capitalist business to conservative Christian movements, and finally, coming full circle, to all the "Christian Warriors" on the Internet.

THEORIES OF RELIGION

At the outset, we must remind ourselves that "religion" is a Western concept. Associating "religion" with churches is another Western notion. European and American philosophers and theologians argue over whether moral principles are tied to religious teachings such as the Ten Commandments, an issue easily resolved by ethnographic experience with communities basing their moral values on the needs of their people rather than a supernatural edict.[2] Western convention equating religion with churches leads many to distinguish "spirituality" from institutionalized "religions"—that is, denominations.

A peculiar statement from a professed historian of religion states, "All history is in some measure a fall of the sacred . . . but the sacred does not cease to manifest itself, and with each new manifestation it resumes its original tendency to reveal itself wholly."[3] Here is one extreme view of religion, a claim that a mystical something is constantly appearing. Whether possibly true, or not, we cannot determine. It may be pertinent that Mircea Eliade, who wrote the statement, was a notoriously careless and unreliable scholar.[4] An anthropological study of religion deals with observable phenomena, human behavior and material objects. Eternal spirit is not reliably observable.

Among theories of religion generally discussed, those that focus on individuals' longing for security, peace of mind, resolution of perceived conflicts, or fear of death miss the critical juncture between individuals and the societies they live in. Christians' anxiety about the fate of their souls is, to an anthropologist, a strange, unnatural belief. That one has a soul, that the soul survives death, that it will ultimately exist eternally either in heaven or in hell, must be taught. Fear of damnation must be taught. The militant Christian Right works constantly to inculcate those beliefs and fear in its communicants; its unremitting, very visible work makes its study highly illuminating for an anthropology of religion. Christian schools and homeschooling encapsulate children in a habitus where repetition makes a stern God, a loving Jesus, and a supernatural Holy Spirit intimately familiar, another trinity arising from Indo-European "magic number" three. If Christians seek reassurance that their souls may be saved, it is because they have been schooled to this. Francis Schaeffer's (Chapter 10) doctrine of the absolute difference between truth and falsehood reinforced the boundaries of the "Christian" community, highlighting the foundations of its ideology. How inwardly focused these congregations are is well described by Gina Welch in her ethnography of Jerry Falwell's Thomas Road Baptist Church.[5]

Thomas Road Baptist Church exemplifies that "elementary form of the religious life" emphasized by Émile Durkheim in his seminal 1912 book: "Since religious force is nothing other than the collective and the anonymous force of the clan [that is, social group], and since this can be represented in the mind only in the form of the totem [or deity], the . . . emblem is like the visible body of the god. Therefore, it is from it that those kindly or dreadful actions seem to emanate, which the cult seeks to provoke and prevent; consequently, it is to it that the cult is addressed."[6] Those Virginia Baptists make the loving Jesus the totem symbolizing their fellowship. Their worldview of oppositional dualism necessarily creates an opposition, Satan. Fighting Satan works, as strongly as loving Jesus, to bind and circumscribe the community.

Claude Lévi-Strauss was one generation removed from his countryman Durkheim. Where Durkheim identified the community as elementary to religion, Lévi-Strauss considered myths an essential societal instrument.[7] It is useful, he felt, to analyze myths as dialectical structures, a thesis contrasted with its antithesis, then the conflict or contradiction resolved, at least for the moment, by a mediating factor or a new thesis. Of course, Lévi-Strauss spoke and thought in an Indo-European language, was educated and practised in its European cultural tradition; therefore, it is not surprising he was comfortable with the dynamic dualism of dialectical analysis plus its resolutions, making up a set of three. Sharing that cultural tradition, Lévi-Strauss's method should be fruitful in analyzing Christianity, particularly that faction, the militant Christian Right, deeply committed to its Indo-European heritage. Conservative talk-radio hosts often follow the formula of stating a thesis, for example that Social Security is socialism, then its antithesis—our grandparents saved to provide for their old age—and the resolution, privatize saving for old age. The Bible is full of myths but, as a book, not coherent due to its being a compendium of a variety of sources. Conservative politics offer better examples in their constant charges against "liberals" and "secular humanism," exaggerating the incompatibility between conservative and opposed policies (Chapter 10). From the point of view of discourse (communication theory), myths are a form of rhetoric where objective truth, or validity, is downplayed while emotional effect is heightened. Certainly for all of us reared in the cultural tradition replete with good guy versus bad guy stories, Fundamentalist rhetoric of absolutes, the totems Jesus versus Satan, seem "natural."

For an anthropologist, theories of religion that lack observed, or even observable, data, such as Sigmund Freud's assumed individual early childhood traumas known only through the psychoanalyst's probing questions, which Freud projected into a "childhood" of the species when a mythic father was murdered by his sons, cannot be accepted.[8] Assumed "psycho-dynamics" of individual experience don't explain manifest behavior. Observed human behavior is so molded by the person's socialization, and expressed or repressed according to the society's mores, that attention to cultural factors is necessary to understand it. "Self-fulfillment" is itself an idea dependent on our culture's concept of autonomous selves struggling to live free. Simple observation of our daily lives demonstrates, rather, the contrary: that we humans strive to be identified as members of groups, whether as saved souls in Thomas Road Baptist Church, outlaw bikers at the massive annual Sturgis rallies, madcaps at the Burning Man festivals, responsible men in Masonic lodges, or good older citizens playing bingo at the local senior center. Each and every group has its customary behavior that signals its ethos; some groups we label "religious," others "civic" or "fringe," but all to some degree ritualize customary behavior and thus function as religions do by binding members for mutual recognition, survival, and benefit.

THE AMERICAN MILITANT CHRISTIAN RIGHT AS A POSTMODERN CASE STUDY

"Postmodern" is a bugaboo word to many anthropologists who equate it with narcissistic indulgence in personal feelings. More properly, postmodern refers to a worldview acknowledging the multiplicity of evolutionary-historical pathways to present societies and accepting that our Western culture's valuing of rational scientific objectivity has tended to devalue other societies' knowledge. Underlying postmodernism is the shift in Western political economies from imperialism and its colonies to ostensible independence for most of the former colonies. That many former colonies are still subject to economic exploitation and covert political intervention doesn't negate the principle that nations ought to be free, not subject to control by a "superior race." In other words, "multiculturalism" is postmodern.

Rejecting the nineteenth-century Western imperialist conviction that European educated men are superior to everyone else, reduces the sacrosanct status of Christianity. Still, studying a major American Christian movement as a persistent cultural tradition, not merely contemporary communities, may seem startling. The popularity of labeling a huge variety of non-Western religious practices "shamanic," in defiance of actual historical and ethnographic accounts of Asian shamans, illustrates the residue of disrespect to other societies' histories not yet expunged from anthropology.[9] A postmodern standpoint demands that I admit I am a "liberal," certainly by Christian Right criteria, but divulging my personal political philosophy does not make this case study "political." To the contrary, the reader can see that—by postmodern standards—refusing to allow the militant Christian Right to be studied from an anthropological approach *would* be political. Multiculturalism enfolds all societies.

There is precedent in American anthropology for this anthropological approach. In 1896, Smithsonian Bureau of American Ethnology staff member James Mooney published his monograph comparing a Paiute Indian prophet to other "messiahs" and prophets, including Jesus of Nazareth. Mooney, son of impoverished Irish immigrants, empathized with American First Nations brutally conquered, as Ireland had been by British colonial power. Far from labeling the Paiute "primitive," he respected the prophet

Wovoka and compared his doctrine favorably with Christianity. More than a century later, Irish American anthropologist Eileen Kane published her memoir of 1964 fieldwork in Wovoka's community.[10] Kane, like Mooney, grew up in a laboring-class family and neighborhood, and like Mooney, came to realize that her family, like the Indians, had been exploited by the politically and economically dominant Anglo American managerial class. Mooney's and Kane's standpoint is critical of Christian America's failure to embrace non-Anglos in the promise of "life, liberty, and the pursuit of happiness." My own critical standpoint is that of an American Jew, whose forebears suffered two thousand years of disenfranchisement, and worse. Indo-European Germanic ideology is by no means the only cultural tradition that persists over millennia. To understand these persistent core cultural systems, they must be compared. From my standpoint, it is obvious that the American militant Christian Right is a cultural tradition well suited to an anthropological analysis.

CONCLUSION

Anthropology, with its scientific methodology and holistic, humanistic approach, can analyze our contemporary society, particularly its subcultures. Working out the *longue durée* history of Indo-European cultural tradition of militancy up to its present expression in the American militant Christian Right illustrates the dynamic between ethos persistence and social adaptation. Socialization of children transmits the worldview, continuously creates the habitus that perpetuates the core culture (Chapter 13), while opportunities such as successful invasions of foreign territories and inventions of industrial technologies ramify and adapt the larger community. To show this cultural process, we need case studies with data spanning many generations. We need historical documents to be read with an anthropologist's sensitivity, plus the archaeology of material culture, sociolinguistics, and ethnographic observation. This case study includes these elements, deployed to illuminate one of the most powerful cultural traditions known to us.

Looking at the many strands interwoven in this cultural tradition, we can appreciate how complex history really is. Beginning with Constantine, whose eulogies cannot be relied upon,[11] an anthropological point of view sees how superficial national conversions to Christianity tended to be (*cuius regio, eius religio*), letting the indigenous Indo-Germanic worldview and ethos persist. Then demographic recovery from the Black Death and development of mercantile capitalism in the late fifteenth century shifted balance of power in Europe from Italy to states north of the Alps, giving opportunity to Martin Luther to articulate rebellion. Again, the anthropological point of view sees the authoritarian structure of the Protestant Reformations, in Luther's case, upholding the German states, and in Calvin's, a theocracy. England's royal Reformation provoked formation of Dissenting communities such as the Puritans who colonized New England. Concomitantly, mercantile expansion created colonial proprietorships in America, legitimized by the astute logics of John Locke, secretary to the British Board of Trade. Both the plantation gentry of the South and the entrepreneurs of the North speculated heavily in land at the ever-moving frontier, invoking "Manifest Destiny" as the United States inaugurated its imperial conquests in 1845. Achieving sea-to-sea dominion, America built the infrastructure of railroads and telegraph that integrated the nation and fostered industrialization. Around 1900, American Protestants diverged into politically conservative and Social Gospel ameliorative factions. The former, coming to be called Fundamentalist evangelicals, preserved the pre-Christian warrior ethos exemplified by Constantine and even Martin Luther. For decades in the twentieth century, John D. Rockefeller, a conservative Baptist, and his son gave millions to influence US policies through research their foundations funded. Andrew Carnegie, from a Dissenter family, used his millions to build public libraries and support research such as Maya archaeology that appeared to be nonpolitical. Rockefeller's philanthropy aimed for a fascist state controlled by an elite of scientists, Carnegie's for uplifting the masses.

The conservative Christian Right is historically correct that the United States was a Christian nation, de facto if not constitutionally. Studying the segment of our population that most vociferously proclaims this, the militant Christian Right, uncovers the economic, political, ecological and demographic factors that favored and supported their ideology, and indicates why they believe themselves beleaguered. The familiarity of this trumpeting elephant in the room of America, its myths and battles filling talk radio, renders its factual study discomfiting. It is, nevertheless, engrossing and the kind of anthropology that the twenty-first century must utilize to mitigate dysfunctional clashes.

NOTES

CHAPTER 1

1. Bourdieu 1977: 78.
2. Lakoff and Johnson 1980.
3. Riesebrodt 2010: 181.
4. Macpherson 1962.
5. Anderson 2006.

CHAPTER 2

1. Diocletian named himself Augustus, or ruler of the eastern sector of the empire, and he named his friend Maximian Augustus, for the western sector, with responsibility for the frontier along the Rhine and for Britain. Each Augustus had a junior emperor called the caesar. Appointment was to be on merit, not heredity. Constantine destroyed the scheme.
2. Stephenson 2010: 185.
3. I am indebted to my colleague Robert L. Hall for this perception.
4. Voltaire remarked of Constantine that he "had a father-in-law and made him hang himself; he had a brother-in-law and caused him to be strangled; he had a nephew of twelve or thirteen years and had him throttled; he had a first-born son and he had his head cut off; he had a wife and he caused her to be suffocated in the bath" (quoted in Doerries 1972: 226–27).
5. Maguire 2008: 87.
6. Kee 1982: 53.
7. Ibid.: 29–30.
8. Ibid.: 20, 57, 96; Stephenson 2010: 156–57; Barnes 2011: 79–80.
9. Kee 1982: 96. Emphasis added.

CHAPTER 3

1. Emile Benveniste, an authority on Indo-European, stated that, for them, "peace intervenes as a sometimes accidental and often temporary solution to a quasi-permanent state of hostility between towns and states" (Benveniste [1969] 1973: 299). Gilbert Rist, a professor of development studies in Geneva, Switzerland, wrote that, for conventional economists, "the non-spoken . . . element underlying economic theory belongs to the *paradigm of war*—war against nature, and war of humans against one another" (Rist 2011: 15, his emphasis).

2. Biological anthropologist Henry Harpending suggests that the ancestral population developed a genetic allele (LCT 13910-T) favoring lactase digestion, which encouraged adult milk consumption. He notes that an economy based on dairying produces five times the amount of calories per acre than beef production. Indo-European milk-drinking pastoralists therefore would have been an expanding as well as healthy population (Cochran and Harpending 2009: 180–85).
3. I use "nation" in its original sense as a political body of persons "born to" (*natio*) the group. A nation may be quite small: a local cultural group rather than a state. The word "nation" is preferable to "tribe" because the latter is now associated with imperial powers' denigration of the nations they have, or are trying to, conquer.
4. "Whig histories" are those written by victors, making their success seem divinely blessed or resulting from their virtues and talents.
5. Hedeager 2011: 214–15; Winn 1995:16 (see picture of Wotan and Thor here).
6. Holand 1957: 103.

CHAPTER 4

1. Quoted in Fletcher 1997: 77.
2. Hillgarth (1969) 1986: 84.
3. Marrin 1971: 57.
4. Quoted in Wright 2001: 169.
5. Quoted in Riley-Smith 2002: 34.
6. McGiffert 2003: 13.
7. Bainton (1950) 1955: 54.
8. The "priesthood of believers"—that every man may form an unmediated relationship with God—was not an original idea of Luther's. He founded his argument for it on the New Testament, First Epistle of Peter 2:9, rather than on its use by the fourteenth-century Lollards and John Wycliffe (and from Wycliffe, Jan Hus [c. 1369–1415], who was burned at the stake as a heretic for his criticisms of the pope and curia).
9. Ekelund, Hébert, and Tollison 2006: 161.

CHAPTER 5

1. Macpherson 1962.
2. Note that "modern" refers to the period roughly from the late seventeenth to the twenty-first century.
3. Quoted in Marius 1999: 431.
4. Quoted in McKim 2003: 235.
5. Philipp Melanchthon (1497–1560), born Philipp Schwartzerd, joined the faculty at Wittenberg in 1518 as professor of Greek and Luther's devoted colleague. Like Luther, he came from a comfortably well-off commoner family. Whereas Luther studied Greek and Hebrew without losing love for his native language, Schwartzerd became so convinced of the superiority of Greek that he translated his surname into Greek. Only scholars know of "Melanchthon"; everyone knows "Luther."
6. Wuthnow 1989: 128.
7. Tawney (1926) 1954: 114.
8. Quoted from "1651 Massachusetts Colony General Court," in Innes 1995: 102–3.

Chapter 6

1. Locke wrote that in civil societies such as Europe, "the chief matter of property being now not the fruits of the earth and the beasts that subsist on it, but the earth itself . . . As much land as a man tills, plants, improves, cultivates, and can use the product of, so much is his property . . . God and his [man's] reason commanded him to subdue the earth . . . He gave it to the use of the industrious and rational (and labour was to be his title to it) . . . So that God, by commanding to subdue, gave authority so far to appropriate: and the condition of human life, which requires labour and materials to work on, necessarily introduces private possessions" (Locke 2003: 113–14).
2. Ibid.
3. Ibid.: 112.
4. Arneil 1996: 69.

Chapter 7

1. O'Sullivan wrote, "the general law which is rolling our population westward, in . . . connexion . . . with that ratio of growth in population which is destined within a hundred years to swell our numbers to the enormous population of *two hundred and fifty millions* (if not more), is too evident to leave us in doubt of the manifest design of Providence in regard to the occupation of this continent" (*Democratic Review*, "Annexation," July 1845, 7 [O'Sullivan's italics], quoted in Hietala 1997: 51).
2. See the last, twenty-seventh "Fact" enumerated in the Declaration of Independence, claiming that King George deliberately sent "the merciless savages on our frontier" to indiscriminately massacre colonists. The king would hardly want to massacre his own subjects and taxpayers; also, the Indians along the thirteen colonies' frontier in 1776 were the Five Civilized Tribes and equally "civilized" Iroquois, all farmers and with leaders developing plantations.
3. Quoted in Fifer 1996: 195. [Fifer does not cite a source for this quote.]
4. Butler 1990: 189.
5. Quoted in Eslinger 1999: 195.
6. Quoted in ibid.: 236.
7. Quoted in Butler 1990: 240.

Chapter 8

1. The nineteenth-century "American system" of mass production is not to be confused with Henry Clay's American System of governmental support of manufacturing by road and canal construction and protective tariffs.
2. Quoted in Weinberg 1935: 112.
3. Ibid.: 61.
4. Ibid.: 126.
5. Ibid.
6. Ibid.: 165.
7. Ibid.:166.
8. Ibid.:163.
9. Ibid.:178.

10. The issue precipitating the Civil War was secession. Not until the Union proved its superior might, during 1863, did Lincoln and others speak more about ending slavery.
11. Quoted in Morison and Commager 1942: 324.

CHAPTER 9

1. Congressional Record, 1956: 13917, Public Law 84–140. See also "History of 'In God We Trust,'" Fact Sheets, US Department of the Treasury, accessed January 14, 2008.
2. Carnegie 1900: 12.
3. Quoted in Chernow 1998: 499.
4. Ibid.:230.
5. Quoted in Nasaw 2006:766–67.
6. Goldman, ed. 1989: 294.
7. Quoted in Brown 1979: 125.
8. Quoted from a 1914 address by Harvard Law School professor Joseph H. Beale, in Lagemann 1989: 74.
9. Quoted in Lagemann 1989: 77.
10. Ibid.: 79.
11. Quoted in Fisher 1993: 58.

CHAPTER 10

1. Quoted in Moberg (1977) 2006: 32.
2. Quoted in Crunden 1982: 200.
3. Ibid.: 217.
4. Ibid.: 224. The "Doxology" is a standard Protestant hymn written in 1674:

> Praise God, from Whom all blessings flow;
> Praise Him, all creatures here below;
> Praise Him above, ye Heavenly Host;
> Praise Father, Son, and Holy Ghost. Amen.

> (from "Doxology" in Wikipedia, accessed April 25, 2008).

5. The 1925 trial in Dayton, Tennessee, of John Scopes, charged with teaching evolution, excited African American leaders who clearly perceived the strong connection between antievolution Fundamentalist Protestants, white supremacy and Jim Crow laws, and degradation of African Americans in the South (Moran 2003: 892).
6. Goldman, ed. 1989: 294.
7. Fosdick 1922.
8. Ibid.
9. Quotes from Packer 2008: 47.
10. Seek God Ministries 2012.
11. Seek God Ministries 2008.
12. Quoted in Bacevich 2005: 128–29.
13. Ronald Reagan, speech to the National Association of Evangelicals, Orlando, Florida, March 8, 1983.
14. Ibid.

15. Concomitantly, a similar rugged cowboy image was the Marlboro Man, promoting cigarettes; on television, Westerns were numerous and popular.
16. Gayner 1995.
17. Bureau of Justice Statistics, press release, August 18, 2003.
18. Southern Baptist Convention 2008.
19. Baptist General Conference 2008.
20. Council on Biblical Manhood and Womanhood 1988.
21. Kotter 2008.
22. Schaeffer 1968: 14–15.
23. Schaeffer 1976: 140.
24. Schaeffer 1980.
25. The extreme of cobelligerency is the project of Richard Wilkins, a professor of law at Brigham Young University. In 2004, he began collaborating with the government of Qatar to bring together Christian and Muslim fundamentalists who agreed with the Mormon *The Family: A Proclamation to the World*: "By divine design, fathers are to preside over their families in love and righteousness and are responsible to provide the necessities of life and protection for their families. Mothers are primarily responsible for the nurture of their children . . . the disintegration of the family will bring upon individuals, communities, and nations the calamities foretold by ancient and modern prophets" (quoted in Goldberg 2008).

CHAPTER 11

1. Mark 19:29: "And every one that hath forsaken houses, or brethren, or sisters, or father, or mother, or wife, or children, or lands, for my name's sake, shall receive an hundredfold, and shall inherit everlasting life." King James Translation, published Nashville, Tennessee, Gideons International.
2. Hickey 2004: 16.
3. Ibid.: xix.
4. Epistle of Paul to the Hebrews 11:17 and 10:9. King James Translation, published Nashville, Tennessee, Gideons International.
5. In modern German, a male sheep is *Widder*. *Ramm* has only the meaning of "ramming" with blows. English apparently dropped the word for male sheep, substituting the word describing the animal's method of fighting.
6. One Norse tale, probably from the Christian medieval period, has a giant stealing Thor's hammer. To get it back, Thor disguises himself as a bride for the giant, who places the hammer on the "bride's" lap as a bride-gift, whereupon the reinvigorated god leaps up and slays the giant with the hammer (Simek 1993: 318).
7. Dumézil 1973:146, note 26. Dumézil considers the Rig-Veda, the "One-legged Goat," associated with a serpent most probably a constellation near Polaris.
8. Simek 1993: 219.
9. Turville-Petre 1964: plate 18; see also plates 15, 16.
10. Simek 1993: 324–25.
11. Turville-Petre 1964: 90.
12. Dumézil 1973: 66.
13. Jewett 1973: 152–53.
14. Shires 2007.
15. Schaeffer 1970: 37, quoted in Shires 2007: 160.

16. Quoted in Crawford 1980: 159, from *Time*, October 1, 1978: 68.
17. Quoted in Burlein 2002: 96.
18. Ibid.
19. Warren 2002: 215.
20. Reagan writing in *Reader's Digest*, October 1979: 115–19, quoted in Crawford 1980: 79.
21. Dobson 1978: 17, 19, 36, 46–47, 171, 174–75. Original emphasis.
22. Ransomed Heart Ministries 2009.
23. Morris 1975: 109.
24. Ibid.: 72, 74–75.
25. Patrick Henry College Student Handbook 2012.
26. Simpson 1970.
27. Transnational Association of Christian Colleges and Schools 2009.
28. Institute for Creation Research 2009.
29. Ibid.: "To Prospective Students."
30. Quoted in Branch 2008.
31. "[B]orn again Christians are not defined on the basis of characterizing themselves as 'born again' but based upon their answers to two questions. The first is 'have you ever made a personal commitment to Jesus Christ that is still important in your life today?' If the respondent says 'yes,' then they are asked a follow-up question about life after death. One of the seven perspectives a respondent may choose is 'when I die, I will go to Heaven because I have confessed my sins and have accepted Jesus Christ as my savior.' Individuals who answer 'yes' to the first question and select this statement as their belief about their own salvation are then categorized as 'born again.' 'Evangelicals' meet the born again criteria plus seven other conditions. Those include saying their faith is very important in their life today; believing they have a personal responsibility to share their religious beliefs about Christ with non-Christians; believing that Satan exists; believing that eternal salvation is possible only through grace, not works; believing that Jesus Christ lived a sinless life on earth; asserting that the Bible is accurate in all that it teaches; and describing God as the all-knowing, all-powerful, perfect deity who created the universe and still rules it today. Being classified as an evangelical is not dependent upon church attendance or the denominational affiliation of the church they attend. Respondents were not asked to describe themselves as 'evangelical.' " Barna Group 2009.
32. "The Barna Group, Ltd. (which includes its research division, The Barna Research Group) conducts primary research, produces media resources pertaining to spiritual development, and facilitates the healthy spiritual growth of leaders, children, families, and Christian ministries. Located in Ventura, California, Barna has been conducting and analyzing primary research to understand cultural trends related to values, beliefs, attitudes, and behaviors since 1984." Ibid.

CHAPTER 12

1. Calian 1975: 30.
2. Quoted in Calian 1975: 26.
3. Ibid.: 15.
4. Beach 1966:14–15.
5. Bob Jones University 2009.

6. See translations used in major denominations at http://en.wikipedia.org/wiki/English_versions_of_the_Nicene_Creed_in_current_use#Lutheran_Service_Book_version_282006.29.
7. Horton 2009.
8. Winston 2009.
9. Regent University 2009.
10. Gyertson 2005: 1, 7.
11. McFarlane 2004: 12.
12. Warren 2002: 268.
13. Abanes 2009.
14. Sataline 2006.
15. *Move Ahead with Possibility Thinking* (1967) and *Self-Love* (1969).
16. Smith 2006. "If Reinventing Jesus Christ is read prayerfully and carefully, one should be able to understand how a very real false Christ is effectively convincing the world and the church into accepting his New Age Peace Plan and his New Gospel/New Spirituality."
17. Lindsay 2007: 162.
18. Ibid.: 194, citing Wuthnow 1998.
19. Kroll 2003:

Church	Attendance*	City, State	Pastor
Lakewood Church	25,060	Houston, TX	Joel Osteen
World Changers	23,093	College Park, GA	Rev. Creflo Dollar
Calvary Chapel of Costa Mesa	20,000	Santa Ana, CA	Pastor Chuck Smith
The Potter's House	18,500	Dallas, TX	Bishop T. D. Jakes
Second Baptist Church	18,000	Houston, TX	Dr. H. Edwin Young
Southeast Christian Church	17,863	Louisville, KY	Bob Russell
First Assembly of God	17,532	Phoenix, AZ	Dr. Tommy J. Barnett
Willow Creek Community Church	17,115	S. Barrington, IL	Bill Hybels
Calvary Chapel of Ft. Lauderdale	17,000	Fort Lauderdale, FL	Pastor Bob Coy
Saddleback Valley Community Church	15,030	Lake Forest, CA	Dr. Rick Warren

*Catholic churches are not tracked for this study. This is all 2003 attendance data and represents total weekend attendance for each congregation. Source: Dr. John N. Vaughan, Church Growth Today.

20. Coolidge 2003.
21. Murphy 2003.
22. Series of news articles, Milwaukee *Journal Sentinel*, March 2009.
23. Pomerantz 2003.
24. Phalon 2002.
25. Colson 2008.
26. Mohler 2008.
27. Carnes 2008.
28. Exodus Mandate Project 2009. "Exodus Mandate Project is a Christian ministry to encourage and assist Christian families to leave government schools for the

Promised Land of Christian schools or home schooling. It is our hope that this fresh obedience in educating our children according to Biblical mandates will prove to be the key for revival in our families, churches and nation." See also "'The Call to Dunkirk' Urges Churches and Ministries to Help Parents Rescue Children from the Corrupt and Decaying Government Education System."

29. North 2001.
30. North and DeMar 1991: 30–31.
31. North 1986: Conclusion. (Online publication unpaged).
32. North 1998.
33. North 1984: 267.
34. North 1983: 406.
35. Kennedy 1982: i–ii.
36. Ibid.: 56, 59, 61. His emphasis.
37. Ibid.: 37–38. His emphasis.
38. Allen 2006: 82; Connolly 2008: 3, 147 notes 2, 4.
39. Larson 2007: 21, 166.
40. Phillips 2006: 130–31.
41. Blank 2006: 178. Original emphasis.
42. Durrenberger and Doukas 2008.
43. Biblical America Resistance Front 2009.

CHAPTER 13

1. American Association of Christian Schools 2009a.
2. Discover Christian Schools 2009a.
3. American Association of Christian Schools 2009b.
4. Sprigg 2009.
5. American Association of Christian Schools 2009c.
6. Home School Legal Defense Association 2009a.
7. Home School Legal Defense Association 2009b.
8. Ibid.
9. Christian Schools International 2009.
10. Their emphasis. http://www.discoverchristianschools.com/Page.aspx?id=157155.
11. Tree of Life Classical & Christian Home Schooling 2009.
12. Discover Christian Schools 2009.
13. Exodus Books 2009.
14. A Beka Book 2009a.
15. A Beka Book 2009b.
16. Crossroads Christian School 2009.
17. Christian Trivium 2009.
18. Veritas Press 2009. The card on Genesis is pictured on the website next to the quoted passage.
19. Wilson 2005: 4. His emphasis.
20. Ibid.: 39.
21. North 2002.
22. North 2001.
23. FAQs, Educational Research Analysts 2009.
24. *Southern Partisan* 1996.
25. *Southern Partisan* 2007.

26. Gottfried 2008.
27. *Southern Partisan* 2007.
28. Glazier 2012: 172.
29. Sebesta 2009.
30. The Mel Gablers' Educational Research Analysts 2009b.
31. Frye 1983.
32. The Institute for Creation Research 2009. The Institute for Creation Research states on its website, "The Bible's text is inspired by God in a way that used selected humans to write its original words (even to each letter in every word) . . . When the Bible mentions a scientific topic, it is scientifically accurate. Likewise, the Bible is historically accurate, mathematically accurate, etc. . . . The Bible proves that it is God's Word by its prediction of events, beyond all possible odds, that are now documented history, including the prophesied events about Jesus as the predicted Messiah."
33. Discover Christian Schools 2009b.
34. Discover Christian Schools 2009c.
35. The Mel Gablers' Educational Research Analysts 2009c. Their emphasis.
36. The Mel Gablers' Educational Research Analysts 2009c.
37. A Beka Book 2009c.
38. Educational Research Analysts 2009e. Original emphasis.
39. Discover Christian Schools 2009c.
40. A Beka Book 2009c.
41. ACE 2009a.
42. ACE 2009b.
43. Blamires (1963) 1978:136–37.
44. Ibid.:137.
45. A Beka Book 2009c.
46. Whitewashed Feminists 2009a.
47. A Chosen Child 2009.
48. Whitewashed Feminists 2009b.
49. Whitewashed Feminists 2009c.
50. Whitewashed Feminists 2009d.
51. Vision Forum 2009a.
52. Vision Forum 2009b.
53. Short 2004.
54. Ekeland 2008.
55. National Home Education Research Institute 2012.
56. Cherokee Christian Schools 2009a.
57. Gamble 2009.
58. Cherokee Christian Schools 2009b.
59. Simek 1993: 272.

CHAPTER 14

1. Warren 2009.
2. Gorra 2009.
3. Curmi 2009.
4. R. Dobson 2008.
5. Motto 2009.

6. Highlands Study Center 2009a.
7. Public Documents Concerning the Defrocking of R. C. Sproul Jr. and the Saint Peter Presbyterian Church Session, April 20, 2009, http://hushmoney.org/RC_Sproul_Jr-defrocking-docs.htm.
8. Highlands Study Center 2009b.
9. In South Dakota, a "prairie muffin" is a cowpat—dung. From personal communication on May 30, 2009, from a colleague, a native of South Dakota who wishes to remain anonymous ("I don't want my mother to think I talk shit," he said).
10. Wick 2007.
11. Kaiser 2009.
12. Eldredge 2009.
13. Freikorps officer Ernst von Salomon, quoted in Theweleit 1987: 60.
14. Quoted in Spiro 2009: 110, 111.
15. Peters 2009a. Note that dictionaries give the origin of the name Saxon as a Latin name for a nation in northern Germany in the fourth century. It has no connection with the biblical Isaac.
16. Peters 2009b.
17. Peters 2009c.
18. Peters 2009d.
19. Weinland 2009.
20. Dragon-Slayer, cover of newsletter, Scriptures for America, http://www.scripturesforamerica.org/newsletters.php.
21. Russakoff and Kovaleski 1995.
22. Morris 2009.
23. Click on the armed knight logo for Cherokee Christian Schools at http://www.cherokeechristian.org. Children's voices yell a war cry.
24. Sanger 2009.
25. Matthew 5:4, King James Translation.

Chapter 15

1. Anderson 2006: 6.
2. The Blackfoot Nation of the northwestern American Plains, for example, recognizes an immaterial almighty power, but moral principles of generosity, honesty, respect for others, honor for worthwhile work, and commitment to family are seen to arise from the community's needs.
3. Eliade 1964: xix.
4. Kehoe 2000: 39–42.
5. Welch 2010.
6. Durkheim (1915) 1963, excerpted in Lessa and Vogt 1979: 34.
7. Lévi-Strauss 1955.
8. Leach 1976: 96.
9. Kehoe 2000: 102.
10. Kane 2010.
11. Stephenson 2010; Barnes 2011: 4.

References by Chapter

Chapter 1

B. Anderson 2006; Bourdieu 1977; Lakoff and Johnson 1980; Malinowski 1926, 1944; Macpherson 1962; M. Mead, ed. 1937; Riesebrodt 2010.

Chapter 2

Anthony 2007; Bahn 2001; Egeler 2009; Frachetti 2012; Kohn 2007; Kristiansen 2009; Kristiansen and Larsson 2005; Winn 1995. *Constantine*: Barnes 1981, 2011; Coleman 1914; Eadie 1977; Grant 1994; Huttmann 1967; Kee 1982; Lieu and Montserrat, eds. 1998; Maguire 2008; Pohlsander 2004; Stephenson 2010.

Chapter 3

Benveniste 1973; Bonfante, ed. 2011; Bowder 1978; Cochran and Harpending 2009; Dumézil 1970, 1983; Fletcher 1997; Gamkrelidze and Ivanov 1995; Hallpike 1986; Harding 2008; Hedeager 2011; Hines 2001; Holand 1957; Lincoln 1986, 1991; Pagels 2012; Rist 2011; Russell 1994; Ward-Perkins 2005; Watkins 1995; Webster and Brown, eds. 1997; Winn 1995; Wolfram 1997.

Chapter 4

Bainton 1955; Bartlett and MacKay, eds. 2000; Bast and Gow, eds. 2000; Dombrowski 1991; Ekelund, Hébert, and Tollison 2006; Forey 1992; Gregary 2000; Hsia, ed. 1988; Hillgarth, ed. 1986; Hoffmeister, ed. 1977; Housley 1006; Jenkins 2010; Kehoe 1986; Lewis 1988; Madden, ed. 2002; Marius 1999; McGiffert 2003; McKim, ed. 2003; Nicholson, ed. 1994; Oberman 1994a, 1994b; O'Flaherty 1980; Riley-Smith 2002, 2005; Scribner, Porter, and Teich 1994; Southern 1995; Strauss, ed. 1971; Tyerman 1998; Wallace 1956; Winks and Wandel 2003; C. Wright 2001.

Chapter 5

P. Anderson 1974, 1992; Craig and Fisher 2000; Duplessis 1997; Green, ed. 1973; McKim 2003; Innes 1995; Mooers 1991; Streeck and Yamamura, eds. 2001; Swatos, ed. 1990; Swatos and Kaelber, eds. 2005; Tawney 1954; Tilly 1990; W. Wright 1988; Wuthnow 1989.

CHAPTER 6

Ameil 1996; Boucher 2007; Butler 1990; Butler, Wacker, and Balmer 20003; Elliott 2007; Fitzmaurice 2007; Gates 1973; Gilje, ed. 1997; Headlee 1991; Kehoe 2009; Kulikoff 1992; Locke 2003; Martin 1991; P. Morgan 2007; Morison and Commager 1942; Norton and Studnicki-Gizbert 2007; Sheridan 2006; R. Wright 2002.

CHAPTER 7

Chaplin 1993; Cumings 2009; Fifer 1996; Fischer and Kelly 2000; Hietala 1997; Kagan 2006; W. Mead 2001; R. Morgan 2007; Nasaw 1979; Wallace 1999; Weinberg 1934.

CHAPTER 8

Fifer 1996; Fones-Wolf 1989; Gates 1973; Goetzmann 1986; Hannah 2000; Headlee 1991; Kiernan 2005; W. Mead 2001; McDougall 1997; Morison and Commager 1942; Philips 1999; Sutton 1998; Taylor 2007; Weinberg 1935; Wrobel 1996.

CHAPTER 9

F. Allen 1934; Berman 1983; Brandeis 1914; Brown 1979; Butler 1991; Carnegie 1900; Chernow 1998; Crunden 1982; Fisher 1993; Gillespie 1991; Goldman 1989; Lagemann 1989; Moody 1919; Nasaw 2006; Nielsen 1972; Olien and Olien 2000; Park and Burgess 1921; Philips-Fein 2009; Ross 1991; Schenkel 1995; Smith and Dalzell 2000.

CHAPTER 10

Bacevich 2005; Berlet and Lyons 2000; Burlein 2002; Crunden 1982; Fosdick 1922; Goldberg 2008; Goldman 1989; Green, Rozell, and Wilcox 2003; Jacoby 2008; Jakobsen and Pellegrini 1999; Larson 1997; Moberg 2006; Moen 1992; Moore 1979; Moran 2003; Packer 2008; Reiss 1982; Schaeffer 1968, 1976; Smith 2000.

CHAPTER 11

Arnold 2011; Berlet and Lyons 2000; Branch 2008; Burlein 2002; Crawford 1980; Dobson 1978; Dumézil 1971, 1973; Faludi 1991; Green, Rozell, and Wilcox 2003; Harding 2000; Heaton 2007; Hickey 2004; Jewett 1973; Larson 1997; Lindsay 2007; Morris 1975; Numbers 1992; Petto 2008; Polomé 1989; Shires 2007; Simek 1993; Simpson 1970; Turville-Petre 1964; Warren 2002; Williams 2010.

CHAPTER 12

B. Allen 2006; Applbaum 2004; Beach 1996; Blank 2006; Calian 1975; Coolidge 2003; Connolly 2008; Dochuk 2010; Dunn, ed. 2009; Durrenberger and Doukas 2008; Gay 1991; Gyertson 2005; Kennedy 1982; Kroll 2003; Larson 2007; Lindsay 2007; McFarlane 2004; Murphy 2003; North 1983, 1984, 1986, 1998; North and DeMar 1991; Phalon 2002; Phillips 2006; Pomerantz 2003.

CHAPTER 13

Blamires 1978; Cummings, ed. 1979; DeMar 1982; Frye 1983; Glazier 2012; Gottfried 2008; Hague, Beirich, and Sebesta, eds. 2008; Lederhouse 1997; North 2001; Orchard 1997; Parrish, ed. 1978; Petto and Godfrey, eds. 2007; Rose 1988; Rosin 2007; Sandler 2006; Sebesta 2009; Sebesta and Hague 2002; Simek 1993; Stewart 2012; Wagner 1990; Wilson 2005.

CHAPTER 14

Bacevich 2005; Burlein 2002; Griffith 1997; Hughes 2009; Lienesch 1993; Maguire 2008; Onians 1951; Sandler 2006; Sharlet 2008; Spiro 2009; Theweleit 1987; Welch 2010.

CHAPTER 15

B. Anderson 2006; Barnes 2011; Durkheim 1915; Eliade 1964; Kane 2010; Kehoe 2000; Leach 1976; Lessa and Vogt 1979; Lévi-Strauss 1955; Mooney 1896; Stephenson 2010; Welch 2010.

References

Abanes, Richard. 2009. Interview with Rick Warren. http://abanes.com/peace.html (accessed March 16, 2009).

A Beka Book. 2009a. Homepage. http://www.abeka.com/OurFoundation.html.

———. 2009b. "Statement." https://www.abeka.com/Distinctives.html (accessed April 15, 2009).

———. 2009c. "Distinctives." https://www.abeka.com/Distinctives.html (accessed April 15, 2009).

ACE Ministries. 2009a. "About Us: Great Command Commission." http://www.aceministries.com/aboutus/Great_Command_Commission-web.pdf (accessed April 15, 2009).

———. 2009b. "About Us." http://www.aceministries.com/aboutus/Default.aspx (accessed April 15, 2009).

A Chosen Child. 2009. http://thechosenchild.blogspot.com (accessed April 20, 2009).

Allen, Brooke. 2006. *Moral Minority: Our Skeptical Founding Fathers*. Chicago: Ivan R. Dee.

Allen, Frederick Lewis. (1935) 1966. *The Lords of Creation*. Paperback edition. New York: Harper.

American Association of Christian Schools. 2009a. "Statement of Faith." http://www.aacs.org/statement-of-faith (accessed March 31, 2009).

———. 2009b. "Statement of Mission." http://www.aacs.org (accessed April 6, 2009).

———. 2009c. "Legislative Update." http://www.aacs.org/legislative-update (accessed April 6, 2009).

Anderson, Benedict. 2006. *Imagined Communities: Reflections on the Origin and Spread of Nationalism*. Second edition. London: Verso.

Anderson, Perry. 1974. *Lineages of the Absolutist State*. London: NLB.

———. 1992. *A Zone of Engagement*. London: Verso.

Anthony, David W. 2007. *The Horse, the Wheel, and Language*. Princeton: Princeton University Press.

Applbaum, Kalman. 2004. *The Marketing Era*. New York: Routledge.

Arneil, Barbara. 1996. *John Locke and America: The Defence of English Colonialism*. Oxford: Clarendon Press.

Bacevich, Andrew J. 2005. *The New American Militarism: How Americans Are Seduced by War*. New York: Oxford University Press.

Bahn, Paul G. 2001. *The Penguin Archaeology Guide*, 52. London: Penguin.

Bainton, Roland H. (1950) 1955. *Here I Stand: A Life of Martin Luther*. New York: Mentor.

————. 1960. *Christian Attitudes toward War and Peace*. Nashville, TN: Abingdon Press.

Baptist General Conference. 2008. http://216.177.136.28/content/view/1533/69 (accessed December 3, 2008).

Barna Group. 2009. "Research." http://www.barna.org (accessed February 3, 2009).

Barnes, Timothy D. 1981. *Constantine and Eusebius*. Cambridge: Harvard University Press.

————. 2011. *Constantine: Dynasty, Religion, and Power in the Later Roman Empire*. Malden, MA: Wiley-Blackwell.

Bartlett, Robert, and Angus MacKay, eds. 1989. *Medieval Frontier Societies*. Oxford: Clarendon Press.

Bast, Robert J., and Andrew C. Gow, eds. 2000. *Continuity and Change: The Harvest of Late-Medieval and Reformation History*. Leiden: Brill.

Beach, Waldo. 1966. *The Christian Life*. Richmond, VA: Covenant Life Curriculum Press.

Benveniste, Emile. (1969) 1973. *Indo-European Language and Society*, translated by Elizabeth Palmer. London: Faber and Faber. First published by Les Editions de Minuit.

Berlet, Chip, and Matthew N. Lyons. 2000. *Right-Wing Populism in America*. New York: Guilford.

Berman, Edward H. 1983. *The Ideology of Philanthropy: The Influence of the Carnegie, Ford, and Rockefeller Foundations on American Foreign Policy*. Albany: State University of New York Press.

Biblical America Resistance Front. 2009. "Statement of Mission." http://www.barf .org (accessed May 26, 2009).

Blamires, Harry. (1963) 1978. *The Christian Mind: How Should a Christian Think?* London: S. P. C. K. Reprint, Ann Arbor, MI: Servant Books. First American edition.

Blank, Steven Gary. 2006. *The Four Steps to the Epiphany*. Third edition. Cafepress.com.

Bob Jones University. 2009. "Creed." http://www.bju.edu/about/creed/atone.html (accessed February 6, 2009).

Bonfante, Larissa, ed. 2011. *The Barbarians of Ancient Europe: Realities and Interactions*. Cambridge: Cambridge University Press.

Boucher, Philip P. 2007. "Revisioning the 'French Atlantic': or, How to Think about the French Presence in the Atlantic 1550–1625." In *The Atlantic World and Virginia, 1550–1624*, ed. Peter C. Mancall, 274–306. Chapel Hill: University of North Carolina Press.

Bourdieu, Pierre. 1977. *Outline of a Theory of Practice*. Translated by Richard Nice. Cambridge: Cambridge University Press.

Bowder, Diana. 1978. *The Age of Constantine and Julian*. London: Paul Elek.

Branch, Glenn. 2008. "A Setback for the ICR in Texas." *Reports of the National Center for Science Education* 28, no. 2: 11–15.

Brandeis, Louis D. 1914. *Other People's Money and How the Bankers Use It*. New York: Frederick A. Stokes.

Brown, E. Richard. 1979. *Rockefeller Medicine Man: Medicine and Capitalism in America*. Berkeley: University of California Press.

Bureau of Justice Statistics. 2003. Press release, August 18, 2003. http://bjs.ojp.usdoj .gov (accessed December 3, 2008).

Burlein, Ann. 2002. *Lift High the Cross: Where White Supremacy and the Christian Right Converge*. Durham, NC: Duke University Press.

Butler, Jon. 1990. *Awash in a Sea of Faith: Christianizing the American People.* Cambridge: Harvard University Press.

Butler, Jon, Grant Wacker, and Randall Balmer. 2003. *Religion in American Life: A Short History.* New York: Oxford University Press.

Butler, Jonathan M. 1991. *Softly and Tenderly Jesus Is Calling: Heaven and Hell in American Revivalism, 1870–1920.* Brooklyn: Carlson.

Calian, Carnegie Samuel. 1975. *The Gospel According to the Wall Street Journal.* Atlanta: John Knox Press.

Carnegie, Andrew. 1900. *The Gospel of Wealth and Other Timely Essays.* New York: Century.

Carnes, Tony. 2008. In Crisis, Wall Street Turns to Prayer. *Christianity Today*, September 19. http://www.christianitytoday.com/ct/2008/septemberweb-only/138-53.0.html (accessed March 19, 2009).

Chaplin, Joyce E. 1993. *An Anxious Pursuit: Agricultural Innovation and Modernity in the Lower South, 1730–1815.* Chapel Hill: University of North Carolina Press.

Chernow, Ron. 1998. *Titan: The Life of John D. Rockefeller, Sr.* New York: Random House.

Cherokee Christian Schools. 2009a. "Information." http://74.125.95.132/u/CherokeeChristian?q=cache:Se0vuCS8PNkJ:www.cherokeechristian.org/pdf_files/Information_Booklet.pdf+warrior&cd=3&hl=en&ct=clnk (accessed April 17, 2009).

———. 2009b. "Do Your Best!" *The Warrior*, March 2, 2009. http://www.cherokee christian.org/pdf_files/ww/7_mar_09.pdf (accessed April 17, 2009).

Christian Schools International. 2009. "Information on Curricula Sets." http://www.csionline.org/csibible/1 (accessed April 7, 2009).

Christian Trivium. 2009. "Latin Trivium." http://www.latintrivium.com (accessed April 8, 2009).

Cochran, Gregory, and Henry Harpending. 2009. *The 10,000 Year Explosion: How Civilization Accelerated Human Evolution.* New York: Basic Books.

Coleman, Chirstopher Bush. 1914. *Constantine the Great and Christianity: Three Phrases: The Historical, the Legendary, and the Spurious.* New York: Columbia University Press.

Colson, Charles. 2008. "God Is in Control During the Financial Crisis." *Christianity Today*, October 2. http://www.christianitytoday.com/ct/2008/october web-only/140-42.0.html (accessed March 19, 2009).

Connolly, William E. 2008. *Capitalism and Christianity, American Style.* Durham, NC: Duke University Press.

Coolidge, Carrie. 2003. "David vs. Goliath." *Forbes* online, September 15.

Council on Biblical Manhood and Womanhood. 1988. "Danvers Statement." Wheaton, IL: Council on Biblical Manhood and Womanhood.

Craig, Lee A., and Douglas Fisher. 2000. *The European Macroeconomy: Growth, Integration and Cycles 1500–1913.* Cheltenham, UK: Edward Elgar.

Crawford, Alan. 1980. *Thunder on the Right: The "New Right" and the Politics of Resentment.* New York: Pantheon.

Crossroads Christian School. 2009. "About Us." http://www.crossroadschristian school.com (accessed March 31, 2009).

Crunden, Robert M. 1982. *Ministers of Reform: The Progressives' Achievement in American Civilization, 1889–1920.* Urbana: University of Illinois Press.

Cumings, Bruce. 2009. *Dominion from Sea to Sea: Pacific Ascendancy and American Power.* New Haven: Yale University Press.

Cummings, David B., ed. 1979. *The Purpose of a Christian School*. Phillipsburg, NJ: Presbyterian and Reformed Publishing.

Curmi, Nick. 2009. "Biola Hosts ACSI Science Fair." Biola University website. http://www.biola.edu/news/articles/2009/090422_sciencefair.cfm (accessed May 2, 2009).

DeMar, Gary. 1982. *God and Government: A Biblical and Historical Study*. Vol. 1. Atlanta: American Vision Press.

Discover Christian Schools. 2009a. "Deuteronomy." http://www.discoverchristian schools.com (accessed March 31, 2009).

————.2009b."Statement."http://www.discoverchristianschools.com/Page.aspx?id =157170 (accessed April 10, 2009).

————. 2009c. "FAQs." http://www.discoverchristianschools.com (accessed March 31, 2009).

————. 2009d. "Ten Differences: Public Schools and Christian Schools." http://www .discoverchristianschools.com/page.aspx?id=302582 (accessed April 14, 2009).

Dobson, James C. 1978. *The Strong-Willed Child*. Wheaton, IL: Tyndale House.

Dobson, Ryan. 2008. "Blessing or Testing?" *Pomomusings.com*. http://pomomu sings.com/2008/01/28/ryan-dobson-on-the-kingdom-of-god (accessed May 2, 2009).

Dochuk, Darren. 2010. *From Bible Belt to Sun Belt: Plain-Folk Religion, Grassroots Politics, and the Rise of Evangelical Conservatism*. New York: W. W. Norton.

Doerries, Hermann. 1972. Constantine the Great. Translated by R. H. Bainton. New York: Harper and Row.

Dombrowski, Daniel A. 1991. *Christian Pacifism*. Philadelphia: Temple University Press.

Dumézil, Georges. 1970. *The Destiny of the Warrior*. Paris: Presses Universitaires de France. Reprint, translated by Alf Hiltebeitel. Chicago: University of Chicago Press. Originally published as *Heur et malheur du guerrier: Aspects mythiques de la fonction guerrière chez les Indo-Européens*.

————. 1971. *Mythe et Epopée*. Vol. 2. Paris: Gallimard.

————. 1973. *Gods of the Ancient Northmen*, translated and edited by Einar Haugen. Berkeley: University of California Press.

————. 1983. *The Stakes of the Warrior*, translated by David Weeks. Berkeley: University of California Press. Originally published as *L'enjeu du jeu des dieux—un héros*, part 1 of volume 2 of *Types épipues indo-européens—un héros, un sorcier, un roi*, of *Mythe et Épopée*.

Dunn, Charles W., ed. 2009. *The Future of Religion in American Politics*. Lexington: University Press of Kentucky.

Duplessis, Robert S. 1997. *Transitions to Capitalism in Early Modern Europe*. Cambridge: Cambridge University Press.

Durkheim, Émile. (1915) 1963. *The Elementary Forms of the Religious Life*, translated by Joseph Ward Swain. London: Allen and Unwin. Reprint, New York: Free Press.

Durrenberger, E. Paul, and Dimitra Doukas. 2008. "Gospel of Wealth, Gospel of Work: Counterhegemony in the U.S. Working Class." *American Anthropologist* 110, no. 2: 214–24.

Eadie, John W. 1977. *The Conversion of Constantine*. Huntington, NY: Robert E. Krieger.

Educational Research Analysts. 2009a. "FAQs." http://www.textbookreviews.org/ index.html?content=resume.htm (accessed April 11, 2009).

———. 2009b. "Areas of Concern." http://www.textbookreviews.org/index.html ?content=about.htm (accessed April 12, 2009).

———. 2009c. "Textbook Reviews." http://www.textbookreviews.org/pdf/NL_5 -02_page_2.pdf (accessed April 13, 2009).

———. 2009d. "Christian High School U.S. History Textbooks Reviewed." http://www.textbookreviews.org/pdf/NL_5-06_front_page.pdf (accessed April 12, 2009).

———. 2009e. "Textbook Reviews." http://www.textbookreviews.org/pdf/nl_5 -08_p1.pdf (accessed April 12, 2009).

Egeler, Matthias. 2009. "Some Considerations on Female Death Demons, Heroic Ideologies and the Notion of Elite Travel in European Prehistory." *Journal of Indo-European Studies* 37, nos. 3–4: 321–49.

Ekeland, Jonathan. 2008. Discover Christian Schools blog. http://discoverchristian schools.blogspot.com/search/label/Worldview (accessed April 16, 2009).

Ekelund, Robert B., Jr., Robert F. Hébert, and Robert D. Tollison. 2006. *The Marketplace of Christianity*. Cambridge, MA: MIT Press.

Eldredge, John. 2009. "Ransomed Heart: John's Blog." http://www.ransomed heartblog.com/john/2008/08/boot-camp-week.html (accessed May 13, 2009).

Eliade, Mircea. 1964. *Shamanism: Archaic Techniques of Ecstasy*. Revised edition, translated by Willard R. Trask. Princeton: Princeton University Press.

Elliott, J. H. 2007. "The Iberian Atlantic and Virginia." In *The Atlantic World and Virginia, 1550–1624*, edited by Peter C. Mancall, 541–57. Chapel Hill: University of North Carolina Press.

Eslinger, Ellen. 1999. *Citizens of Zion: The Social Origins of Camp Meeting Revivalism*. Knoxville: University of Tennessee Press.

Exodus Books. 2009. "Biographies of Great American Saints and Scoundrels." CD description. http://www.exodusbooks.com/details.aspx?id=3281 (accessed April 10, 2009).

Exodus Mandate Project. 2009. http://www.exodusmandate.org (accessed March 22, 2009).

Faludi, Susan. 1991. *Backlash: The Undeclared War against American Women*. New York: Doubleday.

Fifer, J. V. 1996. *The Master Builders: Structures of Empire in the New World—Spanish Initiatives and United States Invention*. Durham, UK: Durham Academic Press.

Fischer, David Hackett, and James C. Kelly. 2000. *Bound Away: Virginia and the Westward Movement*. Charlottesville: University of Virginia Press.

Fisher, Donald. 1993. *Fundamental Development of the Social Sciences: Rockefeller Philanthropy and the United States Social Science Research Council*. Ann Arbor: University of Michigan Press.

Fitzmaurice, Andrew. 2007. "Moral Uncertainty in the Dispossession of Native Americans." In *The Atlantic World and Virginia, 1550–1624*, edited by Peter C. Mancall, 383–409. Chapel Hill: University of North Carolina Press.

Fletcher, Richard. 1997. *The Conversion of Europe; From Paganism to Christianity 371–1386 AD*. London: HarperCollins.

Fones-Wolf, Ken. 1989. *Trade Union Gospel: Christianity and Labor in Industrial Philadelphia, 1865–1915*. Philadelphia: Temple University Press.

Forey, Alan. 1992. *The Military Orders: From the Twelfth to the Early Fourteenth Centuries*. London: Macmillan.

Fosdick, Harry Emerson. 1922. "Shall the Fundamentalists Win?" *Christian Work* 102 (June 10): 716–722. http://historymatters.gmu.edu/d/5070 (accessed April 25, 2008.)

Frachetti, Michael D. 2012. "Multiregional Emergence of Mobile Pastoralism and Nonuniform Institutional Complexity across Eurasia." *Current Anthropology* 53, no. 1: 2–38.

Frye, Roland Mushat. 1983. *Is God a Creationist?* New York: Charles Scribner's Sons.

Gamble, Edward E. 2009. "Why Choose Christian Schooling?" Southern Baptist Association. http://www.sbacs.org (accessed March 31, 2009).

Gamkrelidze, Thomas V., and Vjaceslav V. Ivanov. 1995. *Indo-European and the Indo-Europeans: A Reconstruction and Historical Analysis of a Proto-Language and a Proto-Culture*, translated by Johanna Nichols, edited by Werner Winter. Berlin: Mouton de Gruyter.

Gates, Paul Wallace. 1973. *Landlords and Tenants on the Prairie Frontier*. Ithaca: Cornell University Press.

Gay, Craig M. 1991. *With Liberty and Justice for Whom? The Recent Evangelical Debate over Capitalism*. Grand Rapids, MI: Eerdmans.

Gayner, Jeffrey. 1995. "The Contract with America: Implementing New Ideas in the U.S." The Heritage Foundation. http://heritage.org (accessed December 3, 2008).

Gilje, Paul A., ed. 1997. *Wages of Independence: Capitalism in the Early American Republic*. Madison, WI: Madison House.

Gillespie, Richard. 1991. *Manufacturing Knowledge: A History of the Hawthorne Experiments*. Cambridge: Cambridge University Press.

Glazier, Jack. 2009. "Grand Delusion: An Anthropologist Looks at the Jefferson Davis Bicentennial." Paper presented at Central States Anthropological Society annual meeting, Urbana, Illinois, April 4, 2009.

———. 2012. *Been Coming through Some Hard Times: Race, History and Memory in Western Kentucky*. Knoxville: University of Tennessee Press.

Goetzmann, William H. 1986. *New Lands, New Men: America and the Second Great Age of Discovery*. New York: Viking.

Goldberg, Michelle. 2008. "Proposition 8, The Mormon Coming Out Party." *Religious Dispatches* online magazine. http://www.religiondispatches.org (accessed December 5, 2008).

Goldman, Steven L., ed. 1989. Appendix 1 of *Science, Technology and Human Progress*, 294. Bethlehem, PA: Lehigh University Press.

Gorra, Joseph. 2009. "Craig Hazen Presents Evidence for the Resurrection of Jesus." Biola University website. http://www.biola.edu/news/articles/2009/090501_radio.cfm (accessed May 2, 2009).

Gottfried, Paul. 2008. "Why They Hate the South." *Southern Partisan*. http://www.southernpartisan.net/2008/04/24/why-they-hate-the-south (accessed April 11, 2009).

Grant, Michael. 1994. *Constantine the Great*. New York: Charles Scribner's Sons.

Green, John C., Mark J. Rozell, and Clyde Wilcox. 2003. *The Christian Right in American Politics: Marching to the Millennium*. Washington, DC: Georgetown University Press.

Green, Robert W., ed. 1973. *Protestantism, Capitalism, and Social Science: The Weber Thesis Controversy*. Lexington, MA: D. C. Heath.

Gregory, Brad S. 2000. "Late Medieval Religiosity and the Renaissance of Christian Martyrdom in the Reformation Era." In *Continuity and Change: The Harvest of Late-Medieval and Reformation History*, edited by Robert J. Bast and Andrew C. Gow, 379–99. Leiden: Brill.

Griffith, R. Marie. 1997. "Submissive Wives, Wounded Daughters, and Female Soldiers: Prayer and Christian Womanhood in Women's Aglow Fellowship." In *Lived Religion in America: Toward a History of Practice*, edited David D. Hall, 160–95. Princeton: Princeton University Press.

Gyertson, David J. 2005. "God's Work Stands: Reflections on the Influence of Christianity in Virginia's First Colonial Period and the Implications for the Ministries of the Christian Broadcasting Network and Regent University." Regent University website. http://www.regent.edu/acad/global/about/GWSwithBiblio .pdf (accessed February 6, 2009).

Hague, Euan, Heidi Beirich, and Edward H. Sebesta, eds. 2008. *Neo-Confederacy: A Critical Introduction*. Austin: University of Texas Press.

Hallpike, Christopher R. 1986. *The Principles of Social Evolution*, 329–69. Oxford: Clarendon Press.

Hannah, Matthew G. 2000. *Governmentality and the Mastery of Territory in Nineteenth-Century America*. Cambridge: Cambridge University Press.

Harding, Anthony. 2008. "The Development of Warrior Identities in the European Bronze Age." Paper presented at World Archaeological Congress, Dublin, Ireland, June 30.

Harding, Susan Friend. 2000. *The Book of Jerry Falwell: Fundamentalist Language and Politics*. Princeton: Princeton University Press.

Headlee, Sue. 1991. *The Political Economy of the Family Farm: The Agrarian Roots of American Capitalism*. New York: Praeger.

Heaton, Timothy H. 2007. "A Visit to the New Creation 'Museum.'" *Reports of the National Center for Science Education* 27, nos. 1–2: 21–24.

Hedeager, Lotte. 2011. *Iron Age Myth and Materiality: An Archaeology of Scandiavia AD 400–1000*. New York: Routledge.

Hickey, Steve. 2004. *Obtainable Destiny: Molding and Mobilizing Today's Emerging Apostolic People*. Lake Mary, FL: Creation House Press.

Hietala, Thomas R. 1997. "'This Splendid Juggernaut:' Westward a Nation and Its People." In *Manifest Destiny and Empire: American Antebellum Expansionism*, edited Sam W. Haynes and Christopher Morris, 48–67. College Station: Texas A & M University Press.

Highlands Study Center. 2009a. Highland Ministries blog. http://www.highlands studycenter.org/what.php (accessed May 4, 2009).

———. 2009b. "ETC—Every Thought Captive." http://www.highlandsstudycenter .org/ETC/ETC.php (accessed May 4, 2009).

Hillerbrand, Hans J. 2003 *Encyclopedia of Protestantism*. New York: Routledge.

Hillgarth, Jocelyn N., ed. (1969) 1986. *Christianity and Paganism, 350–750: The Conversion of Western Europe*. Englewood Cliffs, NJ: Prentice-Hall. Reprint, Philadelphia: University of Pennsylvania Press.

Hines, John. 2001. "Demography, Ethnography, and Archaeolinguistic Evidence: A Study of Celtic and Germanic from Prehistory into the Early Historical Period." In *Archaeology, Language, and History: Essays on Culture and Ethnicity*, edited by John Edward Terrell, 153–72. Westport, CT: Bergin and Garvey.

Hoffmeister, Gerhart, ed. 1977. *The Renaisance and Reformation in Germany: An Introduction*. New York: Frederick Ungar.

Holand, Hjalmar R. 1957. *My First Eighty Years*. New York: Twayne.

Home School Legal Defense Association. 2009a. "Statement of Mission." http:// www.hslda.org/docs/nche/000000/00000069.asp (accessed April 6, 2009).

————. 2009b. "Description of Michael Farris." http://www.hslda.org/about/default.asp (accessed April 7, 2009).

Horton, Ron. 2009. "BJU Statement of Christian Education." http://www.bju.edu/academics/edpurpose.html (accessed February 6, 2009).

Housley, Norman. 2006. *Contesting the Crusades*. Oxford: Blackwell.

Hsia, Po-Chia, ed. 1988. *The German People and the Reformation*. Ithaca, NY: Cornell University Press.

Hughes, Richard T. 2009. *Christian America and the Kingdom of God*. Urbana: University of Illinois Press.

Huttmann, Maude Aline. (1914) 1967. *The Establishment of Christianity and the Proscription of Paganism*. New York: Columbia University Press. Reprint, New York: AMS Press.

Innes, Stephen. 1995. *Creating the Commonwealth: The Economic Culture of Puritan New England*. New York: W. W. Norton.

Institute for Creation Research. 2009. "Professional Certificate Program." http://www.icr.edu/home (accessed February 2, 2009).

————. "Statement on Inerrancy." http://www.icr.org/scripture (accessed May 21, 2009).

Jacoby, Susan. 2008. *The Age of American Unreason*. New York: Pantheon Books.

Jakobsen, Janet R., and Ann Pellegrini. 1999. "Getting Religion." In *One Nation Under God?: Religion and American Culture*, edited by Marjorie Garber and Rebecca L. Walkowitz, 101–14. NewYork: Routledge.

Jenkins, Philip. 2010. *Jesus Wars: How Four Patriarchs, Three Queens, and Two Emperors Decided What Christians Would Believe for the Next 1,150 Years*. New York: HarperOne.

Jewett, Robert. 1973. *The Captain America Complex*. Philadelphia: Westminster.

Kagan, Robert. 2006. *Dangerous Nation*. New York: Knopf.

Kaiser, Kyle. 2009. Fight 4 Christ home page. http://www.fight4christmma.com/jointheteam.htm (accessed May 13, 2009).

Kane, Eileen. 2010. *Trickster*. Toronto: University of Toronto Press.

Kee, Alistair. 1982. *Constantine versus Christ: The Triumph of Ideology*. London: SCM Press.

Kehoe, Alice B. 1986. "Christianity and War." In *Peace and War: Cross-Cultural Perspectives*, edited by Mary LeCron Foster and Robert A. Rubinstein, 153–73. New Brunswick, NJ: Transaction Books.

————. 2000. *Shamans and Religion: An Anthropological Inquiry into Critical Thinking*. Long Grove, IL: Waveland Press.

————. 2009. "Deconstructing John Locke." In *Postcolonial Perspectives in Archaeology*, edited by Peter Bikoulis, Dominic Lacroix, and Meaghan Peuramaki-Brown, 125–32. Calgary: Chacmool Archaeological Association.

Kennedy, D. James. 1982. *Reconstruction: Biblical Guidelines for a Nation in Peril*. Fort Lauderdale, FL: Coral Ridge Ministries.

Kiernan, V. G. 2005. *America: The New Imperialism*. London: Verso.

Kohl, Philip L. 2007. *The Making of Bronze Age Eurasia*. Cambridge: Cambridge University Press.

Kotter, David. 2008. "Does Sarah Palin Present a Dilemma for Complementarians?: Part 4." The Council on Biblical Manhood and Womanhood website. http://www.cbmw.org/Blog/Posts/Does-Sarah-Palin-Present-a-Dilemma-for-Complementarians-Part-4.

Kristiansen, Kristian. 2009. "Proto-Indo-European Languages and Institutions: An Archaeological Approach." *Journal of Indo-European Studies Monograph Series* no. 56: 111–40.

———, and Thomas B. Larsson. 2005. *The Rise of Bronze Age Society: Travels, Transmissions and Transformations*. Cambridge: Cambridge University Press.

Kroll, Luisa. 2003. "Megachurches, Megabusinesses." *Forbes* online, September 17. http://www.forbes.com/2003/09/17/cz_lk_0917megachurch_print.html (accessed March 19, 2009).

Kulikoff, Allan. 1992. *The Agrarian Origins of American Capitalism*. Charlottesville: University of Virginia Press.

Lagemann, Ellen Condliffe. 1989. *The Politics of Knowledge: The Carnegie Corporation, Philanthropy, and Public Policy*. Middletown, CT: Wesleyan University Press.

Lakoff, George, and Mark Johnson. 1980. *Metaphors We Live By*. Chicago: University of Chicago Press.

Larson, Edward J. 1997. *Summer for the Gods: The Scopes Trial and America's Continuing Debate over Science and Religion*. Cambridge: Harvard University Press.

———. 2007. *A Magnificent Catastrophe: The Tumultuous Election of 1800*. New York: Free Press.

Leach, Edmund. 1976. *Culture and Communication*. Cambridge: Cambridge University Press.

Lederhouse, Jillian N. 1997. "Caught in the Middle: Evangelical Public Elementary Educators." *Anthropology and Education Quarterly* 28, no. 2: 182–203.

Lessa, William A., and Evon Z. Vogt. 1979. *Reader in Comparative Religion*. Fourth edition. New York: Harper and Row.

Lévi-Strauss, Claude. 1955. "The Structural Study of Myth." *Journal of American Folklore* 68: 428–44.

Lewis, Archibald R. 1988. *Nomads and Crusaders, A.D. 1000–1368*. Bloomington: Indiana University Press.

Lienesch, Michael. 1993. *Redeeming America: Piety and Politics in the New Christian Right*. Chapel Hill: University of North Carolina Press.

Lieu, Samuel N. C., and Dominic Montserrat, eds. 1998. *Constantine: History, Historiography and Legend*. London: Routledge.

Lincoln, Bruce. 1986. *Myth, Cosmos, and Society: Indo-European Themes of Creation and Destruction*. Cambridge: Harvard University Press.

———. 1991. *Death, War, and Sacrifice: Studies in Ideology and Practice*. Chicago: University of Chicago Press.

Lindsay, D. Michael. 2007. *Faith in the Halls of Power: How Evangelicals Joined the American Elite*. New York: Oxford University Press.

Locke, John. 2003. "Two Treatises of Government." In *Two Treatises of Government and a Letter Concerning Toleration*, edited by Ian Shapiro, 3–209. New Haven: Yale University Press.

Macpherson, C. B. 1962. *The Political Theory of Possessive Individualism: Hobbes to Locke*. Oxford: Clarendon Press.

Madden, Thomas F., ed. 2002. *The Crusades*. Oxford: Blackwell.

Maguire, Daniel C. 2008. *Whose Church? A Concise Guide to Progressive Catholicism*. New York: New Press.

Malinowski, Bronislaw. (1926) 1954. "Myth in Primitive Psychology." In *Magic, Science and Religion*. Reprint, Garden City, NY: Doubleday.

———. 1944. *A Scientific Theory of Culture and Other Essays*. Chapel Hill: University of North Carolina Press.

Marius, Richard. 1999. *Martin Luther: The Christian between God and Death*. Cambridge MA: Belknap Press of Harvard University.

Marrin, Albert, ed. 1971. *War and the Christian Conscience*. Chicago: Henry Regnery.

Martin, John Frederick. 1991. *Profits in the Wilderness: Entrepreneurship and the Founding of New England Towns in the Seventeenth Century*. Chapel Hill: University of North Carolina Press.

McDougall, Walter A. 1997. *Promised Land, Crusader State: The American Encounter with the World since 1776*. Boston: Houghton Mifflin.

McFarlane, Scott. 2004. "Six Ways to Get Involved in the 'Business as Missions' Movement." *Regent Business Review* 11: 12–16.

McGiffert, Arthur C. (1911) 2003. *Martin Luther: The Man and His Work*. Reprinted in Martin Tangely, editor, *Martin Luther Overview and Bibliography*, 1–154. New York: Nova Science. Originally published by The Century.

McKim, Donald K., ed. 2003. *The Cambridge Companion to Martin Luther*. Cambridge: Cambridge University Press.

Mead, Margaret, ed. (1937) 1961. *Cooperation and Conflict among Primitive Peoples*. New York: McGraw-Hill. Reprint, New Brunswick, NJ: Transaction.

Mead, Walter Russell. 2001. *Special Providence: American Foreign Policy and How It Changed the World*. New York: Knopf.

Moberg, David O. (1977) 2006. *The Great Reversal*. Reprint, Eugene, OR: Wipf and Stock.

Moen, Matthew C. 1992. *The Transformation of the Christian Right*. Tuscaloosa: University of Alabama Press.

Mohler, Al. 2008. "Speaking Out: A Christian View of the Economic Crisis. Is the Economy Really Driven by Greed?" *Christianity Today*, September 19. http://www.christianitytoday.com/ct/2008/septemberweb-only/140-12.0.html (accessed March 19, 2009).

Moody, John. 1919. *The Masters of Capital: A Chronicle of Wall Street*. New Haven: Yale University Press.

Mooers, Colin. 1991. *The Making of Bourgeois Europe: Absolutism, Revolution, and the Rise of Capitalism in England, France and Germany*. London: Verso.

Mooney, James. (1896) 1973. *The Ghost-Dance Religion and Wounded Knee*. Part 2 of the Fourteenth Annual Report 1892–93, Bureau of Ethnology. Washington, DC: Government Printing Office. Reprint, New York: Dover Publications.

Moore, James R. 1979. *The Post-Darwinian Controversies: A Study of the Protestant Struggle to Come to Terms with Darwin in Great Britain and America 1870–1900*. Cambridge: Cambridge University Press.

Moran, Jeffrey P. 2003. "Reading Race into the Scopes Trial: African American Elites, Science, and Fundamentalism." *Journal of American History* 90: 891–911.

Morgan, Philip D. 2007. "Virginia's Other Prototype: The Caribbean." In *The Atlantic World and Virginia, 1550–1624*, edited by Peter C. Mancall, 307–80. Chapel Hill: University of North Carolina Press.

Morgan, Robert. 2007. *Boone: A Biography*. Chapel Hill, NC: Algonquin Books of Chapel Hill.

Morison, Samuel Eliot, and Henry Steele Commager. 1942. *The Growth of the American Republic*. Third edition, vol. 1. New York: Oxford University Press.

Morris, Henry M. 1975. *The Troubled Waters of Evolution*. San Diego: Creation-Life Publications.

Morris, John D. 2009. "Days of Praise; Mutations." http://www.icr.org/articles/view/1133/286 and http://www.icr.org/mutation (accessed May 21, 2009).

Motto, Ken. 2009. "Spiritual Gifts and Women Pastors." Spiritual Pathways Ministries. http://obadiah1317.wordpress.com/2009/04/19/spiritual-gifts-and-women -pastors-part-five-guest-post-2 (accessed May 3, 2009).

Murphy, Victoria. 2003. "The Good Book." *Forbes* online, April 14.

Nasaw, David. 1979. *Schooled to Order: A Social History of Public Schooling in the United States*. New York: Oxford University Press.

———. 2006. *Andrew Carnegie*. New York: Penguin.

National Home Education Research Institute. 2012. National Center for Education Statistics, The Condition of Education Indicator 6-2009. http://www.nheri.org (accessed April 7, 2012).

Nicholson, Helen, ed. 1994. *The Military Orders: volume 2, Welfare and Warfare*. Aldershot, UK: Ashgate.

Nielsen, Waldemar A. 1972. *The Big Foundations*. New York: Columbia University Press.

North, Gary. 1983. "Levers, Fulcrums, and Hornets." In *Tactics of Christian Resistance*, edited by Gary North, 401–31. Tyler, TX: Geneva Divinity School Press.

———. 1984. *Backward, Christian Soldiers? An Action Manual for Christian Reconstruction*. Tyler, TX: Institute for Christian Economics.

———. 1986. *Conspiracy: A Biblical View*. New York: Dominion. http://onlinebooks .library.upenn.edu/webbin/book/lookupid?key=olbp25279 (accessed March 22, 2009).

———. 1998. "By Law or by Promise?" *Biblical Economics Today* 20, no. 5. http:// reformed-theology.org/ice/newslet/bet/bet98.08.htm (accessed March 22, 2009).

———. 2001. "Where, Exactly, Is the Southern Tradition These Days?" http:// www.lewrockwell.com (accessed March 23, 2009).

———. 2002. "Textbooks and the Southern Tradition." http://www.lewrockwell .com/north/north100.html (accessed March 23, 2009).

———, and Gary DeMar. 1991. *Christian Reconstruction: What It Is, What It Isn't*. Tyler, TX: Institute for Christian Economics.

Norton, Marcy, and Daviken Studnicki-Gizbert. 2007. "The Multinational Commodification of Tobacco, 1492–1650: An Iberian Perspective." In *The Atlantic World and Virginia, 1550–1624*, edited by Peter C. Mancall, 251–73. Chapel Hill: University of North Carolina Press.

Numbers, Ronald L. 1992. *The Creationists: The Evolution of Scientific Creationism*. New York: Knopf.

Oberman, Heiko A. 1994a. *The Impact of the Reformation*. Grand Rapids, MI: Eerdmans.

———. 1994b. *The Reformation: Roots and Ramifications*. Edinburgh: T&T Clark.

O'Flaherty, Wendy Doniger. 1980. *Women, Androgynes, and Other Mythical Beasts*. Chicago: University of Chicago Press.

Olien, Roger M., and Diana Davids Olien. 2000. *Oil and Ideology: The Cultural Creation of the American Petroleum Industry*. Chapel Hill: University of North Carolina Press.

Onians, Richard Broxton. 1951. *The Origins of European Thought*. Cambridge: Cambridge University Press.

Orchard, Andy. 1997. *Dictionary of Norse Myth and Legend*. London: Cassell.

Packer, George. 2008. "The Fall of Conservatism." *The New Yorker* 84, no. 15, May 26, 2008.

Pagels, Elaine. 2012. *Revelations: Visions, Prophecy, and Politics in the Book of Revelation*. New York: Viking Penguin.

Park, Robert E., and Ernest W. Burgess. 1921. *Introduction to the Science of Sociology*. Chicago: University of Chicago Press.

Parrish, William E., ed. (1970) 1978. *The Civil War: A Second American Revolution?* Huntington, NY: Robert E. Krieger. Originally printed by Holt, Rinehart, & Winston.

Patrick Henry College. 2012. Student Handbook, edition 8.2.1. Purcellville, VA: Patrick Henry College.

Peters, Peter J. 2009a. "A Bible Story." Scriptures for America. http://scriptures foramerica.org/book%20files/A%20BIBLE%20STORY_files/A%20BIBLE%20 STORY.htm (accessed May 6, 2009).

———. 2009b. "Dragon Slayer." Scriptures for America. http://www.scripturesfor america.org/newsletters/Volume%203%202009%20for%20web.pdf (accessed May 7, 2009).

———. 2009c. "Scriptures for America Prayer." Scriptures for America. http://www .scripturesforamerica.org/prayer.php (accessed May 7, 2009).

———. 2009d. "Scripture for America Resource Catalog." Scriptures for America. http://www.scripturesforamerica.org/newsletters/Volume%203%202009%20 for%20web.pdf (accessed May 7, 2009).

Petto, Andrew J. 2008. "Dreaming of a White Kitzmas: Books about the *Kitzmiller v. Dover* trial." *Reports of the National Center for Science Education* 28, no. 2: 20–21.

———, and Laurie R. Godfrey, eds. 2007. *Scientists Confront Creationism, Intelligent Design and Beyond*. New York: W. W. Norton.

Phalon, Richard. 2002. "That Old-Time Religion." *Forbes* online, June 10.

Phillips, Kevin. 1999. *The Cousins' Wars: Religion, Politics, and the Triumph of Anglo-America*. New York: Basic Books.

———. 2006. *American Theocracy: The Peril and Politics of Radical Religion, Oil, and Borrowed Money in the 21st Century*. New York: Viking.

Phillips-Fein, Kim. 2009. *Invisible Hands: The Businessmen's Crusade against the New Deal*. New York: W. W. Norton.

Pohlsander, Hans A. 2004. *The Emperor Constantine*. 2nd edition. London: Routledge.

Polomé, Edgar C. 1989. *Essays on Germanic Religion*. Washington, DC: Journal of Indo-European Studies Monograph Number Six.

Pomerantz, Dorothy. 2003. "On a Script and a Prayer." *Forbes* online, March 3.

Ransomed Heart Ministries. 2008. Store. http://www.ransomedheart.com/ministry/ books.aspx (accessed May 13, 2009).

Regent University. 2009. "Vision." http://www.regent.edu/acad/global/faq/ regent.shtml (accessed February 7, 2009).

Reiss, Timothy. 1982. *The Discourse of Modernism*. Ithaca: Cornell University Press.

Riesebrodt, Martin. 2010. *The Promise of Salvation: A Theory of Religion*, translated by Steven Rendall. Chicago: University of Chicago Press.

Riley-Smith, Jonathan. 2002. "Crusading as an Act of Love." In *The Crusades: The Essential Readings*, edited by Thomas F. Madden, 32–50. Oxford: Blackwell. Originally presented as a lecture May 10, 1979, to Royal Holloway College, University of London.

———. 2005. *A History of the Crusades*. Second edition. New Haven: Yale University Press.

Rist, Gilbert. (2010) 2011. *The Delusions of Economics: The Misguided Certainties of a Hazardous Science.* Translated by Patrick Camiller. Paris: Presses de Sciences Po. Reprint, London: Zed. Originally published as *L'économie ordinaire entre songes et mensonges.*

Rose, Susan E. 1988. *Keeping Them out of the Hands of Satan: Evangelical Schooling in America.* New York: Routledge.

Rosin, Hanna. 2007. *God's Harvard: A Christian College on a Mission to Save America.* Orlando: Harcourt.

Ross, Dorothy. 1991. *The Origins of American Social Science.* Cambridge: Cambridge University Press.

Russakoff, Dale, and Serge F. Kovaleski. 1995. "An Ordinary Boy's Extraordinary Rage." The Washington Post, July 2, p. A01.

Russell, James C. 1994. *The Germanization of Early Medieval Christianity: A Sociohistorical Approach at Religious Transformation.* New York: Oxford University Press.

Sandler, Lauren. 2006. *Righteous: Dispatches from the Evangelical Youth Movement.* New York: Viking.

Sanger, David. 2009. "Biblical Quotes Said to Adorn Pentagon Reports." New York Times, May 17, p. A8.

Sataline, Suzanne. 2006. "Strategy for Church Growth Splits Congregants." *Wall Street Journal,* September 5. http://www.post-gazette.com/pg/06248/719178 -84.stm (accessed March 16, 2009).

Schaeffer, Francis A. 1968. *The God Who Is There.* Downers Grove, IL: InterVarsity Press.

———. 1976. *How Should We Then Live?* Old Tappan, NJ: Fleming H. Revell.

———. 1980. "We Don't Have Forever." PCA Messenger. http://www.pcahistory .org/findingaids/schaeffer/index.html.

Schenkel, Albert F. 1995. *The Rich Man and the Kingdom: John D. Rockefeller, Jr., and the Protestant Establishment.* Minneapolis: Fortress Press.

Scribner, Bob, Roy Porter, and Mikulás Teich. 1994. *The Reformation in National Context.* Cambridge: Cambridge University Press.

Sebesta, Edward H. 2009. Breaking the White Nation: Or a Tour of the Red and Blue States. Posted at http://www.templeofdemocracy.com/breaking.htm, accessed 4/11/09.

———, and Euan Haque. 2002. "The US Civil War as a Theological War: Confederate Christian Nationalism and the League of the South." *Canadian Review of American Studies* 32, no. 3: 254–83.

Seek God Ministries. 2008. "New Life." http://www.seekgod.org/newlife.html (accessed May 27, 2008).

———. 2012. "New Life." http://www.seekgod.org/newlife.html (accessed August 1, 2012).

Sharlet, Jeff. 2008. *The Family: The Secret Fundamentalism at the Heart of American Power.* New York: Harper Collins.

Sheridan, Thomas E. 2006. *Landscapes of Fraud: Mission Tumacácori, the Baca Float, and the Betrayal of the O'odham.* Tucson: University of Arizona Press.

Shires, Preston. 2007. *Hippies of the Religious Right.* Waco, TX: Baylor University Press.

Short, Rachel. 2004. "A Patriarchal Vision for a Daughter's Graduation." Vision Forum Ministries website. Posted July 22. http://www.visionforumministries .org/issues/education/a_patriarchal_vision_for_a_dau.aspx (accessed April 20, 2009).

Simek, Rudolph. 1993. *Dictionary of Northern Mythology*. Cambridge, UK: D. S. Brewer.

Simpson, George Gaylord. 1970. "Uniformitarianism. An Inquiry into Principle, Theory, and Method in Geohistory and Biohistory." In *Essays in Evolution and Genetics in Honor of Theodosius Dobzhansky*, edited by Max K. Hecht and William C. Steere, 43–96. New York: Appleton-Century-Crofts.

Smith, Christian. 2000. *Christian America? What Evangelicals Really Want*. Berkeley: University of California Press.

Smith, George David, and Frederick Dalzell. 2000. *Wisdom from the Robber Barons: Enduring Business Lessons from Rockefeller, Morgan, and the First Industrialists*. Cambridge MA: Perseus.

Smith, Warren. 2006. Reinventing Jesus Christ. http://www.reinventingjesuschrist.com (accessed March 16, 2009).

Southern Baptist Convention. 2008. "Baptist Faith and Message, Basic Beliefs Article 6: The Church." http://sbc.net (accessed December 3, 2008).

Southern Partisan. 1996. "The Moral Defense of the Confederate Flag: A Special Message for Southern Christians." 16 (4): 16–21.

———. 2007. http://www.southernpartisan.net/2007/10/24/a-sorry-state (accessed April 11, 2009).

Southern, R. W. 1995. *Scholastic Humanism and the Unification of Europe: Volume 1, Foundations*. Oxford: Blackwell.

Spiro, Jonathan Peter. 2009. *Defending the Master Race*. Burlington: University of Vermont Press.

Sprigg, Peter. 2009. "Free Markets, Not Just Freedom of Religion, Threatened by ENDA." Family Research Council website. http://www.frc.org/get.cfm ?i=PV08D07 (accessed April 6, 2009).

Stephenson, Paul. 2010. *Constantine: Roman Emperor, Christian Victor*. New York: Overlook.

Strauss, Gerald, ed. 1971. *Manifestations of Discontent in Germany on the Eve of the Reformation*. Bloomington: Indiana University Press.

Streeck, Wolfgang, and Kozo Yamamura, eds. 2001. *The Origins of Nonliberal Capitalism: Germany and Japan in Comparison*. Ithaca, NY: Cornell University Press.

Sutton, William R. 1998. *Journeymen for Jesus: Evangelical Artisans Confront Capitalism in Jacksonian Baltimore*. University Park, PA: Pennsylvania State University Press.

Swatos, William H., Jr., ed. 1990. *Time, Place, and Circumstance: Neo-Weberian Studies in Comparative Religious History*. New York: Greenwood.

———, and Lutz Kaelber, eds. 2005. *The Protestant Ethic Turns 100: Essays on the Centenary of the Weber Thesis*. Boulder, CO: Paradigm.

Tawney, Richard H. (1926) 1954. *Religion and the Rise of Capitalism*. Reprint, New York: New American Library.

Taylor, M. Scott. 2007. "Buffalo Hunt: International Trade and the Virtual Extinction of the North American Bison." Working Paper 12969, National Bureau of Economic Research. http://www.nber.org/papers/w/1296.

Theweleit, Klaus. 1987. *Male Fantasies*, translated by Stephen Conway. Minneapolis: University of Minnesota Press.

Tilly, Charles. 1990. *Coercion, Capital, and European States, AD 990–1990*. Cambridge, MA: Blackwell.

Transnational Association of Christian Colleges and Schools. 2009. "Accreditation Standards." http://www.tracs.org/files/accreditation_standards.pdf (accessed February 2, 2009).

Tree of Life Classical and Christian Home Schooling. 2009. "Statement." http://www.treeoflifeathome.com/great_ideas.php (accessed April 8, 2009).

Turville-Petre, Edward O. Gabriel. 1964. *Myth and Religion of the North: The Religion of Ancient Scandinavia*. New York: Holt, Rinehart and Winston.

Tyerman, Christopher. 1998. *The Invention of the Crusades*. Toronto: University of Toronto Press.

Veritas Press. "Classically Cursive Attributes of God." http://www.veritaspress.com (accessed April 10, 2009).

Vision Forum. 2009a. "Beautiful Girlhood." http://www.visionforum.com/beautifulgirlhood/about (accessed April 20, 2009).

———. 2009b. "The All-American Boy's Adventure Catalog." http://download.visionforum.com/documents/catalogs/abc_intro.pdf (accessed April 20, 2009).

Wagner, Melinda Bollar. 1990. *God's Schools: Choice and Compromise in American Society*. New Brunswick, NJ: Rutgers University Press.

Wallace, Anthony F. C. 1956. "Revitalization Movements: Some Theoretical Considerations for Their Comparative Study." *American Anthropologist*, n.s., 58, no. 2: 264–81.

———. 1999. *Jefferson and the Indians: The Tragic Fate of the First Americans*. Cambridge, MA: Belknap.

Ward-Perkins, Bryan. 2005. *The Fall of Rome and the End of Civilization*. Oxford: Oxford University Press.

Warren, Rick. 2002. *The Purpose-Driven Life*. Grand Rapids, MI: Zondervan.

———. 2009. "Rick Warren's Ministry Toolbox: 'Facing the Five Giants.'" http://legacy.pastors.com/RWMT/?id=200&artid=8140&expand=1 (accessed May 4, 2009).

Watkins, Calvert. 1995. *How to Kill a Dragon: Aspects of Indo-European Poetics*. New York: Oxford University Press.

Webster, Leslie, and Michelle Brown, eds. 1997. *The Transformation of the Roman World AD 400–900*. London: British Museum Press.

Weinberg, Albert K. 1935. *Manifest Destiny: A Study of Nationalist Expansionism in American History*. Baltimore: Johns Hopkins Press.

Weinland, Ronald. 2009. Blog. http://www.ronaldweinland.com (accessed May 13, 2009).

Welch, Gina. 2010. *In the Land of Believers: An Outsider's Extraordinary Journey into the Heart of the Evangelical Church*. New York: Henry Holt.

Whitewashed Feminists. 2008a. "My Pearls Experience." Comment by Richard D, July 1, 2008. http://whitewashedfeminist.com/2008/07/01/my-pearls-experience (accessed April 20, 2009).

———. 2008b. "My Pearls Experience." Comment by Anne, July 1, 2008. http://whitewashedfeminist.com/2008/07/01/my-pearls-experience (accessed April 20, 2009).

———. 2008c. "My Pearls Experience." Comment by normalmiddle, July 1, 2008. http://whitewashedfeminist.com/2008/07/09/selling-fear (accessed April 20, 2009).

———. 2008d. Stamp. http://whitewashedfeminist.com (accessed May 26, 2009).

Wick, Carmon. 2007. "Prairie Muffin Manifesto." Buried Treasure Books. http://buriedtreasurebooks.com/PrairieMuffinManifesto.php (accessed May 4, 2009).

Williams, Daniel K. 2010. *God's Own Party: The Making of the Christian Right*. New York: Oxford University Press.

Wilson, Douglas. 2005. *Black and Tan: A Collection of Essays and Excursions on Slavery, Culture War, and Scripture in America*. Moscow, ID: Canon Press.

Winks, Robin W., and Lee Palmer Wandel. 2003. *Europe in a Wider World, 1350–1650*. New York: Oxford University Press.

Winn, Shan M. M. 1995. *Heaven, Heroes, and Happiness: The Indo-European Roots of Western Ideology*. Lanham, MD: University Press of America

Winston, Bruce E. 2009. "From the Dean." Regent University website. http://www.regent.edu/acad/global/about/deanmessage.shtml (accessed February 6, 2009).

Wolfram, Herwig. 1997. *The Roman Empire and Its Germanic Peoples*, translated by Thomas Dunlap. Berkeley: University of California Press.

Wright, Craig. 2001. *The Maze and the Warrior: Symbols in Architecture, Theology, and Music*. Cambridge, MA: Harvard University Press.

Wright, Robert E. 2002. *Hamilton Unbound: Finance and the Creation of the American Republic*. Westport, CT: Greenwood.

Wright, William John. 1988. *Capitalism, the State, and the Lutheran Reformation: Sixteenth-Century Hesse*. Athens: Ohio University Press.

Wrobel, David M. 1996. *The End of American Exceptionalism: Frontier Anxiety from the Old West to the New Deal*. Lawrence: University Press of Kansas.

Wuthnow, Robert. 1989. *Communities of Discourse: Ideology and Social Structure in the Reformation, the Enlightenment, and European Socialism*. Cambridge: Harvard University Press.

———. 1998. *After Heaven: Spirituality in America Since the 1950s*. Berkeley: University of California Press.

INDEX

Printed and bound in Great Britain by
CPI Antony Rowe, Chippenham and Eastbourne